Reading U.S. Latina Writers

Reading U.S. Latina Writers

Remapping American Literature

Edited by Alvina E. Quintana

First published 2003 by
PALGRAVE MACMILLAN™
175 Fifth Avenue, New York, N.Y. 10010 and
Houndmills, Basingstoke, Hampshire, England RG21 6XS.
Companies and representatives throughout the world.

PALGRAVE MACMILLAN is the global academic imprint of the Palgrave
Macmillan division of St. Martin's Press, LLC and of Palgrave Macmillan Ltd.
Macmillan® is a registered trademark in the United States, United Kingdom and
other countries. Palgrave is a registered trademark in the European Union and other
countries.

ISBN 0–312–29413–1 hardback

Library of Congress Cataloging-in-Publication Data

A catalogue record for this book is available from the British Library.

Design by Autobookcomp.

First edition: February 2003
10 9 8 7 6 5 4 3 2 1

Printed in the United States of America.

Contents

The Writers	The Critics	

Contents

Dedicated to my daughters:

Christina Sascha Quintana

And

Nanú Paloma Guerrero

In Memory

Albina Carrasco Quintana

1909–2001

Acknowledgements

I want to begin by thanking the critics who participated in this project. Seeing that the demand for a well-researched Latina teaching resource was great, they graciously agreed to give their time and expertise. For their intellectual stimulation and their unrelenting moral support, my deepest thanks go to my students, colleagues, and friends in English and women's studies at the University of Delaware. Three dedicated research assistants, Lil Crisler, Jennifer Guarino-Trier, and Meredith Klein, deserve recognition for their keen insights and help with bibliographic research. I owe many thanks to Carmen Palomo García and Caridad Souza for sustaining me with their spirituality and feel especially indebted to Anne Thalheimer, Jen Simington, and Gayatri Patnaik, who provided the editorial assistance and unwavering trust that made the fruition of this project possible.

Finally, I wish to thank my beloved family, especially my siblings Beto, Tito, Rosa, and Julieta, who all deserve recognition for their steadfast patience and faith, and my beautiful daughters, Sascha and Nanú, for their unconditional love.

Introduction
Alvina E. Quintana

In English my name means hope.
In Spanish it means too many letters.
—Sandra Cisneros

Students in my women's literature/women's studies courses have occasionally heard me speak of the significance of matriarchal lineage, recalling the opening of Bettina Aptheker's *Women's Legacy,* wherein she traces backward over her female ancestors. Mirroring her introduction, I like to introduce myself in the following way: My name is Alvina and I am the daughter of a woman who was also named Alvina; she was the daughter of a woman by the name of Refujio, who was the daughter of a woman with the same name Refujio, and this woman was the daughter of a woman who went by the name of Guadalupe, a woman who came from a small village just outside of Mexico City.

Like Aptheker, I use this introduction because it enables me to position myself as a cultural critic and raise a number of issues concerning ethnic/cultural heritage, generational traditions, migration patterns, and naming practices. The introduction has proven useful for a variety of my women's studies, literature, and cultural studies courses because it arouses student interest in the relationship between gender, history, culture, and what I often refer to as "the politics of naming." Aside from emphasizing women's cultural legacies, Aptheker's exercise provides a foundation for considering the intersection between mainstream feminism and the interconnections between culture, gender, and history prevalent in contemporary U.S. Latina writing.

Lillian Castillo-Speed's *Latina: Women's Voices from the Borderlands* stresses the fact that Latina literature should not be thought of as new. This point becomes all the more obvious with a quick survey of twentieth-century American history. The cultural nationalist movements of the sixties created the space for literary innovation that ignited a Latino renaissance, a literary boom that in time set the momentum for the creation of an alternative Latina vision, which in essence synthesized issues relevant to both civil rights and women's liberation.

Bridging the Gap Between Theory and Diversity

The 1982 publication of Gloria Anzaldúa and Cherríe Moraga's *This Bridge Called My Back: Writings by Radical Women of Color* signaled a shift in feminist consciousness that challenged an exclusive, white, middle-class, feminist agenda that privileged scholarly writing and overlooked the contributions of "descriptive" women writers of color. Aside from initiating interest in coalition politics among women of color, this groundbreaking anthology opened the floodgate for U.S. Latina literary production.

Sandra Cisneros's 1984 publication *The House on Mango Street* includes a vignette, "My Name," that exemplifies the shift in feminist practice because it uses the figure of the great grandmother as a means for skillfully contrasting Mexican and U.S. perceptions about cultural traditions and gender relations. On a literal level, it emphasizes the practice of cross-generational naming while symbolically casting Cisneros's adolescent character as a female grappling with some of the cultural implications evoked by her name. Interestingly, the short narrative ends with an observation that speaks volumes about the perceptions of many contemporary Latina writers who seek to revise outdated traditions that have, in the past, more often than not rendered them silent. "My Name" ends with a conclusion marked by a contemporary sensibility that is undoubtedly influenced by Esperanza's U.S. birth and subsequent socialization: "I have inherited her name, but I don't want to inherit her place by the window" (12).

The House on Mango Street features the voice of an adolescent narrator who articulates a variety of gender concerns that are in concert with those that inspired the production of *Reading U.S. Latina Writers: Remapping American Literature*. In concrete terms, this teacher's guide should be viewed as a collective effort, on the part of the critics and the writers they feature, to help fulfill U.S. Latina writers' visions of telling stories that will help liberate those who have been left behind.

In more specific terms *Reading U.S. Latina Writers* was conceived to satisfy a double purpose: to provide a pragmatic method for inspiring a deeper awareness about U.S. Latina literature and to establish a prelude for the non-specialist interested in revising course offerings to highlight the burgeoning literary, cultural, and linguistic influences of one of the fastest-growing ethnic groups in the United States. Despite the fact that Latina writing is not new, its transnational focus on dual identity has often diminished its value in university settings, which in the best circumstances relegate it to the margins of both the mainstream American and Latin American literary canons. This oversight on the part of traditional academic practices raises a number of questions increasingly on the agenda for literary and cultural critique. These questions begin with the issue of essentialist considerations: How, for example, do we define U.S. Latina writing; how indeed do we distinguish it from American or Latin American literary production; is it important to make a distinction between U.S. Latina literature written in English and that written in Spanish or Latin American literature translated into English? Are the boundaries that we construct in our academic disciplines arbitrary or essentialist? To put it another way, how can the literature of U.S. Latinas enhance our awareness of gender, regional, and cultural differences within the United States and within the Americas? It seems that we have reached a moment in history when we might turn to the creative writers, who continue to grapple with many of the limitations created by our scholarly constructs.

In *Something to Declare* Julia Alvarez responds to a Dominican writer who has criticized her for not writing in Spanish. "I don't hear the same rhythms in English as a native speaker of English. Sometimes I hear Spanish in English . . . I'm mapping a country that's not on the map, and that's why I'm trying to put it down on paper" (173). Interestingly enough, Alvarez's response reinforces the vision brought forth by Gloria Anzaldúa and Cherríe Moraga's *This Bridge Called My Back* because it represents her attempt to bridge the contradictions in her cultural experience.

Reading U.S. Latina Writers has been fashioned as a tool that will challenge and disrupt the artificial nationalistic and academic barriers that perpetuate provincial thinking about literature. The inclusive focus of the collection is proposed in an effort to disrupt nationalistic boundaries that undermine a transnational mode of analysis of American literature. The "Latina" designation is thus offered as a strategic intervention aimed at highlighting some of the cultural and political similarities that emerge when individuals living in the United States are identified by the mainstream press under a "Hispanic" label, signifying a European language rather than an ethnic or national point of origin. Consider for example, the current preoccupation with celebrities such as Ricky Martin and Jennifer Lopez and the countless allusions that overlook their Puerto Rican heritage by simply using them as examples of what has been referred to as the "Hispanicization of America." Although the terms "Hispanic" and "Latino" both make reference to categories of difference, it is only the latter that allows for a recognition of the cultural hybridization created by the European fusion with Indigenous, Asian, or African peoples.

Finally, it is important to note that *Reading* represents a democratic, rather than a comprehensive, effort, in that each of the contributors was encouraged to frame the Latina literary text of their choice, within a pedagogical context. This volume should thus be viewed as an introductory guide for non-specialist readers. Because the guide is meant to be useful, rather than comprehensive, exhaustive or all-inclusive, it should *not* be thought of as an overview of literary genre or considered as an attempt to construct yet another literary canon.

The seventeen entries included represent examples of Chicana, Cuban American, Dominican Republic American, Panamanian American and Puerto Rican women's writing as well as the experiences of a variety of Latina scholarly critics, who teach university-level women's studies and literature courses both inside and outside of the United States. The text is intended as a user-friendly guide and is organized alphabetically by author rather than chronologically, by literary genre, or by ethnic categories. Because each of the entries includes a historical overview and bibliographic reference section, the volume is also intended to offer a resource for further readings. This collection of works by sixteen writers and seventeen cultural critics attempts to reflect the heterogeneity of U.S. Latina literature. Although it primarily emphasizes U.S. Latina literature written in English, it deliberately concludes with Lesley Feracho's entry, which features the work of Puerto Rican writer Ana Lydia Vega, whose work has been translated into English. This final entry is thus extremely important because it undermines the belief that U.S. Latina writers have confined their literary production to the English language. My hope is that this collection will, in fact, inspire others to produce companion texts featuring U.S. Latina writers who, despite tremendous pressure to culturally and linguistically assimilate, continue to write in Spanish, dispelling the notion that leads Sandra Cisneros's *House on Mango Street* protagonist to formulate a sad conclusion about her name, "In Spanish it means too many letters."

BIBLIOGRAPHIC RESOURCES

Alvarez, Julia. *Something to Declare*. Chapel Hill: Algonquin Books, 1998.

Anzaldúa, Gloria and Cherríe Moraga, eds. *This Bridge Called My Back: Writings by Radical Women of Color*. Watertown, MA: Persephone Press, 1981.

Aptheker, Bettina. *Women's Legacy: Essays on Race, Sex and Class in American History*. Amherst: University of Massachusetts Press, 1982.

Augenbraun, Harold and Margarite Fernández Olmos, eds. *The Latino Reader: An American Literary Tradition from 1542 to the Present*. New York: Houghton Mifflin Co, 1997.

Castillo-Speed, Lillian, ed. *Latina: Women's Voices from the Borderlands*. New York: Simon & Schuster, 1993.

Castro-Klarén, Sara Sylvia Molloy, Beatriz Sarlo, eds. *Women's Writing in Latin America: An Anthology*. Boulder: Westview Press, 1991.

Cisneros, Sandra. *The House on Mango Street*. Houston: Arte Público, 1983.

Correas de Zapata, Celia, ed. *Short Stories by Latin American Women: The Magic and the Real*. Houston: Arte Público Press, 1990.

Eno-Peralta, Nora and Caridad Silva, eds. *Beyond the Border: A New Age in Latin American Women's Fiction*. Miami: University Press of Florida, 2000.

Espada, Martín, ed. *El Coro: A Chorus of Latino and Latina Poetry*. Amherst: University of Massachusetts Press, 1997.

Fernández, Roberta, ed. *In Other Words: Literature of Latinas of the United States*. Houston: Arte Público Press, 1994.

Flores, Lauro, ed. *The Floating Borderlands: Twenty-Five Years of U.S. Hispanic Literature*. Seattle: University of Washington Press, 1998.

Heyck, Denis Lynn Daly, ed. *Barrios and Borderlands: Cultures of Latinos and Latinas in the United States*. New York: Routledge, 1994.

Kanellos, Nicolás, ed. *The Hispanic Literary Companion*. Detroit: Visible Ink, 1997.

Milligan, Bryce, Mary Guerrero Milligan, and Angela de Hoyos, eds. *¡Floricanto Sí!: A Collection of Latina Poetry*. Bryce Milligan, Mary New York: Penguin, 1998.

Olivares, Julián and Evangelina Vigil-Piñon, eds. *Decade II: An Anniversary Anthology*. Houston: Arte Público Press, 1993.

Poey, Delia, ed. *Out of the Mirrored Garden: New Fiction by Latin American Women*. New York: Doubleday, 1996.

Stavans, Ilan, ed. *New World: Young Latino Writers*. New York: Dell (Division of Bantam Doubleday), 1997.

Tashlik, Phyllis, ed. *Hispanic, Female and Young: An Anthology*. Houston: Piñta Books, 1994.

Vigil, Evangelina, ed. *Woman of Her Word: Hispanic Women Write*. Houston: Arte Público, 1987.

Rosa Linda Fregoso

Julia Alvarez, *In The Time of the Butterflies*

New York: Plume/Penguin Press, 1995.

Textual Overview

Julia Alvarez's *In the Time of the Butterflies* is an intricately woven historical novel about the Mirabal sisters, who became symbols in the Dominican struggle for social justice after they were assassinated. In this fictionalized biography, Alvarez explores the tragic odyssey of three women who revolted against the tyrannical government of the dictator, General Rafael Leonidas Trujillo, and whose murder roused opposition to the regime. On November 25, 1960, as they returned from visiting their jailed husbands, Patria, Minerva, María Teresa Mirabal, and their driver, Rufino de la Cruz, were ambushed, tortured, and killed by a government death squad. The story of the murdered Mirabal sisters—known by their nom de guerre, *las mariposas* (the butterflies)—and their surviving sister, Dedé, unfolds against a background of persecution and oppression in the Dominican Republic. Blending fact with fiction, *In the Time of the Butterflies* probes contradictions in the lives of young women living under both a dictatorial state and provincial patriarchal society.

Historical Context

Although the novel spans the period from 1938–1994, the major part of the story takes place during the brutal regime of Rafael Leonidas Trujillo, the general who ruled the Dominican Republic with an iron fist from 1930 until he was assassinated in 1961. Alvarez documents the clandestine activities of the underground revolutionary movement, Movimiento Revolucionario 14 de Junio (MR1J4) founded by Minerva

Mirabal and her husband, Manolo Tavárez. *In the Time of the Butterflies* does an outstanding job of documenting the culture of fear
elaborated by the Trujillo dictatorship, as well as how people resisted
and revolted against a repressive police state in which torture, imprison-
ment, censorship, and assassination were a way of life. Twentieth-
century struggles for decolonization, anti-imperialist, and revolutionary movements for national liberation throughout the Third World,
and especially in Latin America, are crucial for understanding the
political context of the resistance movement in the Dominican Republic.

Biographical Background

In 1960, ten-year-old Julia Alvarez, along with her parents and three
sisters, joined a community of political exiles from the Dominican
Republic living in New York City. Her father, a member of the
clandestine resistance movement MR1J4, had been forced to leave the
Caribbean island after a plot to overthrow the regime was discovered
by the Servicio de Inteligencia Militar (SIM), Trujillo's secret police.
Alvarez's experience growing up in exile as one of four sisters in an
affluent Dominican family became the backdrop for her highly success-
ful first novel, *How the García Girls Lost Their Accents* (named
Notable Book of 1991). A professor at Middlebury College in Vermont,
Alvarez has written two other novels, *¡Yo!* (1997) and *In the Name of
Salomé* (2000), and published two poetry collections, *Homecoming*
(1984) and *The Other Side/El Otro Lado* (1995). She has also pub-
lished a penetrating book of essays, *Something to Declare* (1998). *In the
Time of the Butterflies* was nominated for the 1995 National Book
Critics Award.

Reception of the Text

Most reviewers have applauded Alvarez for charting the important
contributions of women in the formation of the Dominican nation.
Writing in *Women's Review of Books,* Ruth Behar credits Alvarez for
joining other "Latina writers in the feminist quest to bring Latin
American women into the nation and into history as agents, out from
under the shadows of those larger-than-life men who, too often, have
treated the countries under their rule as their personal fiefdoms."
Although most critical responses welcome Alvarez's efforts to "humanize" the mythic and legendary Mirabal sisters, some reviewers have

critiqued *In the Time of the Butterflies* precisely on these grounds, arguing that the novel tends to trivialize their lives. "Unfortunately Alvarez goes too far in her effort to humanize the Mirabals," Barbara Mujica writes in *Americas.* "Smaller-than-life, her characters often get lost in the trivia of their mundane existences." In a similar vein, writing for the *New York Times,* Roberto González Echevarría laments the novel's sentimentalism, its turning of "eulogy" into "melodrama": "There is indeed much too much crying in this novel." Negative reviews, like the one by González Echevarría, typify the critiques often directed against feminist writers who bring to light the abuses women experience in their everyday lives. As he adds: "Ms. Alvarez clutters her novel with far too many misdeeds and misfortunes: rape, harassment, miscarriage, separation, abuse, breast cancer." In contrast to this response, Ilan Stavans reviewed the novel for the *Nation.* In his review, Stavans commends the author for representing the Mirabals' political struggle as "an attack against phallocentrism as an accepted way of life in Hispanic societies."

Major Themes and Critical Issues

The novel's discernible feminist orientation examines the ways in which women's resistance is central to the history and definition of the nation. Like other feminist works, *In the Time of the Butterflies* is oriented toward the project of historical recovery, chronicling the contributions by women that are so often hidden from official state histories or accounts of sociopolitical movements for national independence, liberation, and decolonization. Developing discrete voices and personas for each of the Mirabal sisters, Alvarez explores the relationship between gender and nation through various overlapping themes.

The theme of women's erasure from official history is examined in the first part of the novel. *In the Time of the Butterflies* opens in the present, with the third-person voice of Dedé, "the one who survived to tell the story" (321). Reluctant to participate in the underground resistance, Dedé had remained at home on the night her sisters were murdered. In 1994, at 66 years of age, Dedé ponders her role as "oracle," as "the one to whom people came for the story of the Mirabal sisters." (312). Dedé maintains the family home as a shrine, as a memorial to her sisters, women who risked their lives for the nation. Although Dedé survived to tell the story of her sisters' metamorphosis into international symbols of feminist opposition and resistance, the character is much more than a family chronicler. The distance in the character's third-person reflections on her role as family historian serves the author's aim of examining the historical role of women in the formation and definition of the nation. Dedé is the repository for female memories as much as she serves as witness to women's struggles against public and private forms of patriarchy.

Alvarez foregrounds the feminist concerns with women's agency and subjectivity through the portrayal of complex inner lives of individual characters. Each of the murdered sisters speaks in the first-person about her coming-of-age story, as they struggle to come into voice as women and forge their identities as daughters, sisters, girlfriends, wives, mothers, and ultimately revolutionaries. The first third of the novel conveys each sister's unique personality and struggle to define the personal and political self.

Challenging every form of patriarchal authority, the most committed to the revolution is the outspoken and courageous Minerva, who joins the opposition movement early on in convent school, where she learned about "the secret of Trujillo" (16) from one of her classmates. The youngest, ever-playful and romantic María Teresa, follows in Minerva's footsteps less out of ideological commitment than through falling in love with the "idea" of revolution, as she becomes involved with one of Minerva's underground comrades. Patria, the eldest, most devoutly maternal and family-oriented sister, journeys from traditional Catholicism to revolution after witnessing the massacre of a young rebel. The ever-fearful Dedé, unable to defy a controlling husband, remains on the margins of her sisters' political activism.

The novel raises profound political questions about the position of women in the family and the nation. At the micro-level, Alvarez uses images of an authoritarian father and Catholicism to question the twin pillars of women's oppression in provincial Dominican society. The patriarch of the Mirabal family embodies male privilege in Latin American families, directing his controlling gaze primarily at his most rebellious daughter, Minerva. It is Papí who maintains and reinforces gendered hierarchies, refusing to allow Minerva to attend the university and discouraging boyfriends because, as Minerva explains: "I was *his* treasure, he'd say, patting his lap, as if I were a girl in a jumper instead of a woman" (84). The sexual dynamics of patriarchy, expressed in this veiled reference to incest, are coupled with a more explicit critique of male privilege, especially in references to Papí's philandering as the root of their mother's alienation and depression.

Catholicism also plays a central role in the formation of gender roles, norms, and expectations. Like many young women of the Latin American elite, the Mirabal sisters were educated in a convent boarding school where nuns inculcated the culture's narrow definition of proper womanhood. In convent schools like Imaculada Concepción, the education of young women was aimed less at preparing them for university studies or a career than at grooming them into motherhood and marriage, either in religious (nuns) or secular (wives) form.

By situating issues of familial, gender hierarchies within a broader social context, Alvarez tackles the relationship between private and public forms of patriarchy, especially the manner in which male privilege and entitlement are engrained in state structures. Women's subordination in the sphere of domestic life is mirrored in the public domain, with Trujillo's regime representing patriarchy's most extreme form. The novel shows how domesticity is compounded for women living in a nation so terrorized that people remained silent even in the privacy of the home because, as Patria puts it, "there are ears everywhere" (210). In many ways, Trujillo's patriarchal authority permeated multiple levels of social life, encompassing civil and personal liberties that, in gendered terms, translated into control over women's bodies. The dictator exercised his masculine entitlement ruthlessly, seducing young women like Minerva's classmate, Lina Lovaton, and keeping them as mistresses: "He's got many of them, all over the island, set up in big fancy houses" (23). However, the culture of terror perpetuated under Trujillo's authoritarian rule touched women's lives in other significant ways as well.

In the final third of *In the Time of the Butterflies,* Alvarez expands on the disturbing theme of gender violence. Like other political dissidents, Minerva and María Teresa Mirabal were imprisoned for their anti-Trujillo activities, spending seven months in prison. Two chapters provide graphic descriptions of the treatment of women in Trujillo's prisons. The Mirabal sisters were incarcerated with twenty-four other women in small, crowded steel cells, sleeping on metal shelves (or bunks), eating a "chao" of "watery paste" with "little gelatin things" (233) and repeatedly witnessing the psychological unraveling and breakdown of fellow women inmates. Minerva spent most of her time in solitary confinement for simple acts like voicing her political sentiments. In order to force her husband's confession, María Teresa was tortured by prison guards. The novel ends with the ultimate expression of state violence: the torture and murder of the Mirabal sisters. Although recent feminist works tend to emphasize the saliency of personal, domestic violence in the lives of women (i.e., battery and rape), in this novel Alvarez has expanded the focus on violence against women to include its political dimension: state-sponsored gender violence. As Alvarez so aptly demonstrates, women are the most vulnerable subjects of social repression, subjected to sexual violations in the home as well as in public spaces. Linking in this manner public and private forms of violence, Alvarez probes the historical and systemic elements of sexual violence as endemic in the reproduction and maintenance of gender and sexual hierarchies in the nation.

Pedagogical Issues and Suggestions

In my large lecture course Introduction to Women and Gender Studies, I have taught *In the Time of the Butterflies* twice within a section entitled, "sexual violence as a continuum in women's lives." The novel works remarkably well in supplementing the more impersonal, theoretical social science material on the subject of gender violence. I use the text to probe the connections between state and domestic violence and to explore the ways in which the state is implicated in violence against women. I prepare students for this text with an initial discussion about gender violence sanctioned by the state, including the use of torture, sexual harassment, and rape on the part of agents of the state such as military and paramilitary groups, border patrol, prison guards, and police. This discussion emphasizes state-directed violence against women as a mechanism of social control.

Alvarez's novel also raises the issue of gender violence in the domestic sphere. Although the text does not deal explicitly with violence within the private sphere, its intimation about Mr. Mirabal's incestuous desires for his daughter opens up the space for examining child sexual abuse in the home. In this context, students will be motivated to do research on the prevalence of incest within the family as a form of domestic violence, perpetrated principally by male relatives (fathers, brothers, and uncles) and directed mostly against young girls.

Another topic for discussion in a women/gender studies course is the issue of women's resistance in the Third World. The novel refuses to construct Latin American women only as victims of male oppression or objects of patriarchy. Although, in the end, the Mirabal sisters pay the ultimate price for their resistance, the novel recuperates the history of Latin American women's activism, the fact that Third World women resist despite huge penalties and refuse to give up in the face of harshly oppressive conditions. *In the Time of the Butterflies* also works well for critiquing the tendency among First World or mainstream feminists to view Third World women as victims in need of salvation. One can probe the contradictions in this "rescue narrative" by highlighting the history of activism among Third World women like the Mirabal sisters.

Finally, the text can be used to explore issues of heterogeneity and difference within feminism, especially since another fiction of mainstream feminism is the idea that Third World women are latecomers to the feminist struggle or that their struggles emerged in the "Third Wave" of feminism. *In the Time of the Butterflies* proves otherwise. At the same time, the novel complicates the narrow definition of feminism as dealing exclusively with gender issues. For Third World feminists, women's activism is inseparable from struggles for social and economic justice, for national liberation and decolonization. Like their First World counterparts, women in less affluent parts of the world struggle not just around their gender identities, but as members of oppressed ethnic, racial, religious, and class groups. Thus within a broader discussion of intersectional identities and structures of domination, the novel can be very effective.

Literary Contexts

Like other immigrant writers, Alvarez writes from the cultural space of the borderlands or in-between-ness, as simultaneously an outsider-insider to both U.S. and Dominican cultures. Alvarez's novel belongs in the genre Diaspora literature insofar as it confronts problems of cultural displacement and dislocation resulting from the experiences of migration. Like other Latina writers from immigrant communities, Alvarez makes evident the extent to which the process of identity formation is often rooted in transnational routes and circuits, physical and metaphorical travel across geopolitical borders. In this respect, by reconstructing a story that haunted her since childhood, Alvarez reclaims a Latina transnational identity and in the process comes to terms with her own Dominican-ness. Writing from the cultural space of the borderlands, the author is a bridge between the past and the present, Spanish and English, and, most significantly, between Dominican social history and contemporary English-speaking readers. This is a novel that crosses the border into the geographic space and history of the Dominican Republic and brings subjugated knowledges of women's history and struggle into the consciousness of mainstream readers.

Comparative Literature

Julia Alvarez joins other Latinas writing in English against the backdrop of political turmoil, military dictatorship, and revolution. The text can be taught alongside the genre of political literature that addresses the social consequences of U.S.-supported dictatorships in Latin America, including Demetria Martinez's *Mother Tongue* and Helena María Viramontes's *Moths and Other Short Stories*. The novel's focus on revolutionary activism by upper-class Latin American women merits comparison with *Inhabited Woman,* by California-based Nicaraguan writer Gioconda Belli. Although Janet Jones Hampton compares Alvarez's "grasp of metaphor and humor" with Barbara Kingsolver's prose, the novel also draws heavily from Latin American artistic influences and stylistic innovation. Within a Latin American literary context, *In the Time of the Butterflies* fits in the genre of "novels of dictatorship," such as *The Autumn of the Patriarch* by Gabriel García Márquez, *El Señor Presidente* by Miguel Angel Asturias, *Recurso al Método* by Alejo Carpentier, and *I, the Supreme* by Agusto Roa Bastos.

BIBLIOGRAPHIC RESOURCES

Secondary Sources:

Behar, Ruth. "Revolutions of the Heart." *Women's Review of Books* 12, no. 8 (May 1995): 6–7.

González Echevarría, Roberto. "Sisters in Death." *New York Times Book Review.* 18 December 1994, 28.

Hampton, Janet Jones. "In the Time of the Butterflies." *Belles Lettres: A Review of Books by Women* 10, no. 2 (spring 1995): 6–7.

Martinez, Elizabeth. "In the Time of the Butterflies." *Progressive* 59, no. 7 (July 1995): 39–42.

Mujica, Barbara. "In the Time of the Butterflies." *Americas* (English edition) 47, no. 2 (March-April 1995): 60.

Pritchett, Kay. "In the Time of the Butterflies." *World Literature Today* 69, no. 4 (autumn 1995): 789.

Puleo, Gus. "Remembering and Reconstructing the Mirabal Sisters in Julia Alvarez's *In the Time of the Butterflies.*" *The Bilingual Review/ La Revista Bilingüe* 13, no. 1 (January-April 1998): 11–20.

Roth, Ava. "Sisters in Revolution." *MS* no. 2 (September-October 1994): 79–80.

Selden, Rodman. *Quisqueya: A History of the Dominican Republic.* Seattle: University of Washington Press, 1964.

Stavans, Ilan. "In the Time of the Butterflies." *Nation* 259, no. 15 (November 7, 1994): 52.

Karen Gaffney

Julia Alvarez, ¡Yo!

New York: Plume/Penguin Press, 1997.

Textual Overview

In many ways Julia Alvarez's *¡Yo!* can be read as a sequel to the first novel, *How the García Girls Lost Their Accents*. In the first novel, Yolanda García, one of four daughters, describes her family's experiences living in the Dominican Republic and immigrating to the United States. In the second novel, Alvarez provides Yolanda's family, friends and acquaintances with the chance to tell their version of the story. *¡Yo!* Is divided into sixteen sections, each one offering a different perspective regarding a character's relationship with Yolanda García. The novel thus paints a multifaceted critique that is inspired by Alvarez's creative writing efforts. These narratives brilliantly disclose the pain that comes from leaving one's home and relocating in a hostile environment that is characterized by its race, class, and gender oppression.

Alvarez's cast of narrators portray Yo as an individual who tends to impose her personal values onto others, whether it be an illiterate Dominican woman who needs help writing a letter to her abused daughter in the United States; the daughter of the family's New York City maid, who wants to deny her class background; or her landlady, who is a victim of domestic abuse. The final story brings the novel to full circle with the representation of Papí, the García patriarch, who provides textual closure when he gives Yo his blessing and thereby validates her writing practice.

Historical Context

Like her first novel, *¡Yo!* depicts the García family within a transnational context, influenced by both the United States and the Dominican Republic. Comprising the eastern two-thirds of the island of Hispaniola, with Haiti occupying the western third, the Dominican Republic has undergone a history marked by colonization and rebellion. The divergent geographical characteristics of the two sides of the island directly affected each colony's industry and use of labor. The land on the French side lent itself well to tobacco and sugar plantations, which demanded a large number of slaves vigilantly controlled by a small number of masters. The land on the Spanish side, though, was more suitable for raising cattle, an industry that needed a different type of slavery, one in which there was a more balanced ratio of masters and slaves and more cooperation between them. In 1791, Toussaint Louverture led a slave revolt in the French colony, which eventually became the independent nation of Haiti in 1804. After considerable fighting, the Dominican Republic became an independent country in 1844.

Within the Dominican Republic, the ideology of "antihaitianismo" developed. Basically, this approach focused hatred on anyone or anything French, Haitian, and/or African. Even though most of the Dominican population was biracial, with both African and Spanish heritage, dominant ideology was based on a denial of African presence in the Dominican Republic and an exclusive focus on Haiti. Dominicans declared their roots to be Spanish and Taíno. The Trujillo dictatorship, lasting from 1930 to 1961, reinforced and perpetuated the antihaitianismo ideology. In 1937, Trujillo instituted a massacre to purge the Dominican Republic of Haitians, resulting in the deaths of thousands. With some help from the United States, underground movements attempted to topple Trujillo several times, eventually leading to his assassination in 1961. Many members of the underground movement immigrated to the United States during Trujillo's regime, later followed by a wave of Dominican immigrants after the United States opened its immigration policy in 1965.

Biographical Background

Born in 1950, Julia Alvarez spent most of her first ten years in the Dominican Republic with her mother, father, and three sisters. Her father's involvement in the underground movement against Trujillo forced the family to escape to the United States in 1960. In the late 1960s and early 1970s, Alvarez attended Connecticut College, Middlebury College, and Syracuse University. She then went on to teach creative writing in a variety of high schools and colleges. Since 1988, she has held a position as a professor of English at Middlebury College in Vermont.

Alvarez's first book publication, *Homecoming* (1984) was a collection of poetry. To date, she has published four novels, a children's book, an adolescent novel, a collection of essays, and three collections of poetry. In addition to her two novels about the Garcías, her other novels include *In the Time of the Butterflies* and *In the Name of Salomé*. Alvarez has received a variety of honors and awards, including grants, fellowships, and prizes from organizations such as the Academy of American Poetry, Bread Loaf Writers' Conference, National Endowment for the Arts, PEN, and the American Library Association.

Reception of the Text

Alvarez's work has grown in popularity since the publication of her first poetry collection. The reviews of *¡Yo!* generally praise Alvarez's language, style, and vivid characters and applaud her textual return to the García family, welcoming the multicultural opportunity it provides for readers. Overwhelmingly this novel continues to receive favorable reviews and be seen as an important addition to the growing body of literature by women writers of color in the United States.

In 1992 *Newsweek* (April 20, 1992) Susan Miller proclaims, "A fresh generation of Latino writers is creating a new and distinctive literary landscape," and a few years later, in 1995, Jennifer Mena in *Hispanic* declared "Four Brash Latina Writers Transform the Literary Landscape." Both articles included a discussion of Alvarez's work.

Despite the enormous popular attention to Alvarez's work, scholarly critiques have been limited. To date, there is only a single book-length study of Alvarez, *Julia Alvarez: A Critical Companion,* and a handful of book chapters and essays, most of which focus on her first two novels. Scholarly articles tend to focus on her writing as resistant, with a focus on Alvarez's use of language and multiple voices as well as on her themes of identity, authority, and the politics of language. In an essay from *Something to Declare,* Alvarez describes negative criticism she received from a prominent Dominican writer for writing in English and not in Spanish. Alvarez addresses this criticism by explaining that she considers herself neither Dominican nor American, but a combination of both. Her writing attempts to weave English and Spanish languages in order to reflect her identity as a transcultural writer. Ellen McCracken's *New Latina Narrative: The Feminine Space of Postmodern Ethnicity* does a particularly good job of exploring the issue of transcultural resistance, arguing that while there is a tendency for books by Latina writers to become commodified in terms of their popularity, the books themselves both contain and resist this process of being incorporated into the existing mainstream society. While McCracken's text limits its analysis of Alvarez to her first two books, the theory can also be applied to ¡Yo!.

Major Themes and Critical Issues

The novel's multiple theme and issues facilitate a consideration of the relationship between content and form. Alvarez does an amazing job of conveying her cultural critique by combining her ideas, language, and style. While *How the García Girls Lost Their Accents* begins to experiment with narrative practices, ¡Yo! takes this experimentation to new levels. The very organization and style of the novel provides multiple and conflicting accounts of the same events, forcing readers to ask questions about belief, truth, and narrative/character reliability. Offering conflicting narratives about family history and memory, Alvarez creates a space for cultural difference(s). The novel's unconventional form is first revealed through a table of contents that lists sixteen sections, each conveying dual titles named after a character as well as a literary form. The first chapter, for example, is entitled "The sisters/fiction," while the second is "The mother/nonfiction." This dual naming tactic allows Alvarez to skillfully deconstruct literary genre while also describing the narrative focus. In the first chapter "sisters/fiction" exposes the character's point of view as well as the fictionality of Alvarez's narratives about the García family. By the time the reader finishes these first two chapters the categories of fictive and nonfictive have lost much of their meaning.

This questioning of classifications also extends to an exploration of social categories like race, class, and gender. In *How the García Girls Lost Their Accents,* Alvarez establishes the García family's position at the top of the social ladder in the Dominican Republic. The mother's family (de la Torres) are represented as members of an elite wealthy Spanish class who reside in mansions and employ servants. Acknowledging only their European ancestors, the Spanish conquistadors, they look down on their servants with darker skin, particularly the Haitians. When the Garcías arrive in the United States, however, they are no longer perceived at the top of the racial and class hierarchy but are instead socially positioned under a Hispanic rather than Anglo banner, as part of the working class rather than the middle class or upper class. This shift in classification itself reveals the relativity of social groupings, thereby reinforcing their fictive nature. If two countries can construct these categories differently, where in one a Spanish ancestry is racialized and in another it is not, we must consider how these categories are socially rather than biologically created or natural.

After living in the United States for several years, the García family attempts to re-assert their power in the United States by hiring a dark-skinned maid from the Dominican Republic. Their nickname for her, Primitiva, reveals their racialized perception, which in literal terms labels her as wild, primitive, and inferior. Several years later, the family welcomes the new generation of domestic help, allowing the maid's daughter, Sarita, to also move into their home. Sarita finds her mother "imprisoned," with a room in the basement (a literal manifestation of her inferior position) and only Sundays off. The literary term assigned to this story is "report" because the story focuses on Yo's ethnographic report on Sarita for a college class. Yo's ability to write a report on Sarita reveals her power over Sarita, her ability to label her and speak in her behalf. Alvarez, however, resists this authority by giving Sarita the first person voice in this story. This story, like many in this novel, thus reveals the author's attempt to navigate the complex relationship between power and voice.

Pedagogical Issues and Suggestions

If students read ¡Yo! as a singular text, it should be contextualized with reference to *How the García Girls Lost Their Accents*. Without this emphasis students will be confused and wonder why Yo does not receive her own section within the novel. Even a cursory review of the first novel will be helpful in that students will begin to comprehend how *García Girls* can easily be viewed as a book devoted entirely to Yolanda García's perspective. It is also useful to have students read an interview with Alvarez, like "Something to Declare" at www.salon.com, where the author discusses the intense negative response her family had to the publication of her first novel, because these concerns tie in directly to Alvarez's themes of voice and power.

In addition to these types of content-based issues, students will want to discuss the form of the novel. It may be very different from anything they have read, with the novel's multiple narrators/short story approach. Spending some time on the table of contents with particular attention to the literary terms used to label each section is always useful during the initial class discussion of the novel. This approach provides students with an opportunity to reflect on the multiple meanings of the stories, in terms of both content and form. Another interesting class discussion can focus on Alvarez's shifting point of view and use of first- and third-person narration in these chapters. Some of the text's narrators speak in first person, and some speak in third person, and there is no obvious pattern to these differences. Students can, however, develop insightful arguments speculating about a pattern and its relationship to the relative power of the narrator.

Aside from these more general issues and questions, it is important to address the specific stories themselves. A variety of classroom exercises work very well for diving into specific characters. For example, students can role play a conversation about Yo between two characters who, although represented in individual sections within the novel, may not necessarily know each other. What do their perceptions of Yo have in common and how do they differ? It can also be helpful to incorporate an in-class writing exercise, in which students write from the perspective of one of the characters in order to flesh out their relationship with Yo. It can be particularly helpful to have students do this exercise with characters who do not have their story told in the first person. These kinds of exercises encourage students to engage with the novel directly and to consider the process that leads to their knowledge about individual characters and whether or not they agree with their assumptions. In addition discussion questions might include:

> Is there a particular pattern to the three main divisions of Part I, Part II, and Part III?
>
> Are you left with a favorable or unfavorable impression of Yo?
>
> Why does the novel close with Yo's father?
>
> Does the final chapter empower or disempower Yo?
>
> In an essay, Alvarez describes her writing by stating: "I'm mapping a country that's not on the map" (*Something to Declare* 173). How does this mapping process work within her novel?
>
> How would you define a novel? Does ¡Yo! fit this definition?
>
> Why do you think Alvarez experiments with literary form?
>
> How does each story relate to power relations?
>
> Describe the different levels of Yo's empower and disempowerment.
>
> How do other people she encounters experience either a gain or loss in power (particularly the maid's daughter, the stranger, the landlady, and the stalker)?

Literary Contexts

One of the reasons that Alvarez's work does so well in the classroom is that she writes and speaks about her creative process and thus gives students a window into much more than her individual writing practice. In a few key essays and interviews, Alvarez describes the length of time it took to develop her literary voice. She describes how the bias against bilingualism in the United States made her feel silenced. Alvarez's *Something to Declare* describes her first experience in an American school, when the children made fun of her accent: "'No speak eengleesh,' they taunted my accent" (140). She worked very hard to master written and spoken English, becoming quite successful at both. She did so, though, at the expense of silencing her Spanish: "As a young writer, I was on guard *against* the Latina in me, the Spanish in me because as far as I could see the models that were presented to me did not include my world. In fact, I was told by one teacher in college that one could only write poetry in the language in which one first said Mother. That left me out of American literature, for sure. And so I thought that if I wanted to write literature, with a capital L, I had to hide my ethnicity, I had to lose my accent" ("Local Touch, Global Reach" 68). Alvarez reveals how this experience debilitated and silenced her, noting that it was not until much later, when she discovered Asian American writer Maxine Hong Kingston's *The Woman Warrior,* that she felt inspired to write. In her own terms she states that the book "gave me permission to be myself on paper" (69). Since then Alvarez has been able to use creative writing to explore the relationship between language, power, and identity politics.

Comparative Literature

Because *¡Yo!* is emblematic of an emergent body of literature by women writers of color in the United States, it can be easily incorporated within a course on similarly resistant novels like those of Amy Tan and Louise Erdrich, who also focus on multiple narrators and intergenerational dialogue. This novel also fits beautifully within other literature courses, including the more basic introduction to literature class, the more advanced survey of American literature course, as well as courses that emphasize literary genre. Because *¡Yo!* can be taught as both a collection of short stories and a novel, it allows students to consider the meaning of genre distinctions and literary definitions, linking them with issues of authority and the division between fiction and nonfiction. Within the context of a traditional American literature survey course, it resembles more canonical American novels, because it addresses questions such as: What is the American experience? What does it mean to be American? Because of this similarity, the novel can be taught alongside works such as *The Grapes of Wrath, The Great Gatsby,*

Death of a Salesman, Absalom, Absalom!, Invisible Man, and *The Glass Menagerie.* Incorporating ¡*Yo!* into this type of a course enriches the discussion, allowing for questions concerning the politics surrounding cultural and American identity formation(s).

BIBLIOGRAPHIC RESOURCES

Primary Sources

Alvarez, Julia. *How the García Girls Lost Their Accents.* Chapel Hill: Algonquin Books, 1991.
———. ¡*Yo!.* Chapel Hill: Algonquin Books, 1997.
———. "Local Touch, Global Reach: Address to the Texas Library Association, April 4, 1998." *Texas Library Journal* (summer 1998): 68–74.
———. *Something to Declare.* Chapel Hill: Algonquin, 1998.

Secondary Sources

Alvarez, Julia. "Something to Declare." Interview by Dwight Garner. *Salon* 25 September 1998. Accessed November 1, 2001 http://www.salon.com/mwt/feature/1998/09/25feature.html.
———. "Conversation with Julia Alvarez." Interview by Heather Rosario-Sievert. *Review: Latin American Literature and Arts* (spring 1997): 31–37.
———. "A Clean Windshield." Interview in *Passion and Craft: Conversations with Notable Writers.* Bonnie Lyons and Bill Oliver, eds. Urbana: University of Illinois Press, 1998. 128–144.
Christian, Karen. *Show and Tell: Identity as Performance in U.S. Latina/o Fiction.* Albuquerque: University of New Mexico Press, 1997.
McCracken, Ellen. *New Latina Narrative: The Feminine Space of Postmodern Ethnicity.* Tucson: The University of Arizona Press, 1999.
Mena, Jennifer. "Women on the Verge." *Hispanic* (March 1995): 22–26.
Miller, Susan. "Caught Between Two Cultures." *Newsweek* (April 20, 1992): 78–79.
Ortiz-Márquez, Maribel. "From Third World Politics to First World Practices: Contemporary Latina Writers in the United States." *Interventions: Feminist Dialogues on Third World Women's Literature and Film.* Bishnupriya Ghosh and Brinda Bose, eds. New York: Garland Publishing, Inc., 1997. 227–244.

Pons, Frank Moya. *The Dominican Republic: A National History.* Princeton: Markus Wiener Publishers, 1998.

Sagás, Ernesto. *Race and Politics in the Dominican Republic.* Gainesville: University Press of Florida, 2000.

Sirias, Silvio. *Julia Alvarez: A Critical Companion.* Westport: Greenwood Press, 2001.

Stefanko, Jacqueline. "New Ways of Telling: Latinas' Narratives of Exile and Return." *Frontiers: A Journal of Women Studies* (1996): 50–69.

Wucker, Michele. *Why the Cocks Fight: Dominicans, Haitians, and the Struggle for Hispaniola.* New York: Hill and Wang, 1999.

Ifeoma C. K. Nwankwo

Veronica Chambers, *Mama's Girl*

New York: Riverhead Books, 1996.

Textual Overview

Mama's Girl (1996) is Veronica Chambers's critically and popularly acclaimed second novel. The first, directed at a preteen to early teen audience, told the story of Marisol and Magdalena, best friends of Panamanian descent who must negotiate their connections to both their relatives' Panamanian memories and their own American lives. That novel is full of laughter, code-switching, and cultural referents from both Panama and Brooklyn. Her third novel, *Quinceanera Means Sweet 15,* is a sequel to the first and again features Marisol and Magdalena, now adolescents. Marisol spends a year in Panama that forces her to evaluate the significance of her Panamanian background and to confront the new Magdalena she finds upon her return.

Mama's Girl, a 1997 Book of the Month Club selection, is a personal memoir that tells of a young woman's coming of age both through and despite her relationship with her mother. Although the text is Chambers's memoir, it reads like a novel portraying a young protagonist. The young woman tells her own story of coming of age in the 1970s and 1980s with the concomitant chronological and cultural references. She is a child of a Panamanian–West Indian mother and a Dominican father, and she struggles to become an intelligent, strong, and driven young woman in the face of her father's abuse and absence, her stepmother's abuse, and above all her mother's withholding of love. She works to please her mother, without her mother's acknowledgement, while her brother, who almost seems to be working to displease her mother, becomes the object of her mother's attention. Significantly, as if to announce her determination to win this struggle, the beginning of the text is set in the girl's world, the world she shares with her "girls," the world of double-dutch girls. The beginning pronounces the value of the girls' worlds, and the girls' knowledge at the same time subtly calls for the equal valuation of girls' and boys' worlds and knowledge. *Mama's Girl* begins

> Ten years before Air Jordans, I learned to fly. It's like the way brothers pimp-walk to a basketball hoop with a pumped-up ball and throw a few shots, hitting each one effortlessly. Like a car idling before a drag race, there is an invitation, perhaps even a threat, in the way their sneakers soft shoe the pavement and the ball rolls around in their hands. As double-dutch girls, we had our own prance . . . We knew the corners where you could start a good game. Like guys going up for a layup, we started turning nice and slow. Before jumping in, we would rock back and forth, rocking our knees in order to propel ourselves forward; rocking our hips just to show how cute we were. (2)

As this beginning shows, the text's language is refreshingly clear and alive, reflecting the youthful exuberance of the young protagonist as well as her playful precocity. Throughout the text we see a young girl who is, at times, put in adult situations but who always refuses to become hardened or embittered. She remains a girl who has crushes, best friends, and, most importantly, dreams. Despite the fact that her mother tells her "Don't always be pushing yourself ahead" (53), she insists on doing so. As she does so, though, she must also deal with the significance of her actions for her relationship with her mother. She feels guilty for not being satisfied with that which satisfied her mother. She feels anger because her mother never recognizes or appreciates her achievements or her struggles. She feels desperation because she wants her mother's love so very badly. At the same time, she understands her mother, loves her mother, and recognizes that she must make peace both with her mother and with the elements of her mother that are within her in order to become a whole person.

Historical Context

Chambers's text speaks from and of three primary histories, the Panamanian–West Indian, the African American, and the U.S. Latino/a. In terms of Panamanian–West Indian history, *Mama's Girl* speaks implicitly to the origin of Panamanian–West Indian communities and more explicitly to the Panamanian–West Indian experience in the United States today. Between 1904 and 1914, tens of thousands of people were brought from the British Caribbean to Panama to build the Panama Canal, the waterway that was to create a watery shortcut between the Atlantic and Pacific Oceans and by extension revolutionize the American economy. Historian George Westerman estimates the number at 31,071 (24). The canal builders worked under torturous conditions, with death always hovering over their heads in the forms of yellow fever, malaria, and dangerous working conditions. There was also another factor that, although not explicitly fatal, profoundly shaped their lives: racism. The segregation of the "Gold Roll" (white) employees and the "Silver Roll" (black) employees recreated the contemporaneous Jim Crow system in the United States. Although both groups often did the same work, the blacks were paid less, given worse housing, and denied privileges accorded to the white employees. The black workers had to drink from the "silver roll" fountains and use the "silver roll" bathrooms. Despite the horrible conditions, a strong Panamanian–West Indian community formed that embraced and exemplified the traditions and languages of both elements of its history. The community, however, has still had to contend with individual and institutional racism both at home and abroad. Although Chambers does not deal explicitly with this history in the text, it underscores the sentiments, attitudes, and cultures of her older characters, including Mama's Girl's mother.

The text more directly engages the present-day stories of Panamanian–West Indians in the United States who are simultaneously African American and Latino/a. The language and cultural referents of *Mama's Girl* reflect all three of these backgrounds. As Chambers explained to the National Endowment for the Arts, "Although I am identified as African-American, both of my parents are black Latinos from Panama. I would like to explore more of my Latino heritage not only because of my own interests, but because of the paucity of material available. I'd like to use the fellowship to write literary essays about the Afro-Latino experience here and abroad."

Biographical Background

Veronica Chambers grew up in Brooklyn, New York in the 1970s. She graduated Summa Cum Laude with a B.A. from Simon's Rock College. In addition to the novels *Marisol and Magdalena, Mama's Girl,* and *Quinceanera Means Sweet 15,* Chambers coauthored *Poetic Justice: Filmmaking in South Central* with filmmaker John Singleton and *Amistad Rising: The Story of Freedom,* a children's book. Her work has appeared in several popular magazines, including *Esquire, USA Weekend, Glamour,* and *Vogue.* She was promoted to general editor at

Newsweek in May 1999. Before joining *Newsweek*, Chambers served as senior associate editor for *Premier* magazine and assistant editor for *Essence*. Currently, Chambers is executive editor of *Savoy* magazine. She lives in Brooklyn, New York. Chambers, in an article for *Essence*, cowritten with Haitian American writer Edwidge Danticat and African American writer Sheneska Jackson, describes her relationship with writing by saying

> Although I have always loved writing, I never imagined I could be a writer. I went to college at age 16 with peers who had started writing novellas at the age of 12. I, on the other hand, had a vague notion that I might be a lawyer, an ambition fueled by two things: I was a young Black woman with a deep passion for justice; I was also a poor Black woman from Brooklyn, and I wanted to be paid in full. As far as I knew most writers lived in abject poverty. I'd been far too poor to get the romantic notion of living hand-to-mouth for the sake of "art." But language beguiled me . . . When a friend suggested that I get an internship at a magazine, I decided to try it out . . . I've been in love with writing ever since.

Reception of the Text

Chambers's work has been acclaimed for her content as well as her style. As mentioned above, *Mama's Girl* was a Book of the Month Club selection in 1997. The praise for her text comes from a wide range of sources. Jeris Cassel in the *Library Journal* lauds Chambers for presenting "an honest, open, and ultimately warm memoir of her relationship with her mother" and for capturing "the reader's sympathies not by recounting negative circumstances but by stressing the need to rise above them and make one's own choices." Clare McHugh for *People* says "Chambers shows just how keenly she shares her mother's identity in this intensely personal and perceptive memoir." Dottie Kraft for the *School Library Journal* notes that "her autobiographical account reads beautifully and smoothly but far from easily as readers may keep asking themselves how this person was able to overcome so much in her life." Her work poses a special challenge, however, to those who aim to categorize her work as purely African American or Latino/a. The reception of Chambers's work highlights the especially complex situation of Panamanian–West Indians in the United States. Her work has been celebrated variously as giving "voice to the first generation of African-Americans to come of age in the post-

Civil rights era" and *"Un gran libro para que la gente joven lea, entienda y se relacione con la familia y amigos intimos, dentro del contexto de dos culturas"* (Nana's Book Warehouse, 2002). *Mama's Girl* is almost always classified as African American, particularly by mainstream book review journals. Jill Petty of *Ms.*, however, stands out in her attentiveness to the tensions and/or interactions between her mother's Panamanian background and her own American present, saying "Even when Chambers was a little girl, indifference was not all that separated mother and daughter. Her mother, from Panama, spoke Spanish; Chambers did not."

Major Themes and Critical Issues

The dominant theme of this work, as the title suggests, is the mother-daughter relationship. Mama's girl's search for identity is bound up in her search for her mother's love. Another key, and perhaps even more important, theme underlies this one: the father-daughter relationship. Young Veronica also desperately wants her father's love, and it is this unfulfilled desire that, one could argue, has the most profound impact on her life. She wants her father's love first, then realizes that she is not going to get it, then comes to expect that her mother will give enough love for both parents.

Cultural, linguistic, and ideological differences between immigrant parents and their children also figure prominently in the text. On one hand Veronica hungrily consumes knowledge passed down by her grandmother about *polleras* (carnival dresses) and other aspects of Panamanian culture. She tells us in a pleasant, almost celebratory tone of the Panamanian commonplaces that are shared by her mother and her friends. She says

> They would come through the front door wearing the "home clothes" that my mother wore on weekends . . . Their hair would be dutifully curled in rollers and covered with big silk scarves, never the cloth bandannas that American women wore . . . "Wa-pin" they would say . . . It was shorthand for "What's happening?" and with that phrase, they would make themselves at home. My mother would offer them sorrel or ginger beer if we had any, and they would sit at the dining room table, their conversation weaving quickly in and out of Spanish. They would talk about friends from home and friends who were in Brooklyn with equal passion, as if Brooklyn were only an extension of Panama, a suburb that was just a train ride away. (45)

On the other hand, though, she expresses her frustration at not being able to understand the conversations between her mother and her mother's Latina friends. For young Veronica, the linguistic distance between her and her mother reflects the emotional and psychological distance between them. When her mother tells her that she "stayed in a marriage that was miserable" because of Veronica and her brother, Veronica immediately turns to language in her attempt to process this information: "I went to my room and cried all night . . . I knew then that as good as my Spanish was, there were things I'd been missing. For the first time, I felt as separate from my mother as I once had from my father" (97).

A third theme that underpins *Mama's Girl* is cross-cultural identity. Veronica is both Latina and African American as well as both Panamanian and American. The cultural referents of the text reflect these multiple cultures. Her skin color, her experiences, as well as her mother's experiences determine which of these referents she identifies most with. She tells of her mother's experience with racial prejudice from within the Latino/a community:

> I turned to ask my mother, but she had walked to the back of the store where an old Puerto Rican woman sat behind a counter. "May I help you?" the woman said in English with a heavy accent. "*Estoy buscando algo para limpiar la casa,*" my mother replied. Immediately, the woman relaxed. It was a scene I had witnessed many times before. Latinos would look at my mother's black skin and brush her off. Then, when she began speaking in Spanish, their attitude would change. I knew, from my little Spanish, that "*limpiar la casa*" meant to "clean the house," but why had my mother come to a card store for Mop & Glo? (30)

The answer to her question is that her mother wanted to go to a store in her community run by people with whom she identified, other Latinos/as. Veronica's identification with African Americans is clear when she speaks of writing about Martin Luther King and Shirley Chisolm and Rosa Parks during black history month. She says "watching footage of the bus boycotts, the sit-ins, and the marches on Channel 13, I would wonder if I would have been brave" (52). She understood that "there was no excuse for me not to be, as the old women in the neighborhood put it, 'a credit to my race.'" Veronica understands and embraces her special position as a representative of the African American community even as she also embraces her Panamanian cultural heritage. This cross-cultural complexity distinguishes Chambers from the vast majority of contemporary Latina and African American writers and makes the book an especially apt way to encourage students to consider cross-cultural engagements as normal and necessary.

Pedagogical Issues and Suggestions

Mama's Girl is a text that, because of its style and content, almost teaches itself. Students enjoy reading Chambers's clear yet lively prose and often connect profoundly to the text's content. Young Veronica's love-hate relationship with her mother resonates especially powerfully with young people who are also engaged in a search for self through and despite their parents. Students from high school seniors to college seniors, regardless of their background or level of historical knowledge, will doubtless be eager to discuss the text, with or without the teacher. Given that, the challenge that comes with teaching this text is keeping the discussion focused on the specific issue the teacher wants to discuss, particularly if that issue is neither mother-daughter relationships nor the pains and pleasures of growing up.

One way of facing that challenge is teaching it alongside texts that focus on the same issue or theme. For example, the text can usefully be taught alongside other works from any literary tradition that thematically represent mother-daughter relationships, such as Paule Marshall's *Brown Girl, Brownstones,* Cristina García's *Dreaming in Cuban,* or Amy Tan's *Joy Luck Club* and Edwidge Danticat's *Breath, Eyes, Memory* (recommended for college students in their second year and beyond only). Teachers may wish to have students compare each daughter's relationship to her mother's history. Potential discussion questions for this theme are:

What is passed down from mother to daughter in these texts?
How does the daughter's acceptance or rejection of this history affect her relationship with her mother?
How does her acceptance or rejection shape her perception or definition of herself?
Does the daughter repeat any of her mother's patterns?
What does that say about what and how women pass down and inherit their identities and/or histories?
What does the author want us to think about mother-daughter relationships and how does she encourage us to do so?

Another possible theme around which texts can be clustered is the theme of women writing autobiography. Other texts with which

Mama's Girl could be read include Audre Lorde, *Zami, A New Spelling of My Name* (recommended for college students in their second year and above), Esmeralda Santiago, *When I Was Puerto Rican,* or Maxine Hong Kingston, *The Woman Warrior.* Potential discussion questions for this theme are:

> Why does the writer seem to feel that it is important for her to tell her own story?
> Which aspects of her life does she seem to emphasize?
> Why does she choose those?
> What does she seem to have left out of the autobiography?
> What do those silences tell us about her?
> What is her relationship to writing?
> How does her willingness to express herself in writing compare to her willingness to express herself through speech?
> Are there factors that prevent her from writing and/or claiming her voice?
> How does she overcome them?

Literary Contexts

Chambers's work crosses the boundaries of several literary traditions, including Latina literature, African American literature, and Panamanian–West Indian literature. She draws on all three traditions in *Mama's Girl.* Her emphasis on the implications of the cultural and linguistic difference between her and her mother for their relationship recalls Latina works like Julia Alvarez's *How the García Girls Lost their Accents,* in which young women endeavor to find their own identities, their own relationship to the homeland, and their own connection to their own homeland in the face of their parents' imposition of values and traditions. This tension has been a recurring theme in Caribbean American literature as well. Paule Marshall's *Brown Girl, Brownstones,* for example, tells the story of a Barbadian American daughter who struggles to develop her own identity in the face of her mother's overbearing nature and history of pain.

As several of the reviewers mention, Chambers's work also stands out as an exemplar of the next generation of writing about the African American experience. Chambers is, in fact, included in an anthology that announces the arrival of a new generation of African American writers: *Step Into a World: A Global Anthology of the New Black Literature,* edited by Kevin Powell (2000). Her work can be understood as part of the tradition of black women's autobiographies begun by

Mary Prince, the first woman slave narrator in the Americas. As Mary Prince defied the demand that black women bear slavery in silence, as African American and Caribbean women writers have refused to remain silent, so does Chambers speak her experience as a complex being. Significantly, though, Chambers has also made a concerted effort to treat the Latina aspect of her identity and to speak to other young black Latinas. That her more explicitly Latina works, *Marisol and Magdalena* and *Quinceanera Means Sweet 15,* are those directed at young women speaks to her intention to teach and provide models for young black Latinas.

An understanding of the Panamanian–West Indian literary tradition can also be helpful for readers of Chambers's work. This tradition is a relatively young one that includes Carlos Guillermo Wilson's novel, *Chombo* (1981). The term "chombo" is a derogatory term for black Panamanian–West-Indians. Wilson's use of the term serves a dual purpose that calls attention to the racism it represents as well as the individual's ability to use the word to take charge of one's own social predicament. Wilson is one of the preeminent figures in Panamanian–West Indian literature, having produced this pathbreaking novel as well as acclaimed books of poetry and short stories. Carlos Russell is another of the founding fathers of this tradition. His books of poetry, *An Old Woman Remembers* (1983) and *Miss Anna's Son Remembers* (1976) are written in the voices of an old woman who lived during the canal-building era and of her son, who is a modern-day Panamanian–West Indian. The old woman shares her memories of a range of aspects of life in the Canal Zone. Her son does the same for present day Panamanian–West Indian life, speaking about both the challenges and joys of that experience. *Miss Anna's Son Remembers* is one of very few Panamanian–West Indian texts written in a woman's voice, from the perspective of a woman, or with a woman as the protagonist. The other is a play by Melva Lowe de Goodin, entitled *De/From Barbados a/to Panama,* which presents the story of a student, Manuelita Martin, who decides to write a class paper on her great-grandparents' experiences in the canal-building era. The play alternates between scenes from the present day and the canal-building era. This play and Chambers's work are groundbreaking in Panamanian–West Indian literature because of their woman-centered orientation. In recognition of her importance as a Panamanian–West Indian writer, Chambers was invited to be the keynote speaker for the University of Panama's conference on Panamanian and West Indian literature in May 2001. The conference was, not coincidentally, chaired and organized by Melva Lowe de Goodin.

Comparative Literature

Mama's Girl is in many ways reminiscent of mainstream American coming-of-age stories, including Judy Blume's *Are You There God? It's Me, Margaret,* which, like *Mama's Girl,* tells the story of a young person growing into herself and confronting the wide variety of challenges concomitant with that growth. She has crushes. She has "friend drama." She has fights with her brother. She goes to college and makes new friends. Like this novel, *Mama's Girl* simultaneously speaks to young people where they are and provides them with models for moving forward.

At the same time, though, *Mama's Girl* also echoes texts like Jane Austen's *Pride and Prejudice* and Emily Bronte's *Wuthering Heights* in that all three texts aim to foreground the voices and experiences of young women who are supposed to be silent, young women who are supposed to keep their experiences private. Chambers's style is also reminiscent of Austen's and Bronte's in its simplicity and directness. *Mama's Girl* also recalls Louisa May Alcott's *Little Women* through its content and style but is significantly different from Alcott's work in that it provides insight into the mind of only one young woman.

Mama's Girl is also an interesting counterpoint to traditional male autobiographies, such as those by Benjamin Franklin. As the story of a young woman of color, the text can be used to highlight the different meanings of American-ness and the variety of experiences that fall under the rubric of "American." Another text with which *Mama's Girl* could usefully be compared is James Joyce's *Portrait of the Artist as a Young Man.* In addition to enabling students to compare across genders and time periods, this juxtaposition would allow students to gain an understanding of parallels between the experiences of marginalized people in the United States and abroad. Students can then be asked to contrast the reception of these texts, an exercise that would almost certainly provoke a lively discussion, given the similarities between the texts in terms of content.

BIBLIOGRAPHIC RESOURCES

Primary Sources

Alcott, Louisa May. *Little Women.* Boston: Roberts Brothers, 1869.

Alvarez, Julia. *How the García Girls Lost Their Accents.* New York: Plume, 1992.

Austen, Jane. *Elizabeth Bennet; or, Pride and Prejudice.* New York: Oxford University Press, 1999.

Blume, Judy. *Are You There God? It's Me, Margaret.* Scarsdale: Bradbury Press, 1970.

Bronte, Emily. *Wuthering Heights.* New York: Oxford University Press, 1999.

Chambers, Veronica and John Singleton. *Poetic Justice: Filmmaking in South Central.* Los Angeles: Delta, 1993.

———. *Marisol and Magdalena: The Sound of Sisterhood.* New York: Hyperion, 1995.

———. *Mama's Girl.* New York: Riverhead Books, 1996.

———.and Paul Lee (Illustrator). *Amistad Rising: The Story of Freedom.* New York: Harcourt, 1998.

———. *Quinceanera Means Sweet 15.* New York: Hyperion, 2001.

Danticat, Edwidge. *Breath, Eyes, Memory.* New York: Vintage, 1994.

García, Cristina. *Dreaming in Cuban.* New York: Knopf, 1992.

Joyce, James. *Portrait of the Artist as a Young a Young Man.* New York: Modern Library, 1928.

Kingston, Maxine Hong. *The Woman Warrior: Memoirs of a Girlhood Among Ghosts.* New York: Knopf, 1976.

Lowe de Goodin, Melva. *De/From Barbados a/to Panama.* Panama City: Editora Geminis, 1999.

Lorde, Audre. *Zami, A New Spelling of My Name.* Freedom, CA: The Crossing Press, 1982.

Marshall, Paule. *Brown Girl, Brownstones.* New York: Random House, 1959.

Powell, Kevin, ed. *Step Into a World: A Global Anthology of the New Black Literature.* New York: John Wiley & Sons, 2000.

Prince, Mary. *The History of Mary Prince, A West Indian Slave.* New York: Oxford University Press, 1988.

Russell, Carlos. *Miss Anna's Son Remembers.* Brooklyn: Bayano Publications, 1976.

———. *Cuentos del Negro Cubena.* Guatemala: Landivar, 1977.

———. *Pensamientos del Negro Cubena.* Los Angeles: n.p. 1977.

———. *An Old Woman Remembers.* New York: Caribbean Diaspora Press, 1983.

Santiago, Esmeralda. *When I Was Puerto Rican.* Reading, MA: Addison-Wesley, 1993.

Tan, Amy. *The Joy Luck Club.* New York: Putnam, 1989.

Wilson, Carlos Guillermo (Cubena). *Chombo*. Miami: Universal, 1981.

Secondary Sources

Cassel, Jeris. Review of *Mama's Girl*. *Library Journal* 121, no. 12 (July 1996): 126.

Chambers, Veronica. National Endowment for the Arts. Writer's Corner. Author's Statement. Accessed March 2002. *http://arts.endow. gov/explore/Writers/Chambers.html.*

———, Edwidge Danticat, and Sheneska Jackson. "Three Young Voices." *Essence* 27, no. 1 (May 1996).

Chancy, Myriam. *Searching for Safe Spaces: Afro-Caribbean Women Writers in Exile*. Philadelphia: Temple University Press, 1997.

Davies, Carole Boyce. *Black Women, Writing, and Identity* New York: Routledge, 1994.

Kraft, Dottie. Review of *Mama's Girl*. *School Library Journal* 42, no. 7 (July 1996): 109.

McHugh, Clare. Review of *Mama's Girl*. *People Weekly* 46, no. 1 (July 1, 1996): 29.

Nana's Book Warehouse. Review of Veronica Chambers, *Marisol and Magdalena*. Accessed March 2002. *http://www.angelfire.com/ biz2/nanasbooks/magdal.html*

Petty, Jill L. Review of *Mama's Girl*. *Ms.* 7, no. 1, (July/Aug 1996): 84.

Review of "Veronica Chambers' *Mama's Girl*." In *Reading Group Choices*. Nashville: Paz & Associates, 1997.

Westerman, George W. *Los Inmigrantes Antillanos* (Panama: G.W. Westerman, 1980).

Theresa Delgadillo

Denise Chávez, *Face of an Angel*

New York: Farrar, Straus, and Giroux, 1994.

Textual Overview

This 1994 novel by Denise Chávez tells the story of a woman's coming of age; that is, it portrays a woman in the process of coming into awareness and full possession of her body, intellect, and soul. The principal narrator and protagonist of *Face of an Angel* is Soveida Dosamantes, head waitress at El Farol Restaurant in Agua Oscura, New Mexico. Her story begins with the recognition of the significance of her "telling," an act of witnessing that she is personally called to and that her grandmother sanctions. Soveida first recounts the unions of her great-grandparents, grandparents, and parents. Then, over the next 457 pages, we follow Soveida from her 1950s childhood through the religious and bodily mysteries of girlhood, rebellious young adulthood, working life, dating, two marriages, the writing of a book, her return to school, and approaching motherhood. Soveida's uniquely humorous and compelling voice guides us through the experiences, adventures, and crises she faces as a working-class Chicana struggling to redefine her relationship to traditions. Through these life events and the self-reflexive act of writing her story, Soveida achieves a feminist sense of self as a member of multiple communities. She also both relies on and redefines the meaning of female communities.

Because relationships are so central in Soveida's life, *Face of an Angel* tells not only Soveida's stories but the stories of her coworkers Milia, Eloisa, and Pito; her cousin Mara; her boss Larry; her friend Lizzie; her mother's servant/companion Oralia; her own cleaning helper Chata; her boyfriends Jester, Veryl, Ivan, J. D., and Tirzio; her mother Dolores; and her grandmother Lupe. This constellation of stories reveals the constraints, struggles, and misperceptions that Soveida shares and faces with her relatives and coworkers, especially the women. Chávez tells us that about her characters, stating, "They've got messy lives." For

Soveida and those around her, the struggle of daily life is not just getting through a hard work day but figuring out how to challenge the hierarchies of gender, race, and class that limit their lives, that is, how *not* to be submissive workers, second-class citizens, or victimized women. For example, workers at El Farol, the restaurant where Soveida works, engage in fights to retain their rights to a free meal, fair overtime, and decent working conditions. Meanwhile, Soveida's mother, Dolores, works to overcome her subservience to her husband and discovers herself in the process. Soveida's journey intersects with these and others, leading her to greater inner strength and the ability to invent the life she needs.

Historical Context

Face of an Angel foregrounds the history of the borderlands in its setting, characters, and themes. Agua Oscura, New Mexico, the novel's fictional town, is in the southern part of the State, which, as Chávez herself describes it, is largely desert—a hot, hard, and energetic place that borders both Mexico and Texas. The El Farol Restaurant, where much of the novel occurs, conveys, in its décor and food, references to the variety of cultures and populations that inhabit the borderlands. Just as border crossings to and from Mexico form part of Soveida's great-grandparents' story, so, too, do they continue to shape Soveida's life and relationships. The disparities created and maintained by the border pop up continually in character's lives as limited options, prejudices, and identity conflicts. Therefore, one important historical context for *Face of an Angel* includes the 1848 Treaty of Guadalupe Hidalgo and the 1854 Gadsden Treaty (through which Mexico ceded to the United States what are now the states of California, Arizona, New Mexico, Nevada, Utah, and portions of Wyoming, Colorado, Kansas, and Oklahoma) and the inequalities they engendered for those residing in the annexed territories.

Larry Larragoite's insistence that he is a white Spanish man and not Mexican invokes yet another history: Not only were New Mexico's earliest colonial settlements Spanish (predating English settlements on the East Coast of what is now the United States), but the area retained a strong Spanish influence after independence and then annexation. However, the state's Native American pueblos are even older than Spanish colonial settlement and remain vibrant communities today. *Face of an Angel* references these Native American pueblos in the character of Oralia Milcantos.

Finally, the emergence of a Chicana feminist movement in the 1960s and 1970s and its continuing influence forms an equally important context for reading this novel. In its treatment of the growing awareness of issues of gender and sexuality and its attention to a multiply defined Chicana context, *Face of an Angel* creates both a feminist fiction and an allegory of the development of the Chicana feminist movement in the latter half of the twentieth century.

Biographical Background

Denise Chávez was born in Las Cruces, New Mexico in 1948, where she currently resides. She was raised by her devoutly religious mother and attended Catholic elementary and high school—a life she has described as extremely sheltered. As a student in a Catholic high school for girls, Chávez was attracted to the dramatic arts, an interest that she continued to pursue in college and beyond. She received a B.A. in drama from New Mexico State University in 1971, an M.F.A. in drama from Trinity University in 1974, and an M.A. in creative writing from the University of New Mexico in 1982.

Chávez's professional career includes numerous publications, productions of plays, awards, and varied teaching appointments. While her work has been based in the Southwest, primarily New Mexico and Texas, Chávez has performed and taught across the United States and internationally. To date, over twenty of her plays have been produced. In addition to *Face of an Angel* she has published short stories, essays, children's books, and some plays. Her work appears in over fifteen anthologies, including collections of women's literature, Latina/o literature, and Western literature. She has taught playwriting, literature, theater, and creative writing at Northern New Mexico Community College, University of Houston, and New Mexico State University. In addition she has served as artist-in-residence in the New Mexican communities of Aztec, Socorro, Alamogordo, Carlsbad, and Las Cruces. She has also been a writer-in-residence at *La Compañia de Teatro de Albuquerque* and Theatre-in-the-Red in Santa Fe, New Mexico.

Reception of the Text

Face of an Angel received wide praise from virtually every quarter of the country. From mainstream news magazines to publishing industry

periodicals to feminist journals, reviewers welcomed the novel's intimate voice, rich language, and compelling characters. A sign of its wide
appeal, notes Julio Moran, writing in the *Los Angeles Times,* is that the
novel became a selection for both the Book of the Month Club and the
Quality Paperback Book Club.

Reviewers recognized in Chávez's treatment of the interlinked issues
of race/ethnicity, gender, sexuality, and class a long-silenced but powerful voice and an important story. Alice Joyce in *Booklist* describes *Face
of an Angel* as "an exceptional novel" with "one luminous vignette
after another" that "merits a place in all fiction collections because of
the profound respect and understanding of Chicano culture communi-
cated." The reviewer notes that Soveida Dosamantes, the narrator and
central protagonist, is a "friend to all 'women who serve." *Newsweek*'s
Susan Miller praises the novel for its "vivid portraits of Chicano family
life," its experiments in "cross-fertilization of language and cultures,"
and its articulation of a Latina voice that has "for too long been mute."
Lisa Degliantoni of the *Library Journal* highly recommends the novel
for Latin American, women's, and fiction collections, noting that
"Chávez has written a book about growing up with a double heritage
and learning to shed the constraints of tradition and fear." Jennifer
Mena of *Hispanic* magazine applauds the novel as one of many that are
changing the face of American literature and its reviewer embraces
Chávez as someone "telling our stories." Irene Campos Carr, writing
for *Belles Lettres: A Review of Books by Women,* describes *Face of an
Angel* as a novel "rich in family gossip" that is "engrossing, amusing,
and definitely one to be savored." William Nericcio of *World Literature
Today,* calls the novel "an anti-sentimental family history" and compares it favorably with several major U.S. and Latin American novels.
The reviewer applauds the novel's "powerful glosses" on "the volatile
bonds linking grandmothers, mothers, and daughters." *The Village
Voice* reviewer, Laurie Muchnick, also acclaims the many interlinked
stories in *Face of an Angel,* characterizing it as "a grand, intimate,
contradictory jumble of stories, history, and advice as narrated by
Soveida Dosamantes." Muchnick observes that Soveida doesn't just
work as a waitress but develops a theory of it in writing her *Book of
Service.* Finally, Muchnick says that Denise Chávez "whispers in the ear
of her readers things no decent woman would reveal. I think she would
consider that high praise."

The novel has also been well received by critics and scholars of
Chicana/o and Latina/o literature. For example, Marilyn Mehaffy and
Ana Louise Keating note Chávez's innovative incorporation of "struc-
tural frameworks more commonly identified with dramatic and

performative arts" in *Face of an Angel.* David King Dunaway finds that the novel has an "unabashedly Hispanic worldview" that is grounded in the landscape and cultures of the desert of southern New Mexico, both Chávez's home and the setting for *Face of an Angel.* Important critical interviews with Chávez that focus on *Face of an Angel* are in Deborah L. Madsen, "Denise Chavez" and Bridget Kevane's and Juanita Heredia's "The Spirit of Humor: Denise Chávez." Scholars of Chicana/o literature such as Alvina Quintana and Tey Diana Rebolledo have written on Chávez's work (see bibliography for further information). Finally, at least ten master's and doctoral thesis in recent years devote significant attention to *Face of an Angel.*

Major Themes and Critical Issues

A novel as large and complex as *Face of an Angel* provides fertile ground for the discussion of multiple issues, but in this brief section I will examine only three of its overarching themes. First is the issue of service—as idea and as action, in both personal and professional spheres. This theme is most overtly expressed in Soveida's occupation as a waitress and her engagement in the project of writing *The Book of Service: A Handbook for Servers,* fourteen chapters of which appear intermittently throughout the novel. Ostensibly a guide to waitressing, *The Book of Service* becomes a treatise on the broader question of service. As Soveida describes her final product: "It's about service. What it means to serve and be served. Why is it that women's service is different from men's?" (451). Other questions about service that crop up for characters in *Face of an Angel* include:

Is it denigrating or honorable to serve?
How do we serve God?
How do we serve ourselves?
Is service an excuse for inaction?
Are those who serve entitled to fair pay and benefits?
How do we protect those who serve from exploitation?
Does serving reconfirm our humanity?

Face of an Angel honors a series of female characters whose service in life remains largely unacknowledged and/or poorly compensated. In speaking the stories of many women as well as her own, Soveida Dosamantes addresses another important theme in this novel: overcoming the silence about women's lives. Often described as an "earthy" novel, *Face of an Angel* tells it all, challenging both the shame and invisibility surrounding women's lives. And "all" includes bodily secrets, troubled relationships, and the ins and outs of women's labor. When Soveida gives *The Book of Service* to her successor at El Farol Restaurant, Dedea, she charges her with the task of adding her insight, observations, and experience to the book, that is, to continue writing the story of women's service.

In the first chapter, "A Long Story," Soveida's grandmother, Lupe, encourages her to tell all her story and to "tell it while you can," regardless of the embarrassment or pain it might bring to others, especially family (4). Lupita's words are a call to testify and underscore a recurring motif in the protagonist's life—the relationship between silence and victimization in women's lives. In the telling of hers and other stories, Soveida is transformed. Because much of the narrative centers on home and family life, Soveida's fictional *testimonio* reclaims the domestic sphere as site of struggle, resistance, and transformation.

The search for a feminist spirituality, which includes the revaluation of the female body—as the title of the novel tellingly signals—constitutes a third set of overarching issues in the novel. Soveida's journey requires her to confront received religious knowledge that may underwrite her subordination. But she must also craft a new religious understanding, build a new spirit, and transform her soul. The angel motif linked with the visual image of a *milagro* that appears at the beginning of each section both guides the narrative and underscores these interlinked themes. Just as the chapters progress through the hierarchy of angels, and the images of *milagros* chart a parallel progression through the body, so does the narrative create a journey from innocent and romantic identification with religious ritual to uncritical acceptance of religious doctrine to a more critical assessment of and participation in spiritual practices and beliefs. The spiritual journey is completely intertwined with Soveida's road to accepting and taking responsibility for her own body and its desires, from her need to overcome a socially and religiously imposed shame and denial, as well as her recognition that satisfying herself at another woman's expense can not be borne for long.

Pedagogical Issues and Suggestions

At 497 pages in hardcover, *Face of an Angel* is a big book to teach. While many divide reading and discussion into smaller units in order to succeed in teaching large novels to college undergraduates, some high school teachers and even some college teachers may choose to teach just a single chapter or combine a few chapters.

If assigning the entire novel, instructors may consider dividing the reading and discussion into three separate units as follows: a) "Angels" and "Archangels" introduce themes of border, family, traditions, gendered norms, and religion; b) "Principalities," "Powers," "Virtues," and "Dominations" present Soveida's life as an adult woman—waitress, lover, friend, wife, daughter—and her growing awareness of the importance of service; c) "Thrones," "Cherubim," and "Seraphim" focus on maturation, the building of a feminist community, death, and renewal of life. Questions for discussion might include:

> Why does Soveida start her story with her great-grandparents? What does this tell us both about Soveida and her community in New Mexico?
>
> This novel emphasizes women's work of various sorts, but what does it tell us about the relationship between work and identity? Work and community? Work and knowledge?
>
> How does religion influence Soveida's life?
>
> What do she and others value and reject about their religious upbringing?
>
> Many characters struggle with bodily desires, limitations, and vulnerabilities. Why is the physical body so important in this novel, and what, in different settings, does it signify?
>
> Although there are few likeable male characters, women in this novel are not blameless for their own victimization. Why do women keep serving men who treat them badly?

For instructors interested in teaching an excerpt from the novel, choosing two or three related chapters might work best. For example, assigning "The Memory of Waits," "The Mouse Woman," and "Chata" together presents the opportunity to explore the idea of service at the center of the novel. Because these three chapters focus on women working and women passing on knowledge of work to other women, they also highlight the ways that women's communities are forged through service. Questions for discussion might include:

> Is service synonymous with work? Or is it more akin to a worldview?
>
> How does gender, ethnicity, and class affect each character's views of service?
>
> What knowledge do Milia, Oralia, and Chata pass on to Soveida?

How are Milia, Soveida, Oralia, and Chata related to each other and what is the meaning of that relationship?

Some students may feel challenged by the way this novel blends English and Spanish together. For Chávez, not italicizing the Spanish words was a political decision. As she says, "It's time for readers to pick up a little Spanish." While both high school and college students should not hesitate to use a Spanish/English dictionary, many of the Spanish words and phrases become understandable in context or are translated.

Literary Contexts

Face of an Angel belongs to the emergent area of Chicana and Latina literature, a body of work that has steadily and increasingly gained national and international attention since the 1960s. There is also a transnational context for reading *Face of an Angel*. As Sonia Saldívar-Hull suggests, literature created by Chicanas often articulates and enacts "bridge feminism," a term that refers to the seminal collection of feminist writings edited by Cherríe Moraga and Gloria Anzaldúa in 1981, *This Bridge Called My Back*. That collection, and the movement it participated in, initiated a cross-cultural feminist dialogue that aimed to build alliances and solidarity among women of color. That cross-cultural awareness, as Saldívar-Hull notes, increasingly became a transnational awareness of the solidarity necessary among women of color in the Americas.

In its persistent concern with dismantling the social borders that parallel the physical border between Mexico and the United States as well as in its treatment of the difficulties faced by Mexican women, *Face of an Angel* aligns itself with Chicana texts that enact a bridge feminism. However, its articulation of alliance with women of the Americas, and in significant measure its literary genealogy, also becomes manifest in its form. The novel adopts a Latin American narrative form—the *testimonio*—made increasingly popular by working-class and poor women as a way to tell the stories of their and their communities' combined ethnic, racial, class, and gender oppression. *Face of an Angel* positions Soveida, and her life story, as representative of a multigenerational community of New Mexican, working-class Chicanas attempting to shift the direction of their lives. As such it becomes a fictional *testimonio*.

Comparative Literature

As a fictional *testimonio* that chronicles the lives of Chicana workers and reveals the multiple oppressions that these women struggle against, *Face of an Angel* can be fruitfully read against Latin American *testimonios* such as the autobiographical *An Indian Woman in Guatemala* or Domitilia Barrios de Chungara's *Let Me Speak!* In both texts, the narrative of a woman's life and her eventual confrontation with ideologies and hierarchies of domination describes, in rich detail, women's work and roles in sociohistorically specific terms. They also represent the journeys of many women. These three texts share not only a continent but a legacy of conquest and colonialism, a history of border crossings, and a struggle with Spanish and *mestizo* cultural inheritance. In very different ways, they also each address the particular challenges that women face.

With respect to U.S. literature, assigning *Face of an Angel* and Zora Neale Hurston's *Their Eyes Were Watching God* in the same course might provide the opportunity for several productive discussions. In these texts female protagonists engage in a search for self that requires a challenge to prevailing gender norms and intertwines with communal and relationship issues. As women of color, each protagonist must negotiate a place for a gendered as well as racially/ethnically defined self. Since neither Soveida nor Hurston's Janie automatically enjoys the right to speak their own truths/lives, their stories raise questions about women's silences. Formally, each text frames its story as a call from others to speak and each narrative presents itself as a woman speaking and/or writing her story.

BIBLIOGRAPHIC RESOURCES

Primary Sources

Anzaldúa, Gloria. *Borderlands/La Frontera: The New Mestiza.* 2d. ed. San Francisco: Aunt Lute Books, 1999.
———— and Cherríe Moraga, eds. *This Bridge Called My Back: Radical Writings By Women of Color.* Watertown, MA: Persephone Press, 1981.
Barrios de Chungara, Domitila, with Moema Viezzer. *Let Me Speak!: Testimony of Domitila, a Woman of the Bolivian Mines.* Trans. Victoria Ortiz. New York: Monthly Review Press, 1990.

Chavez, Denise. *Novitiates,* Dallas, Dallas Theatre Center, 1971.

———. *The Flying Tortilla Man,* Espanola, New Mexico, Northern New Mexico Community College, 1975.

———. *The Adobe Rabbit,* Taos, Taos Community Auditorium, 1979.

———. *Sí, Hay Posada,* Albuquerque, Nuestro Teatro, 1980.

———. *How Junior Got Throwed in the Joint,* Santa Fe, State Penitentiary of New Mexico, 1981.

———. "The Step: Monologue for a Woman." *New America.* Vera Norwood, ed. Albuquerque: University of New Mexico Press, 1982.

———, and Chávez and Nita Luna. *Hecho en México.* Albuquerque, Kimo Theatre, 1983.

———. *El Mas Pequeno de Mis Hijos,* Albuquerque, Kimo Theatre, 1983.

———. *Plaza,* Albuquerque, Kimo Theatre, 1984; New York, Festival Latino de Nueva York, September 1984; Edinburgh, Scotland Arts Festival, September 1984.

———. *The Last of the Menu Girls.* Houston: Arte Publico Press, 1986.

———. *Novenas Narrativas,* Tour of Southwestern and U.S. cities, 1986–87.

———. "The King and Queen of Comezon" and "Love Poem." *Las Mujeres Hablan.* Tey Diana Rebolledo et al., ed. Albuquerque: El Norte Publications, 1988.

———. "La Comadre Braulia." *Sin Embargo/Nevertheless: A Woman's Journal.* Rowena A. Rivera, ed. Albuquerque: University of New Mexico Press, 1988.

———. "Novena Narrativas y Ofrendas Nuevomexicanas." *Chicana Creativity and Criticism: Charting New Frontiers in American Literature.* Maria Herrera-Sobek and Helena Maria Viramontes, eds. Houston: Arte Público P, 1988.

———. *Women in the State of Grace,* Grinnell, Iowa, Grinnell College, 1989; produced nationally since 1993.

———. "Heat and Rain: Testimonio." *Breaking Boundaries: Latina Writing and Critical Readings.* Asuncion Horno-Delgado et al., eds. Amherst : University of Massachusetts Press, 1989.

———. "Plaza." *New Mexico Plays.* David Richard Jones, ed. Albuquerque: University of New Mexico Press, 1989.

———. "Chata." *Iguana Dreams: New Latino Fiction.* Delia Poey and Virgil Suarez. eds. New York: Harper Perennial, 1992.

————. "Saints." *Mirrors beneath the Earth: Short Fiction by Chicano Writers.* Ray Gonzalez, ed. East Haven, CT: Curbstone Press, 1992.

————. *The Woman Who Knew the Language of Animals/La Mujer Que Sabía El Idioma de Los Animales.* New York: Houghton Mifflin, 1993.

————. *Face of an Angel.* New York: Farrar, Straus, and Giroux, 1994.

————. "The McCoy Hotel." *Growing up Chicana/o.* Tiffany Ana Lopez, ed. New York: William Morrow, 1995.

————. "The Wedding." *Daughters of the Fifth Sun: A Collection of Latina Fiction and Poetry.* Bryce Milligan et al., eds. New York: Riverhead Books, 1995.

————. "Grand Slam." *Latina: Women's Voices from the Borderlands.* Lillian Castillo-Speed, ed. New York: Simon and Schuster, 1995.

————. "Missss Rede!" *Walking the Twilight II: Women Writers of the Southwest.* Kathryn Wilder, ed. Flagstaff: Northland, 1996.

————. "The Closet." *The Floating Borderlands: Twenty-five years of U.S. Hispanic Literature.* Lauro Flores, ed. Seattle: University of Washington Press, 1998.

————. "The Last of the Menu Girls." *Norton Anthology of American Literature.* Nina Baym, ed. 5th ed. New York: Norton, 1998.

————. *Loving Pedro Infante.* 1st ed. New York: Farrar, Straus, and Giroux, 2001.

————. *Por el Amor de Pedro Infante: Una Novella.* Trans. Ricardo Aguilar Melantzón and Beth Pollack. New York: Vintage Español, 2002.

Hurston, Zora Neale. *Their Eyes Were Watching God.* 1937. Perennial Library Series. Series ed. Henry Louis Gates, Jr. New York: Harper and Row, 1990.

Menchú, Rigoberta. *I, Rigoberta Menchú: An Indian Woman in Guatemala.* 1983. Intro by Elisabeth Burgos-Debray, ed. Trans. Ann Wright. London: Verso, 1984.

Secondary Sources

Interviews

"Carrying the Message: Denise Chávez on the Politics of Chicana Becoming." By Marilyn Mehaffy and AnaLouise Keating. *Aztlan* 26, no.1 (2001): 127–56.

"Denise Chávez." By Annie O. Eysturoy. In *This Is about Vision: Interviews with Southwestern Writers.* William Balassi, John F. Crawford, and Annie O. Eysturoy, eds. Albuquerque : University of New Mexico Press, 1990. 157–69.

"Denise Chávez." By Larry Ahrens. *Writing the Southwest.* Audiocassette. Albuquerque: University of New Mexico Press, 1988.

"Denise Chávez: Chicana Woman Writer Crossing Borders." By Elizabeth Brown-Guillory. *South-Central-Review* 16, no.1 (1999): 30–43.

"Denise Chávez: 'It's All One Language Here.'" By William Clark. *Publishers Weekly* 241, no. 33 (1994): 77–78.

Interview of Denise Chávez. By Theresa Delgadillo. Las Cruces, New Mexico, March 14, 1999.

"The Spirit of Humor: Denise Chávez." By Bridget A. Kevane and Juanita Heredia. *Latina Self-Portraits: Interviews with Contemporary Women Writers.* Bridget A. Kevane and Juanita Heredia, eds. Albuquerque: University of New Mexico Press, 2000.

"Denise Chávez." By David King Dunaway and Sara L. Spurgeon. *Writing the Southwest.* Ed. Sara L. Spurgeon. New York: Plume, 1995.

Articles

Budd, Benita. "Playwright Sees through Eyes of Mexican Workers." *Performance* (April 8, 1983): 6.

Candelaria, Cordelia Chávez. "The 'Wild Zone' Thesis as Gloss in Chicana Literary Study." In *Chicana Critical Issues.* Norma Alarcon, ed. Berkeley: Third Woman Press, 1993. 21–31.

Carr, Irene Campos. Review of *Face of an Angel. Belles Lettres: A Review of Books by Women* 10, no.2 (1995): 35.

Castillo, Debra A. "The Daily Shape of Horses: Denise Chávez and Maxine Hong Kingston." *Dispositio* 16, no. 41 (1991): 29–43.

———. "In a Subjunctive Mood: Denise Chávez, Maxine Hong Kingston, and the Bicultural Text." *Talking Back: Toward a Latin American Feminist Literary Criticism.* Ithaca: Cornell University Press, 1992.

Castillo-Speed, Lillian. "Chicana/Latina Literature and Criticism: Reviews of Recent Books." *WLW Journal* 11, no.3 (1987): 1–4.

Chabram-Dernersesian, Angie. "I Throw Punches for My Race, but I Don't Want to Be a Man: Writing Us—Chica-nos (Girl, Us)/ Chicanas—into the Movement Script." In *Cultural Studies.* Lawrence Grossberg, Cary Nelson, and Paula A. Treichler, eds. New York: Routledge, 1992. 81–95.

Degliantoni, Lisa. Review of *Face of an Angel*. *Library Journal* 119, no.13 (1994): 124.

García, Alma M. *Chicana Feminist Thought: The Basic Historical Writings*. New York: Routledge, 1997.

Gonzalez, Maria. "Love and Conflict: Mexican American Women Writers as Daughters." *Women of Color: Mother-Daughter Relationships in 20th-Century Literature*. Elizabeth Brown-Guillory, ed. Austin: University of Texas Press, 1996. 153–71.

Graeber, L. Review of *Face of an Angel*. *New York Times Book Review*, 17 December 1995: 36.

Heard, Martha E. "The Theatre of Denise Chávez: Interior Landscapes with 'Sabor Nuevomexicano.'" *Americas Review* 16, no. 2 (1988): 83–91.

Hedges, Elaine and Shelley Fisher Fishkin, eds. *Listening to Silences: New Essays in Feminist Criticism*. New York: Oxford University Press, 1994.

Houston, Robert. Review of *Face of an Angel*. *New York Times Book Review* 25 September 1994: 20.

Joyce, Alice. Review of *Face of an Angel*. *Booklist* 91, no. 2 (1994): 110–11.

Kelley, Margot. "A Minor Revolution: Chicano/a Composite Novels and the Limits of Genre." *Ethnicity and the American Short Story*. Julia Brown, ed. New York: Garland, 1997. 63–84.

Kevane, Bridget. "The Hispanic Absence in the North American Literary Canon." *Journal of American Studies* 35, no. 1 (2001): 95–109.

Madsen, Deborah L. "Denise Chávez." *Understanding Contemporary Chicana Literature*. Columbia: University of South Carolina Press, 2000. 135–65.

Martínez, Oscar J., ed. *U.S.-Mexico Borderlands: Historical and Contemporary Perspectives*. Jaguar Books on Latin America, no. 11. Wilmington, Delaware: Scholarly Resources, 1996.

McQueen, Lee. Review of *Loving Pedro Infante*. *Library Journal* 126, no. 6 (2001): 132.

Mena, Jennifer. "Women on the Verge: Four Brash Latina Writers Transform the Literary Landscape." *Hispanic* 8, no. 2 (1995): 22–25.

Miller, Susan. Review of *Face of an Angel*. *Newsweek* (October 17, 1994): 77–78.

Moran, Julio. "My Dream Was to Work at the Dairy Queen." *Los Angeles Times*. 9 November 1994: E1, E4.

Moscoso, Eunice. Review of *Face of an Angel*. *Hispanic* 8, no. 2 (1995): 80–82.

Muchnick, Laurie. Review of *Face of An Angel*. *Village Voice Literary Supplement* 8 November 1994: 17–8.

Nericcio, William. Review of *Face of an Angel*. *World Literature Today* 69 (1995): 792.

Papers, Denise Chávez 1965–1987. Center for Southwest Research, General Library, University of New Mexico Press.

Quintana, Alvina E. *Home Girls: Chicana Literary Voices*. Philadelphia: Temple University Press, 1996.

Rebolledo, Tey Diana."Tradition and Mythology: Signatures of Landscape in Chicana Literature." *The Desert Is No Lady: Southwestern Landscapes in Women's Writing and Art*. Vera Norwood and Janice Monk, eds. New Haven: Yale University Press, 1987. 96–124.

————. *Women Singing in the Snow: A Cultural Analysis of Chicana Literature*. Tucson: University of Arizona Press, 1995.

Saldívar-Hull, Sonia. *Feminism on the Border: Chicana Gender Politics and Literature*. Berkeley: University of California Press, 2000.

Sandoval, Chela. *Methodology of the Oppressed*. Minneapolis: University of Minnesota Press, 2000.

Barbara Brinson Curiel

Sandra Cisneros, *Woman Hollering Creek and Other Stories*

New York: Random House, 1991.

Textual Overview

Woman Hollering Creek (1991), Sandra Cisneros's third book, addresses many topics and concerns raised in her earlier works of poetry and fiction. While representing the experiences of Latinas at different life stages, Cisneros focuses on linguistic, cultural, and artistic hybridity and represents the persistence of Mexican culture in the lives of Mexican Americans. Most of the protagonists in this collection are girls and women confronted with confining gender roles and definitions of so-called "proper womanhood." Most successful in overcoming these gender constraints are the many artist protagonists, who through creativity and innovation liberate themselves from the traditional "mythic" roles allotted to women within the culture.

Historical Context

This collection presents the vitality of the U.S.-Mexico border. The Treaty of Guadalupe Hidalgo settled the Mexican War in 1848 and awarded the United States with the region now known at the American Southwest. The region's historical connections to First and Third Worlds, and the vigorous economic development of the Southwest in the late nineteenth and the twentieth centuries, has created a constant influx of immigrants into the region from Latin America and especially from Mexico. This constant stream of Latin American immigration, coupled with the discrimination and marginalization of Latino peoples in the United States, has reinforced Latino cultural practices and the Spanish language in the United States. Cisneros's writing highlights the migration, poverty, discrimination, and cultural vitality and fluidity that characterizes Chicano culture.

Biographical Background

Sandra Cisneros was born in 1954 in Chicago to a Mexican immigrant father and a Mexican American mother. Her father, who came to the United States as a young adult, moved his family every few years between Chicago and in Mexico City during Cisneros's early childhood. In 1966, when Cisneros was eleven, her family bought a run-down but permanent home, which ended their frequent migration between Mexico and the United States. This house and the Puerto Rican neighborhood in which it was located became the backdrop for Cisneros's first book, *The House on Mango Street* (1984). Her collection of poems *My Wicked Wicked Ways* appeared in 1987 and was followed by *Woman Hollering Creek* (1991) and another collection of poems, *Loose Woman* (1995).

Cisneros holds a B.A. degree in English from Loyola University and an M.F.A. in creative writing from the University of Iowa Writer's Workshop. She was recipient of two National Endowment for the Arts Fellowships and, in 1995, the prestigious MacArthur Foundation Fellowship. She has taught as a professor of creative writing at a number of universities, including: the University of California at Berkeley, University of California at Irvine, University of Michigan at Ann Arbor, and University of New Mexico at Albuquerque. She has contributed to numerous periodicals, including *Imagine, Glamour, The New York Times, Los Angeles Times, Village Voice,* and *Revista Chicano-Riqueña.*

Reception of the Text

When the *Los Angeles Times Magazine* published the title story of *Woman Hollering Creek* as part of its summer fiction issue in 1990, Miguel Sanchez Gracia's letter to the editor characterized the story as a "masterpiece of derogatory terms against Hispanic immigrants" and accused Cisneros of gloating in her story over the "mistaken habits" of working-class Latinos whose labor ironically helps to finance the university educations of their better-off kin. Gracia accused Cisneros of portraying unsavory sides of Latino culture and slandering fellow Latinos. This type of critique concerning the appropriateness of the author's perspective, though not so common in print, regularly emerges in response, not only to Cisneros's work but also to other feminist writers of color who critique issues of gender equity and male privilege. Some readers prefer to see stereotypical Latino representations of romantic or idealized cultural traditions. Cisneros's writing, like that of many other feminist writers, challenges confining and debilitating cultural representations that perpetuate views and subsequent practices that systematically devalue and oppress women.

In contrast to this predictable critique, poet and novelist Barbara Kingsolver reviewed *Woman Hollering Creek* for the *Los Angeles Times* in 1991, immediately after its publication. In her appraisal Kingsolver credits Cisneros for successfully translating her poetic language into prose and provides numerous examples of the book's linguistic innovation and vitality. She argues that these stories are not so much prose as expanded poems with dialogue.

Major Themes and Critical Issues

The stories in *Woman Hollering Creek* are divided into three sections. The first, entitled "My Lucy Friend Who Smells Like Corn," portrays young girls struggling for a sense of belonging and connection within an inhospitable world of indifferent family members, callous teachers, and confining cultural traditions that value and distrust idealized forms of feminine beauty. As in *The House on Mango Street,* patriarchal notions of family are demystified and problematized in feminist terms. In the section's title story, Esperanza, the young protagonist, seeks refuge from her grandmother's house, where she sleeps "alone on the fold-out chair in the living room" (4). Like many of the other female characters portrayed in this text, Esperanza seeks to escape a confining, culturally coded domestic condition that is symbolically represented by her grandmother's house. Ultimately she finds comfort in the sustaining connections she makes with other females. Her idealization of her girlfriend Lucy's house, occupied by many sisters and a mother becomes apparent when she comments "there ain't no boys . . . Only girls and one father who is never home hardly"(4).

"Mexican Movies" and "Barbie-Q" girls also absorb and comment critically upon popular models of womanhood and manhood from both the United States and Mexico. In "Mexican Movies" the children observe traditional gender roles both on the screen and through the behavior of their parents in the audience. On screen, "Pedro Armendariz [is] in love with his boss's wife, only she's nothing but trouble" (12) and "Pedro Infante . . . sings riding a horse and wears a big sombrero and . . . the ladies throw flowers from a balcony" (12). Idealized through the mass media, these distinct gender role models are mirrored by the parents. When the narrator's baby brother begins to cry, she complains, "Papa doesn't move when he's watching a movie and Mama sits with her legs bunched beneath her like an accordion because she's afraid of rats"(13). The responsibility of tending to the baby's needs falls upon the daughter in light of the parent's impasse— the mother stuck in fear and the father in his sense of masculine entitlement.

In "Barbie-Q" deprived girls are seduced by the politics of the advertising industry with dreams of glamour, romance, and success embodied by Barbie, the American icon of feminine perfection. They internalize the promises of professional and romantic success that are supposed to come with the right wardrobe, and yet at the same time they create their own subversive understanding of Barbie and female success. For example, with their Barbie dolls, the girls create a homosocial ideal: "Ken's invisible, right? Because we don't have money for a stupid boy doll when we'd both rather ask for a new Barbie outfit next Christmas" (14–15). They also improvise a doll dress from an old sock and buy a fire-damaged doll sold at a discount, even though one of her feet has melted. They realize the capitalist version of feminine perfection is flawed at its foundation, yet the girls still find Barbie to be full of glamorous possibility.

The second section, "One Holy Night," features a series of adolescent protagonists confronted with the issues of identity and sexuality. The title story also introduces the critical representation of romantic love that reappears throughout the book. "One Holy Night" probes the contradictions between romantic expectations and social reality in the life of the protagonist. The eighth-grade protagonist expects metaphysical transformation from her first sexual encounter: "I wanted it come undone like gold thread, like a tent full of birds" (28). This expectation is at first fulfilled when she believes that her sexual initiation has made her "wise" (31). By the end of the story, however, she is pregnant, shamed, and exiled to relatives in Mexico. There, when other girls ask her what sex with a man is like, she replies, "It's a bad joke. When you find out you'll be sorry." (35). The fact that her lover turns out to be a serial killer of young girls who has seduced her with a fabricated mythic identity of royal Mayan descent further legitimates her sense of having been duped.

The final section, "There Was a Man, There Was a Woman" features adult women protagonists. Their struggles are related to those represented in the earlier sections because like them, they seek autonomy from patriarchal control in history, religious ritual and everyday life. Cisneros also undermines the cultural and social notions that consider single womanhood to be taboo by representing single women as independent, successful, and powerful. Conventional romantic love, courtship, and marriage, however, thematically connect the section's major stories.

In the book's title story Cisneros revises the Mexican myth of *La Llorona* (the Weeping Woman), an icon of female suffering and rage on par with the Western myth of Medea. Like many other Chicana writers and visual artists, Cisneros rewrites the principal icons of Mexican womanhood: *La Llorona, La Virgen de Guadalupe, La Adelita,* and *La Malinche* in order to reinscribe them in powerful and active—rather than suffering and passive—terms. This story also addresses the themes of romantic expectation and domestic violence in women's lives on both sides of the U.S.-Mexico border.

In "Woman Hollering" Cleófilas, the protagonist, gets her ideas about romantic love from television soap operas, movies, songs, and romance novels. She has internalized the definition of love promoted on the soap operas, which she articulates as "to suffer for love is good. The pain all sweet somehow" (45). However, when she marries Juan Pedro and moves with him to the U.S. side of the border, her dream of romantic fulfillment through marriage turns into a nightmare of poverty, isolation, and violence. Like the protagonist in "One Holy Night," Cleófilas comes to the realization that her acculturation in the popular mythology of romantic love has left her vulnerable, and she is pressed by her husband's violent outbursts to reach out to other women for help. She deliberately chooses the shame of returning to her father's house with her small child, her pregnant belly, and no husband rather than continue to risk her life as a married woman.

The characters Graciela and Felice are portrayed as Latinas who reject the traditional models of female passivity and suffering. Felice, who drives Cleófilas to the bus station, is a single woman comfortable driving a pickup truck. Cleófilas ponders in wonder: "the pickup was hers. She herself had chosen it. She herself was paying for it" (55). They drive over the Woman Hollering Creek, whose name has puzzled

Cleófilas throughout the story. She has wondered whether the woman who hollers does so out of "pain or rage" (56). When the pickup is over the creek, Felice yells "as loud as any mariachi" in a celebratory way. (55). This outcry ignites Cleófilas's awareness and she realizes that it is possible for women to use their voices to express their emotions whether they be pain, rage, or loud laughter. At the end of the story, Cleófilas is surprised to find a cry "gurgling out of her own throat . . . like water" (56). Cleófilas returns to Mexico with a new self-knowledge and an awareness of other women who have renegotiated Latina womanhood in their own way. Other stories in this section represent the protagonists as artists, active cultural agents for change who creatively challenge impractical convention. Many of these protagonists are single women in relationships with married men. Their critique of romance, courtship, and marriage hinges on a confrontation between romantic expectation and social reality. For example, Lupe, the protagonist of "Bien Pretty," recalls the beginning of her failed affair with her married lover: Her Prince Charming arrived not on a white horse but in an exterminator's van. Cisneros brings romantic conventions down from the lofty and idealized levels typical in art, literature, and popular culture to the more banal realities of everyday life.

Lupe gradually heals from her inevitably failed romance by listening to and gaining strength from, as if for the first time, other women's voices within her community. Challenging the romantic model omnipresent in soap operas, Lupe replaces resigned and suffering images of womanhood with images of the empowered women in her own life. This enables her to reimagine the woman in love, to allow for the possibility of both passion and power. In critiquing masculine dominance in Mexican and Chicano culture, Cisneros finds a solution that comes from a devalued part of the culture itself. Cisneros locates a woman-affirming part of her own cultural experience.

At the end of the story Lupe completes a painting she had envisioned when she first met her lover: a new version of the popular painting of the Prince Popocatépetl and Princess Ixtaccíhuatl volcano myth. The classic positioning of these two figures—the man on top and the woman dead or sleeping beneath him—reinforces the traditional association between men and dominance over women. The original myth is also a tragedy in which love causes suffering.

In Lupe's new version of this popular painting, the lovers' positions are reversed.

Lupe's revised representation expresses the kind of passion and power she desires for herself and for other women. Placing the Princess Ixta in the upright position and Prince Popo reclining disconnects the traditional associations between men and activity and women and passivity.

Pedagogical Issues and Suggestions

Students' critical reception of this text may rely on their ability to question stereotypical representations of Latinos and Latinas in U.S. culture. In all disciplines, but especially in women's studies, it is important to underscore the similarities as well as the differences among women's experiences across sociocultural categories and to discourage students from seeing certain kinds of women's oppression as problems that occur only in racialized or ethnic groups. This is particularly the case in the representation of domestic violence, teen pregnancy, and other experiences often associated by the mass media with poor and racialized communities. Cisneros's analysis, although culturally specific, also emphasizes commonalities among women who challenge oppressive situations through artistic expression, relationships and collaboration with other women, and an unflinching critique of cultural definitions of "proper" womanhood.

The text can be used to prompt students to think about how the cultural models for womanhood are operative in their own lives. It can be used to get students to write about the gender icons that have influenced them, as well as to prompt them to revise these myths to generate their own more useful concepts of gender. Students can also use these narratives as models for their own parodies or critiques of confining cultural forms: soap operas, historical narratives, romance novels, folk stories, movies, toys, and popular visual arts are all appropriated in various critical ways by Cisneros. These cultural forms and objects can also be used by students to reshape the world through writing in ways that express their utopian ideals.

Literary Contexts

In *Understanding Contemporary Chicana Literature* Deborah Madsen points out that Chicano literature is part of the resurgence of writing by

American women of color that surfaced after the 1960s Civil Rights movement. However, it is important to add that the Chicano literature produced in this period predominantly featured a masculinist representation of community and identified racial formation/relations as the community's principle cultural concern in the United States. In the face of this, Chicana writers developed a distinctive feminist perspective that connected gender oppression with racial and class oppressions. Consciousness of the overlapping axes of race, class, and gender became the foundation for feminists of color.

Madsen lists the characteristic concerns of Chicana literature as the reconstruction of Chicana literary history through the validation of popular speech and the reinvention of traditional icons and forms. She states "in important ways the subject of Chicana writing is the Chicana subject . . . This is a literature that embodies the quest for self-definition"(5).

Comparative Literature

This text fits well into a variety of contexts, but within a course on women's culture it can be taught successfully alongside a variety of canonical and noncanonical works about women's development and cultural production. Cisneros's fluid appropriation of traditional forms and texts can be compared to the narrative quilt work of African American artist Faith Ringgold. Cisneros's representation of girlhood and young womanhood in the United States can be taught alongside works such as Willa Cather's *O Pioneers!* and *My Antonia,* and women's literary classics such as Charlotte Perkins Gilman's *The Yellow Wallpaper* and Kate Chopin's *The Awakening.* Her strong sociocultural critique of women's place fits well with works by other women writers of color, like Harriet Jacobs's *Incidents in the Life of Slave Girl* and Maria Campbell's *Halfbreed,* as well as with immigrant narratives like Anzia Yezierska's *Bread Givers.*

In Chicano studies courses, *Woman Hollering Creek* obviously can be easily included in courses on literature, women, and border studies because it fruitfully represents the hybridity and suppleness of border cultures. In courses on the American short story, it can be used to talk about narrative innovation, the appropriation and revision of other sources, and international influences on the contemporary American narrative.

BIBLIOGRAPHIC RESOURCES

Primary Sources

Cisneros, Sandra. *The House on Mango Street.* Houston: Arte Público, 1983; New York: Vintage Books, 1991.

————.*My Wicked, Wicked Ways.* Berkeley, CA.: Third Woman Press, 1987; New York: Alfred A. Knopf, 1992.

————.*Woman Hollering Creek and Other Stories.* New York: Vintage, 1991.

————.*Loose Woman.* New York: Vintage Contemporaries, 1995.

Secondary Sources

Brady, Mary Pat. "The Contrapuntal Genographies of *Woman Hollering Creek* and Other Stories." *American Literature* 71, no. 1 (March 1999): 117–50.

Carbonell, Ana Maria. "From Llorona to Gritona: Coatlicue in Feminist Tales byViramontes and Cisneros." *MELUS* 24, no. 2 (1999): 53–74.

Curiel, Barbara Brinson. "The General's Pants: A Chicana Feminist (Re)Vision of the Mexican Revolution in Sandra Cisneros's "Eyes of Zapata." *Western American Literature* 35, no. 4 (winter 2001): 403–427.

Doyle, Jacqueline. "Haunting the Borderlands: La Llorona in Sandra Cisneros's *Woman Hollering Creek.*" *Frontiers* 16, no.1 (1996): 5–35.

García, Alesia. "Politics and Indigenous Theory in Leslie Marmon Silko's 'Yellow Woman' and Sandra Cisneros's *Woman Hollering Creek. Folklore, Literature, and Cultural Theory: Collected Essays.* Cathy L. Preston, ed. New York: Garland, 1995. 3–21.

Gonzalez, Maria. "Love and Conflict: Mexican American Women Writers as Daughters." *Women of Color: Mother-Daughter Relationships in Twentieth-Century Literature.* Elizabeth Brown-Guillory, ed. Austin: University of Texas Press, 1996. 153–71.

Gracia, Miguel Sanchez. Letter to the editor. *Los Angeles Times Magazine.* 19 August 1990, 4.

Griffin, Susan E. "Resistance and Reinvention in Sandra Cisneros's *Woman Hollering Creek.*" *Ethnicity and the American Short Story.* Julia Brown, ed. New York: Garland, 1997. 85–96.

Madsen, Deborah L. *Understanding Contemporary Chicana Literature.* Columbia: University of South Carolina Press, 2000.

Mullen, Harryette. "'A Silence Between Us Like a Language': The Untranslatability of Experience in Sandra Cisneros's *Woman Hollering Creek.*" *MELUS* 21 (1996): 3–20.

Payant, Katherine B. "Borderland Themes in Sandra Cisneros's *Woman Hollering Creek.*" *The Immigrant Experience in North American Literature: Carving Out a Niche.* Katherine B. Payant and Toby Rose, eds. Westport, CT: Greenwood, 1999. 95–108.

Saldivar-Hull, S. "Women Hollering Transfronteriza Feminisms." *Cultural Studies* 13, no.2 (1999): 251–262.

Thomson, Jeff. "What Is Called Heaven: Identity in Sandra Cisneros's *Woman Hollering Creek.*" *Studies in Short Fiction* 31, no. 3 (summer 1994): 415–24.

Wyatt, Jean. "On Not Being *La Malinche:* Border Negotiations of Gender in Sandra Cisneros's "Never Marry a Mexican" and "Woman Hollering Creek." *Tulsa Studies in Women's Literature* 14, no. 2 (1995): 243–271.

Frances R. Aparicio

Judith Ortiz Cofer, *Silent Dancing: A Partial Remembrance of a Puerto Rican Childhood*

Houston: Arte Público Press, 1990.

Textual Overview

The book *Silent Dancing* is a collection of poems and short stories that together constitute an autobiographical narrative. Based on the memories of Cofer's childhood, the poems and stories are reflections and remembrances about her experiences growing up in two places, Puerto Rico and New Jersey. The memories focus mostly on the women in her family, her grandmother and mother in particular, and also on the figure of her father, who served in the U.S. Navy. The movement between her hometown of Hormigueros, Puerto Rico, with the traditional cultural and gender values embodied in its inhabitants, and Patterson, New Jersey, where she lived six months per year and faced different gender values, an urban culture, and the reality of being an ethnic minority, becomes a recurring structure throughout the book.

Judith Ortiz Cofer writes about the ways in which the women in her family and in her town negotiated their power and freedom with the traditional values and expectations inherent in the traditions of the times; about how women told stories that became cautionary tales against men and thus articulated the various gender ideologies with which the women in the family struggled; about her experiences in school both on the island and in New Jersey; about how she negotiated her identity with and through English and Spanish; about how her class identity in her hometown in Puerto Rico shifted when she moved to New Jersey; about the ways in which her mother and father adjusted to life in the United States and reacted to racism and discrimination; and about her experiences as a young adolescent in love.

Overall, the book offers a profound reflection on the power of memory, which has the potential to sustain and nurture someone throughout the difficult situations that result from change and displacement. It is a reflection on mother-daughter relationships as well as a commentary on how U.S. Puerto Ricans negotiate between two cultures and create new identity paradigms, or "habits of movement," as Cofer refers to the constant migration between Puerto Rico and the United States.

Historical Context

Judith Ortiz Cofer grew up in the 1950s and early 1960s, a historical period in Puerto Rico characterized by industrialization on the island and the mainland and by a significant migration flux from Puerto Rico to the United States. Puerto Rico has maintained a colonial relation to the United States since 1898. Puerto Ricans were granted U.S. citizenship by birth through the Jones Act of 1917 as a means for recruiting Puerto Ricans into the U.S. army during World War I. Because of their U.S. citizenship Puerto Ricans have, unlike other U.S. Latino minorities, been permitted to travel back and forth between the mainland and the island. This transnational flow has been informed mostly by the labor needs of the U.S. economy, which has led to the recruitment of cheap labor from the island, as well as by the U.S. government's concern for establishing population control on the island. Migration was one of the measures used to depopulate the island, in addition to the sterilization of a significant number of Puerto Rican women.

The fact that Judith Ortiz Cofer's father served in the U.S. Navy is an example of the ways in which the U.S. presence and institutions affected the lives of Puerto Ricans and their families. While Puerto Ricans were drafted into the Army and the Navy, these positions also guaranteed a certain social status and economic privilege, particularly among the working-class and the poor. Thus, Cofer's family was considered privileged in their hometown of Hormigueros, while in Patterson, New Jersey, they lived in "El Building" among many working-poor Puerto Rican families who were considered uneducated and inferior by the dominant society, even though these very families were essential to the growing industrial economy of the Northeast. Numerous Puerto Rican women, for instance, worked in the garment industry and were the backbone of its production. By the 1980s, most of these factories had moved to developing countries, and the industrial economy shifted to a service economy, leaving many of these women unemployed and in need of job retraining.

Finally, it is also important to consider that in the context of education and schooling, Judith Ortiz Cofer's stories—"Primary Lessons" and "One More Lesson"—present reflections about schools on the island and on the mainland. While the systems differed as to the ways in which they normalized dominant ideologies of race, class, language, and social norms, both of the educational experiences offer evidence of the ways in which a colonial education was implemented among Puerto Ricans. Just as on the island English was established as a main language of instruction and was an obligatory subject next to Spanish, on the mainland Spanish was considered an obstacle to academic success. Thus in both cases, the values and ideologies of a colonial education were being enacted.

Biographical Background

Born February 24, 1952, in Hormigueros, Puerto Rico, Judith Ortiz Cofer moved to the United States in 1956 at the age of four. Her family first settled in New Jersey and later moved to the South. She received her bachelor's degree from Augusta College in 1974 and earned her master's degree at Florida Atlantic University in 1977. She also attended Oxford University in 1977. From 1978 to 1981, she was the poetry editor for the *Florida Arts Gazette.* She now lives on a farm in rural Louisville, Georgia, and is the Franklin professor of English and the director of the creative writing program at the University of Georgia.

She has received many awards for her numerous books and essays. In 1989 she was nominated for the Pulitzer Prize for her first novel, *The Line of the Sun.* That same year she received a National Endowment for the Arts fellowship in poetry. She was awarded a PEN/Martha Albrand Special Citation in nonfiction for *Silent Dancing,* the Anisfield Wolf Book Award for *The Latin Deli,* and her work has been selected for the Syndicated Fiction Project. She has received several other fellowships from the NEA and the Witter Bynner Foundation for poetry. Her book *An Island Like You: Stories from the Barrio* was named a Best Book of the Year in 1995–1996 by the American Library Association. She is the 1998 recipient of the Christ-Janner Award in Creative Research from the University of Georgia. Her works include *Latin Women Pray* (1980); *The Native Dancer*

(1981); *Among the Ancestors* (1981); *Peregrina* (1986); *Terms of Survival* (1987); *The Line of the Sun* (1989); *Silent Dancing: A Partial Remembrance of a Puerto Rican Childhood* (1990); *The Latin Deli* (1993); *An Island like you: Stories of the Barrio* (1995); and *The Year of our Revolution: New and Selected Stories and Poems* (1998). Her poems have been published in the *Apalachee Quarterly, Kalliope, Kansas Quarterly, Poem, Prairie Schooner,* and *Southern Humanities Review.*

Reception of the Text

Silent Dancing has been very well received in mainstream literary circles as well as among U.S. Latino literary critics. While Cofer's autobiographical stories and poems have captured the attention of major critics, and the mainstream has also praised Cofer for the quality of her style and use of language, U.S. Latino critics have focused much more on the cultural reflections in which *Silent Dancing* invites readers to engage, particularly on the cultural displacement of Puerto Ricans, the colonial conditions that have fueled P.R. transnational migration, and the ways in which Cofer and her family were subjects of racism and marginalization in New Jersey. One of the most interesting issues regarding the reception of this and other Latina autobiographical narratives is the degree to which they are more often appraised for their sociological or anthropological value and overlooked in terms of their aesthetic merit.

Major Themes and Critical Issues

Silent Dancing foregrounds a number of themes and issues related to gender and culture among U.S. Puerto Ricans. It also explores other general issues, such as childhood, development, and the role of oral tradition and memory in fiction. Stories such as "Casa" and "Tales Told under the Mango Tree" demonstrate the important role that oral traditions and *cuentos* (stories) had in the transmission of a sort of organic feminist knowledge among the women in the family. These were the narratives that helped younger women make decisions about relationships, traditional gender roles, and societal expectations and that would also suggest ways of transgressing such norms. The stories

"More Room," *"Quinceanera,"* "Marina," "Silent Dancing," and "Some of the Characters" serve as examples of how women in real life internalized, negotiated, and transgressed gender norms. For instance, in "More Room" Cofer celebrates how her grandmother asked her spouse to build an additional room to the house, in which he would sleep. This was her method of birth control at a time when women did not have other options available. Issues about sexuality, reproduction, and the ways in which traditional societies marginalize women who transgress expected gender roles reappear throughout the poems and short stories.

In terms of cultural identity, *Silent Dancing* explores the conflicts and negotiations that individuals confront as a result of migration. These conflicts include the relationship of language to identity, as in the use of English and Spanish; the ways in which Cofer and her family were discriminated against in the United States; and even the daughter's disavowal of her mother's tropical body movements and fashion style in the context of urban Patterson, where she did not fit in. The larger historical context that informs these identity negotiations among bicultural U.S. Puerto Ricans is the colonial relationship of the United States to Puerto Rico, a political structure that has affected the daily lives of all Puerto Ricans.

Finally, the book itself, as a collection of "partial remembrances," explores the complexities of memory and remembrance. While childhood is another important topic in this collection, it is clear by the end of the book that Cofer questions how we remember our childhood and whether our memories are even valid as reality and history. Rather, she proposes that we construct our own memories as a result of our own psychological needs of the present. Childhood, then, is not just the accumulation of experiences during our early years but indeed the composite picture that we create as we remember ourselves and as others remember us.

Pedagogical Issues and Suggestions

Clearly, the most central focus throughout this book is the way in which young adults are socialized into gender norms and roles and the way in which they also transgress or reject such roles. An explanation of how gender roles are established through social institutions such as family, religion, cultural myths and traditions, schooling and education, and the media will be an important preface to a larger class discussion on gender roles. Students may be asked to write an essay in which they reflect on their own gender socialization. They can focus on one real life experience in which they experienced either a conflict with or an internalization of a particular gender role. By reflecting on how they negotiated this role, and the factors and influences that led them to make a particular decision regarding gender, they will be able to understand some of the motivations that led Cofer to write about her own childhood. Students could write a memoir or even a poem to articulate this experience.

Oral traditions are also a very important component of *Silent Dancing*. A class activity in which students share in small groups an important myth, story, or fable from their own cultural heritage and discuss the impact it has had on their own values would be a valuable exercise for understanding Cofer's book. Students may talk not just about a myth or traditional text but also about the impact of a film, song, or religious practice in their lives.

In order to discuss bilingualism and the experience of learning a second language as an immigrant, the teacher may invite an individual who speaks a foreign language to come to the class unannounced and present in that language. The individual will ask students questions and prompt them to respond, reproducing in the class the stress and sense of alienation that is usually experienced by immigrant students when they are faced with learning in a language that is foreign to them. The whole class can discuss this experience afterward.

In teaching *Silent Dancing* there is the risk of perceiving the Puerto Rican culture and the U.S. culture as fixed opposites: one is traditional and rural, the other is modern and urban. Because Cofer's writing locates Puerto Rican culture in a small town in the countryside, readers may surmise that all Puerto Ricans share those same traditions. However, urban culture in San Juan, Puerto Rico, and other smaller cities on the island shares many of the modernizing influences that we see in the United States.

Media has played a central role in this modernization as has transnational migration itself. Most Puerto Ricans on the island have families, relatives, or friends who have moved to the United States. Many Puerto Ricans themselves have lived in the United States at some point in their lives. This means that cultural practices, behaviors, and values are not as fixed as they appear. They are constantly changing and being redefined by individuals themselves; by historical processes such as industrialization, migration, and political forces; and by institutions such as schools, the State, religion, and the family. Thus, it will be useful to avoid questions or discussions that would attempt to contrast the cultures or define them in fixed ways.

Literary Contexts

The first edition of *Silent Dancing* appeared in 1990 and the second in 1991. By the early 1990s, Latina writers were beginning to receive more mainstream attention than ever before, and their fictional and nonfictional works and poetry constituted a Latina boom that proposed feminist perspectives and new ways of conceptualizing the bicultural identity of U.S. Latinos. Gloria Anzaldúa's *Borderlands/La Frontera,* published in 1987, became a sort of manifesto for Latinas and for Latina lesbians. Because Anzaldúa explored in very complex and painful ways the processes by which Chicanas (Mexican-American women) were subordinated and oppressed by both traditional Mexican culture and U.S. imperialism and colonialism, her text opened the path for other Latina voices to emerge in the literary context. Thus, Cofer's text appeared at a moment when Latina autobiographical explorations were being published and widely read.

Sandra Cisneros's *The House on Mango Street,* Cherríe Moraga's *Loving in the War Years,* and Ana Castillo's earlier works were now catching the attention of mainstream publishers. These women explored larger issues of biculturalism and cultural hybridity, linguistic colonialism, gender, sexism and sexuality, and the larger experiences of their colonized communities as ethnic minorities in the United States. These topics have all been central to the U.S. dominant society as it comes to accept and give meaning to its own cultural diversification. These texts helped to offset the invisibility of U.S. Latino writers both in the United States literary canon as well as in the Latin American context. Since the mid-1990s, many of these texts by Latina authors have been translated into Spanish and distributed and marketed in Latin America and Spain.

Comparative Literature

Judith Ortiz Cofer's *Silent Dancing* contributes to the larger genre of the autobiography. In the United States, the tradition of the autobiography goes back to colonial times. The autobiography has been a favorite genre in U.S. society because it reaffirms the ethos of individualism and of hard work, in other words, the American Dream. Thus, the Latino and Latina autobiographical narratives that reaffirm this myth, such as Richard Rodríguez's *Hunger of Memory* and Esmeralda Santiago's *When I was Puerto Rican,* have been much more successful in terms of sales and readership than those works which critique and challenge mainstream American ideology. Cofer's book, while it does not offer a particular perspective on social mobility or on the American Dream, has been equally successful in establishing a wide readership. This may be the result of its dual emphasis on childhood experiences and gender inequality framed and influenced by Virginia Woolf and U.S. feminism. In this regard, it is closely connected to this particular audience of feminist readers, Latinas, and youth.

BIBLIOGRAPHIC RESOURCES

Primary Sources

Anzaldúa, Gloria. *Borderlands/La Frontera: The New Mestiza*. San Francisco: Spinsters/Aunt Lute, 1987.

Cherríe Moraga, *Loving in the War Years: Lo Que Nunca Pasó Por Sus Labios*. Boston: South End Press, 1983.

Cisneros, Sandra. *The House on Mango Street*. Houston: Arte Público, 1983.

Rodriguez, Richard. *Hunger of Memory: The Education of Richard Rodriguez*. Boston: D. R. Godine, 1982.

Santiago, Esmeralda, *When I Was Puerto Rican*. New York: Vintage, 1994.

Secondary Sources

Berg, Christine G. "'That ain't nothing but gin-talk': Storytelling in Judith Ortiz Cofer's *Silent Dancing* and August Wilson's 'Fences.'" Paper presented at the seventh National American Women Writers of Color Conference. Salisbury, MD: October 1, 1997.

"Book Marker: Judith Ortiz Cofer." *Latingirl*. (August-September 1999): 82.

Bruce-Novoa, Juan. "Ritual in Judith Ortiz Cofer's The Line of the Sun." *Confluencia: Revista Hispánica de Cultura y Literatura* 8, no.1 (fall 1992): 61–69.

———. "Judith Ortiz Cofer's Rituals of Movement." *The Americas Review* 19, no. 3–4 (winter 1991): 88–99.

Cofer, Judith Ortiz. "Puerto Rican Literature in Georgia? An Interview with Judith Ortiz Cofer." By Rafael Ocasio. *Comparative and Cultural Studies* 16, no. 41 (1991): 71–93.

————. Interview by Rafael Ocasio. *The Kenyon Review.* 14, no. 4 (fall 1992): 43–50.

————. "The Infinite Variety of the Puerto Rican Reality: An Interview with Judith Ortiz Cofer." By Rafael Ocasio. *Callaloo: A Journal of African-American and African Arts and Letters* 17, no. 3 (summer 1994): 730–42.

————. "An Interview with Judith Ortiz Cofer." By Jocelyn Barkevicius. *Speaking of the Short Story: Interviews with Contemporary Writers.* Farhat Iftekharuddin, Mary Rohrberger, and Maurice Lee. eds. Jacksonville, MS: University of Mississippi Press, 1997.

————. "And May He Be Bilingual: Notes on Writing, Teaching, and Multiculturalism." *Women/Writing/ Teaching.* J. Schmidt, ed. Albany, NY: State University of New York Press, 1998. 103–108.

Fabre, Genevieve. "Liminality, In-Betweenness and Indeterminacy: Notes toward an Anthropological Reading of Judith Ortiz Cofer's *The Line of the Sun.*" *Annales du Centre de Recherches sur l'Amerique Anglophone.* 18 (1993): 223–32.

Faymonville, Carmen. "Motherland versus Daughterland in Judith Ortiz Cofer's *The Line of the Sun.*" *The Immigrant Experience in North American Literature: Carving Out a Niche.* Katherine B. Payant and Toby Rose, eds. Westport, CT: Greenwood Press, 1999.

Foster, Elaine Dunphy. Review of *The Year of Our Revolution: Love and Revolution in the 1960s.* New York: Penguin, Putnam Books for Young Readers *Multicultural Review.* (June 1999)

Good, Jennifer. Review of *The Year of Our Revolution: Love and Revolution in the 1960s.* New York: Penguin, Putnam Books for Young Readers, Auburn, AL: ALAN Reviews. (September—December 2000).

Gregory, Lucille H. "The Puerto Rican 'Rainbow': Distortion vs. Complexities." *Children's Literature Association Quarterly* 18, no.1 (spring 1993): 29–35.

Grobman, Laurie. "The Cultural Past and Artistic Creation in Sandra Cisneros's *The House on Mango Street* and Judith Ortiz Cofer's *Silent Dancing.*" *Confluencia: Revista Hispánica de Cultura y Literatura* 11, no.1 (fall 1995): 42–29.

"Judith Cofer Named Franklin Professor." *The Franklin Chronicle* 3 (spring 2000): 1, 6.

Kallet, Marilyn and Judith Ortiz Cofer, eds. *Sleeping with One Eye Open: Women Writers and the Art of Survival.* Athens, GA: University of Georgia Press, 1999.

Lee, Sarah. "A Contradiction in Terms: Athens Author Judith Ortiz Cofer Celebrates Her Multi-Cultural Heritage." *Athens Daily News / Athens Banner Herald.* Sunday, 26 November 2000, 1E.

Maldonado, Sheila. Review of *The Year of Our Revolution: Love and Revolution in the 1960s.* New York: Penguin, Putnam Books for Young Readers. *Latingirl: The Hispanic Teen Magazine* (April/May 1999).

Maldonado-De Oliveira, Deborah. *The Flying Metaphor: Travel, Cultural Memory, and Identity in Three Puerto Rican Texts.* Ph.D. diss., Rochester: University of Rochester, November 2000.

Matuz, Roger, ed. *Contemporary Southern Writers.* Detroit, MI: St. James Press, 2000. 78–81.

"A MELUS Interview: Judith Ortiz Cofer." By Edna Acosta-Belén. *MELUS: The Journal of the Society for the Study of the Multi-Ethnic Literature of the United States* 18, no. 3 (fall 1993): 83–97.

Noguera, Nancy Soledad. *Noción, desplazamiento y género en la escritura autobiográfica de Esmeralda Santiago y Judith Ortiz Cofer.* Ph.D diss. New York: New York University, October 2000.

Pacheco, Teresa. Review of "Woman in Front of the Sun: On Becoming A Writer," by Judith Ortiz Cofer. Athens, GA: *The Georgia Library Quarterly* (winter 2000): 29.

Rangil, Viviana. "Pro-Claiming a Space: The Poetry of Sandra Cisneros and Judith Ortiz Cofer." *Multicultural Review* 9, no.3 (September 2000): 48–51, 54–55.

"Speaking in Puerto Rican: An Interview with Judith Ortiz Cofer." By Rafael Ocasio and Rita Ganey. *The Bilingual Review* 17, no. 2 (May-Aug.1992): 143–46.

"Three Books Published By UGA Press Win Honors." *Athens Banner-Herald and Athens Daily News* (Athens, GA) 27 March 2001.

Norma Cantú

Montserrat Fontes, *First Confession*

New York: W.W. Norton, 1991.

Textual Overview

It is the summer of 1947 in a Mexican border town, and nine-year-old Andrea Durcal and Victor Escalante are preparing to make their first holy communion, which will require their first confession. In search of sins to confess, the children reflect on a series of transgressions that include childhood sinful behaviors such as lying and stealing and the adult sins that include murder and adultery. This process allows the secrets and lies that pervade the adult experience to seep into the innocent yet complex world the children inhabit. The children seem intrigued by the mortal and venial sins that are out of the realm of their youthful sensibilities.

This novel is more complex than it may initially appear because the plot shifts from childhood into adulthood, when Victor commits suicide. Andrea, as the adult narrator, contends with the guilt and the pain both of the past and the present. Her absolution involves her total separation from the past, which includes both a geographical distancing from the border and Victor and a distancing from her "inner child." The plot twists and turns, leading the reader to the first confession, which concludes the main text. In the epilogue we learn of Victor's suicide and the emotional, mental, and spiritual issues that Andrea must negotiate in order to come to wholeness. The novel's title alludes to a series of "confessions" that are introduced in the epilogue and developed more fully as the plot unfolds.

Historical Context

The novel's setting, the border between Mexico and the United States, provides Fontes with an apt metaphor for the children's in-between state as they go from innocence to experience and are introduced to sinful behavior. That U.S. border literature often neglects the perspective of the Mexican side of the border is brought forth by Fontes's vivid picture of post-war behavior on both sides of the border. The decadence of the elites in the U.S. Mexican border town contrasts sharply with the destitute, the beggars, and the children who live along the Rio Grande (Rio Bravo in the book) on the Mexican side of the border.

Fontes achieves historical verisimilitude with specific references to political and cultural events in Mexico. As a child Andrea witnesses her father's sorrow when the famous bullfighter Manolete is gored to death. Victor's father, a medical doctor, goes to a northern city in the United States to study a medical specialization. Although not explicitly referenced within the text, it is interesting to ponder whether the polio scare of the 1940s and 50s motivates his study in the United States.

Because neither of Andrea's parents is from the border, the family is ostracized when the father kills a night watchman in a drunk driving accident. The novel hangs much on one pivotal summer in the protagonist's life: It encapsulates her loss of innocence, her coming to terms with the good and bad in the world, as well as her place in a socially layered household that includes servants. Although sociocultural aspects are rarely represented outside of the historical border reality, Fontes's interweaving of historical events allows her to situate the narrative and illustrate the complexity of border existence.

Biographical Background

Fontes was born in Laredo, Texas, on September 5, 1940, and raised across the river in Nuevo Laredo, Tamaulipas, until the age of nine. As was and remains the custom for prosperous Mexican families, she was sent to Catholic school in Laredo and later in Mexico City. After graduation from high school in Mexico City, she moved to California and attended Los Angeles City College and California State University at Los Angeles, earning her B.A. in English in 1966, followed by an M.A. in 1967. From 1969 to 1970, she worked as a composition instructor at the University of California at Los Angeles campus. Aside from this she also taught at Rio Hondo College (1969–77), Markham

Junior High School (1968–73), and University High School (1974–95) and remained a teacher in the Los Angeles area until her retirement in 2000.

In hopes of realizing her dream of becoming a writer, Fontes attended a creative writing extension course at UCLA in 1980 and joined a writing group that met twice a month. The first draft of *First Confession* was completed in 1984, although it was not published until 1991. Two of Fontes's novels, *Dreams of the Centaur* and *First Confession* have been listed in the California Advanced Placement reading list. Under the pseudonym Jessie Lattimore and in collaboration with Norine Dresser, Fontes also published a novel, *High Contrast*. She has also written an opera libretto that has yet to be produced. Most recently, she has written the screenplay for *First Confession* and is currently working on another novel.

Fontes, obviously influenced by the historical and political events that shaped the society she lived in as a child in Nuevo Laredo, Tamaulipas, represents the cultural clashes between Mexicans and Americans, between the poor and the elites, between men and women. The interest in Chicana literature that began in the mid-eighties clearly contributed to the publication of *First Confession* in 1991. After its publication and favorable, if sporadic, critical reception, Fontes was inspired to continue to write and published *Dreams of the Centaur* in 1996.

Reception of the Text

Although the critical reception for the novel has been slight, scholarly considerations concerning the novel's merits and contribution to borderland literature has contributed to an increased interest in Fontes's work.

Major Themes and Critical Issues

The novel's major themes center on a combination of bildungsroman/ borderland concerns. Sexuality, violence, and class and racial differences revolve around the axis formed by two characters, Victor and Andrea. The anglicized Mexican elite, the professional and upper class, coexist alongside a poverty-ridden subordinate underclass. As the novel concludes in the sixties, the gulf between the rich and the poor grows larger. The theme of social justice pervades the narrative, as the children rationalize a theft that seems to resemble the redistribution tactics of Robin Hood. The novel closes with Andrea coming to terms with Victor's suicide and with her own past. Fontes's narrative closure invites readers to join her as she explores the duality of life—the poverty and the affluence as well as the various spiritual and social complexities that emerge from this binary. Critics have noted Fontes's ability to accurately portray the post-war historical era and depict a child's point of view through an adult narrator's voice.

The novel also represents the role of religion or morality in a way that challenges our understanding of organized religion, as the character's privileged states allow for religious license. The educational and class systems appear as problematic social structures that support the elites' position regardless of its excesses. Fontes also points to traditions that perpetuate unequal gender roles. She also offers a perspective that allows readers to compare and contrast life on the Mexican side of the U.S.- Mexico border with that on the U.S. side.

Pedagogical Issues and Suggestions

Teaching *First Confession* must include lessons on Mexican culture and history. The best way to prepare is to read up on the presidency of Miguel Alemán, who was president during the prosperous and defining period of Mexican history: 1946 to 1952. Other cultural signifiers offer room for discussion: the reference to Manolete, the famous bullfighter who was gored to death in the summer of 1947; the conflict between the two groups of servants in the household and the murder of one of them; and the status of workers in general—at the restaurant, the factory, and home. Useful strategies for generating discussion include the following topics that can either be used before, during, or after students have read the novel:

> Think back to when you were nine and identify an event in your life that shaped and defined your understanding about life.
> Can you characterize the kinds of experiences that influence and inform nine year olds today? Be specific.
> Can you describe some typical summer activities for this age group?
> Can you recall a first communion experience? How old were you?
> Why is it that the nine year old, Andrea, has not gone through the first communion ritual?

Students will also benefit from a discussion of narrative structure, which will enable them to understand the issues revolving around "authenticity" and "difference." Topics that elicit discussion in terms of the structure:

> What does the epilogue offer the reader and why does Fontes include it?
> Isolate the setting, the characters, the plot, and the theme and discuss how each of these elements of fiction is shaped by the tone and the style of the narrator's voice.

Literary Contexts

In the summer of 1947, the U.S.–Mexico borderlands underwent a number of cultural and social upheavals, such as the threat of a polio epidemic, extreme poverty, and relentless heat. Unlike the protagonist of Roberta Fernandez's *Intaglio: A Novel in Six Stories,* also set around the same time, Andrea does not romanticize her border life experience. Rather than pursue this nostalgic approach, Fontes raises issues related to class and cultural differences by depicting the political background that allows the family to live on the border, where they work to earn enough capital to migrate to Mexico City. This narrative is in many ways reminiscent of Canseco del Valle's *Orquidea Negra,* a novel published in the 1950s and also set in the immediate post–World War II era in Nuevo Laredo, Tamaulipas. *Orquidea*'s romantic tone is, however, contrasted with Fontes's realism, which seems more appropriate for representing the contemporary geopolitical situation of the border area.

Comparative Literature

In terms of borderlands literature, *First Confession* stands out, for few if any texts of the border exist that represent the Mexican perspective. In terms of class and geographic perspective, *First Confession* breaks with earlier texts about the border. Like regional U.S. literatures from the South or the Northeast it deserves a place in the literary canon. Coming-of-age stories like James Baldwin's *Go Tell It on the Mountain* and immigrant narratives such as Willa Cather's *My Antonia* offer excellent companion readings for Fontes's text. Additionally, the work of Eudora Welty, Flannery O'Connor, and William Faulkner offer parallel texts of regional, religious, and social dramas that shape the characters who inhabit their fictitious worlds. The issues of inclusion and exclusion as well as the class stratification that surfaces in any analysis of these texts also emerges in Fontes's novel.

BIBLIOGRAPHIC RESOURCES

Primary Sources

Anzaldúa, Gloria. *Borderlands La Frontera: The New Mestiza.* 1st. ed. San Francisco: Aunt Lute Press, 1987.

Canseco del Valle, Margarita. *Orquidea Negra.* Monterrey, Nuevo León, MX: Impresora del Norte, 1971.

Cantú, Norma E. *Canícula Snapshots of a Girlhood en la frontera.* Albuquerque: University of New Mexico Press, 1997.

Fernandez, Roberta. *Intaglio: A Novel in Six Stories.* Houston: Arte Público Press, 1994.

Garza-Falcón, Leticia M. *Gente Decente: A Borderlands Response to the Rhetoric of Dominance.* Austin: University of Texas Press, 1998.

González, Genaro. *Only Sons.* Houston: Arte Público Press, 1994.

Gonzalez, Jovita and Eve Merriam. *Caballero: A Historical Novel.* College Station: Texas A & M University Press, 1996.

Islas, Arturo. *Rain God: A Desert Tale.* New York: Avon Books, 1991.

———. *Migrant Souls.* New York: Avon Books, 1991.

———. *La Mollie and the King of Tears: A Novel.* Albuquerque: University of New Mexico Press, 1996.

Paredes, Américo. *George Washington Gomez: A Mexicotexan Novel.* Houston: Arte Público, 1990.

Rios, Alberto Alvaro. *Curtain of Trees.* Albuquerque: University of New Mexico Press, 1999.

Saenz, Benjamin Alire. *Carry Me Like Water: A Novel.* New York: Harper Collins, 1996.

Secondary Sources

Martínez, Oscar. *Border People: Life and Society in the U.S. Mexico Borderlands.* Tucson: University of Arizona Press, 1994.

Saldívar-Hull, Sonia. *Feminism on the Border: Chicana Gender Politics and Literature.* Berkeley: University of California Press, 2000.

Zamora O'Shea, Elena. *Mesquite: A Story of the Early Spanish Settlements Between The Nueces and the Rió Grande.* College Station: Texas A & M University Press, 2000.

Tiffany Ana Lopez

Maria Irene Fornes, *The Conduct of Life*

In *Maria Irene Fornes: Plays*, New York: Performing
Arts Journal, 1986.

Textual Overview

The Conduct of Life (1985) is one of Maria Irene Fornes's most
critically acclaimed plays. This work brings together issues of politics,
gender, and sexuality to show how forms of national and domestic
violence often exist in direct relationship to one another. The play
centers on Orlando, a career military officer who interrogates and
tortures prisoners at the command of an unseen fascist regime in an
unspecified Latin American country. His goal is to steadily rise in
military rank and obtain "maximum power." In the opening scene,
Orlando vows "to eliminate all obstacles," including his wife and his
own excessive "sexual passion." Unapologetic, he graphically describes
the torture he inflicts. Fornes's purposefully disturbing dialogue illustrates the rapid pace at which Orlando becomes desensitized to the
violence demanded by his military employment and his ensuing brutal
treatment of the women in his home. Clearly obsessed with the power
he gains from interrogation and torture, Orlando cannot separate the
boundaries between military and domestic spaces. He kidnaps a homeless twelve-year-old girl named Nena and keeps her locked in the
basement, where he methodically sexually abuses her. Fellow soldier
and friend Alejo witnesses Orlando's disturbing violent behaviors in
both spaces. Yet, regardless of his revulsion to Orlando's acts, he
remains a passive bystander.

The housekeeper, Olimpia, also witnesses Orlando's acts of violence
toward both Nena and Leticia, Orlando's wife. Like Alejo, neither
Olimpia nor Leticia do anything to disrupt Orlando's rule. Olimpia
fears losing her job; Leticia resists losing the comforts of married life.

Though Olimpia cannot stop the abuse, she befriends Nena in an attempt to make her life more comfortable and human. Leticia initially defends Orlando despite her own experiences of his horrific emotional and physical abuse. She admits worrying about his nocturnal outbursts, which she believes are the result of his feeling haunted by the terrible things he does for the military. Though she learns of Orlando's terrible kidnapping and torture of Nena, Leticia refuses to intervene; she instead strives toward an absurd sense of acceptance concerning Nena's presence in her household. Yet nothing appeases Orlando. His violence and abuse culminate in his formal interrogation of Leticia. Unable to withstand this campaign of terror in her home, Leticia shoots him and immediately presses the gun into Nena's hands. This closing image focuses on the three female characters and their daunting task of rebuilding life without Orlando in the political state that created him.

Historical Context

With her first play, *Tango Palace* (1963), Fornes garnered national recognition as an award-winning dramatist in American avant-garde theater. Throughout her career, Fornes has eschewed the use of categories such as feminist, lesbian, or Latina. While she writes about identity issues, she completely disavows identity politics. Her writing principally focuses on questions concerning the disintegration of society, as exemplified with earlier works such as *A Vietnamese Wedding* (which dealt with the Vietnam War [1967]), *The Danube* (nuclear disarmament [1982]), *Mud* (domestic abuse [1983]), and *Abingdon Square* (the repression of female sexuality [1985]). Consistently, her plays portray women in a wide variety of social roles, with female characters always placed at the very center of her theatrical universe.

Importantly, the 1980s marks an interesting shift in Fornes's career concerning the critical reception of her plays, the thematic content of her work, and her evolving role as a teacher and dramatist. In this often-described "decade of the Hispanic," Fornes cofounded the Hispanic Playwrights Lab at International Arts Relations (INTAR) in New York City and, from that space, wrote several plays the themes of which directly speak to Latino cultural and political concerns. *The Conduct of Life* (1985) is the first play Fornes wrote after founding the lab and was actually begun during one of its writing exercises. Notably, this work explores the kind of political crisis that gave rise to a new generation of Latin American immigrants.

Throughout her career, Fornes has consistently focused on the most pressing political issues of a given moment. Therefore, her attention to Latina/o cultural concerns should be understood as part of an ongoing conversation that crosses several cultural borders. Susan Sontag wrote the introduction to the collection *Maria Irene Fornes: Plays,* and her essay "Fascinating Fascism" provides a vital context for understanding Fornes's deliberately graphic portraits of political, sexual, and domestic violence in *The Conduct of Life.* Reading Fornes alongside other plays contemporaneously produced by Lab participants, most notably Cherríe Moraga's *Giving Up the Ghost* and Migdalia Cruz's *The Have-Little,* wonderfully illustrates the ways Latina writers address questions of violence both as a collective and as distinct voices.

Biographical Background

Fornes was born in 1931, in Havana, Cuba, in the midst of the Depression. In 1945, at the age of fifteen, she emigrated to the United States and became a naturalized citizen in 1951. Her immigration story very much distinguishes her from self-proclaimed Cuban exile playwrights because she came to New York well before Castro's rise to power and not for economic or political reasons but because her father had died and her mother always wanted to live in the United States. Notably, the perceived influences of Cuba on Fornes's work do not follow a predictable or coherent pattern concerning nostalgia or political exile.

In interviews and her own writings Fornes works to complicate simple readings that attempt to position her as representative of all Cuban writers. She acknowledges the importance of her Cuban background yet refuses an obvious relationship between her work and Cuba. She declares herself equally Latin, European, and American, each of these cultures having historically, economically, and culturally shaped Cuba, and by extension herself as a writer. Notably, Fornes began her career as a painter. While studying in France, she became motivated to explore playwrighting after attending a production of *Waiting for Godot.* Although she did not understand French, Fornes was deeply moved by the images and acting, finding theater, like painting, a powerfully evocative artistic medium. Many of her most famous workshop exercises require students to work from an image in a photograph or a pivotal visual memory.

Fornes has written and directed over thirty plays. *The Conduct of Life* stands among her most celebrated plays. Her work has predominantly been produced in New York, mainly off- and off-off-Broadway, in such historic locations as the Judson Poets' Theatre and New Dramatists, as well as the Actors' Workshop in San Francisco and the Firehouse Theatre in Minneapolis. In addition to her own work, Fornes has also directed plays by classic world dramatists, such as Calderon, Ibsen, and Chekhov, as well as several contemporary playwrights, including Cherríe Moraga. Among her many distinctions, including being a finalist for a Pulitzer Prize, she has been the recipient of nine Obie Awards, several National Endowment for the Arts awards, a Guggenheim grant, and a Lila Wallace Reader's Digest Literature Award. From 1973 to 1979, she was the managing director of the New York Theatre Strategy. Since 1981, she has directed the INTAR Hispanic Playwrights-In-Residence Laboratory. She has also been a Theatre Communications Group/PEW Artist-in-Residence at The Women's Project & Productions (note: Pew is the surname of the original donor for the Pew Foundation).

Presently, she conducts playwright workshops in theaters and universities in the United States and abroad. The 1999–2000 season of the prestigious Signature Theatre Company was devoted entirely to Fornes's body of work and included the world premiere of *Letters from Cuba,* which garnered Obie Awards for her writing and direction. The Signature season also featured *Mud, Drowning,* and the New York premiere of *Enter the Night.* Significantly, Fornes is one of the few dramatists working outside of mainstream American Broadway theater to see two collections of her plays published. She is the only Latina dramatist have her work widely anthologized in collections not exclusively devoted to writing by women of color.

Reception of the Text

Numerous articles and essays have been written about *The Conduct of Life* by theater scholars and feminist critics interested in the provocative ways Fornes engages issues of feminism, fascism, and violence. Because she prefers to direct her own work, Fornes frequently writes into her scripts quite elaborate stage directions. As theater critic Scott Cummings notes, stage directions are paramount to the production of this particular play (Robinson 1999). Drama scholar W. B. Worthen notes the significance of set design in emphasizing "the interdependence of politics, power, and gender" that charge the play. In her 1997 Los

Angeles production of *The Conduct of Life*, Dona Guevara-Hill pre-
miered a new ending that Fornes had boldly rewritten. Like other
productions, the set illustrated the ways geographic spaces, political
activity, and personal conduct are intimately connected.

Major Themes and Critical Issues

The major themes that characterize *The Conduct of Life* include:
fascism, political violence, sexual violence, violence against women,
bearing witness to violence, homelessness, child abuse, patriarchal
systems of power, culturally damaging definitions of feminism and
femininity, and terror as a means to control women and other disen-
franchised communities. Significantly, the play begins with the image of
Orlando doing jumping jacks in military breaches, vowing to obtain
"maximum power." Fornes very precisely scripts the ways he should
move when he physically abuses Nena. Orlando's monologues about
torture are directly related to his increasing acts of violence throughout
the play. Through his character, Fornes shows how state violence and
domestic violence operate in tandem in a struggle for power that
depends on assigning negative value to the bodies of women, children,
and feminized men.

The play engages several debates that characterize the 1980s. Prominent figures such as Robin Morgan, Susan Griffin, Andrea Dworkin,
and Catherine MacKinnon attacked pornography as a major catalyst
for violence against women. They argued that pornography, like rape,
is about violence, not sex. Morgan's writing situated pornography as a
form of terrorism designed to maintain patriarchy. Dworkin and
MacKinnon lobbied for the legal regulation and practical elimination of
pornography, viewing such action not as censorship but as an intervention in the preservation of women's civil rights. To them, all representations of violence against women, without exception, are purposefully
designed to keep women in a constant state of terror. Other feminists,
such as those involved in FACT (Feminist Anti-Censorship Taskforce),
opposed violence against women yet refused to advocate censorship.
These groups feared that vague and rigid definitions would foster an
unintentional alliance with political conservatives and extremists who
would then use anti-porn ordinances to attack feminist bookstores or
ban visually explicit texts about women's health. Such critics found it
more productive to explore the dynamics of power and gender manifested in the influential albeit troubling images of popular culture.

With *The Conduct of Life,* Fornes complicates facile arguments that approach all representations of violence as destructive. Clearly, there are certain instances when images of violence serve an important purpose. In her essay "Fascinating Fascism," Susan Sontag expresses concern about the 1980's visual quest for "fresh" images in art and advertising, a search that sparked the promotion of black leather and other props of sadism and fascism as extremely fashionable modes of expression devoid of historical context. *The Conduct of Life* asks readers and audiences to make unsettling connections, to actively witness violence in a specific context as opposed to blindly accept it as part of the cultural scenery. In this way, Fornes turns the debate away from the issue of pornographic and violent images in and of themselves and toward the question of who is producing the images and for what purposes.

During the 1980s, media coverage focused on horrific acts of political violence in Argentina, Chile, Honduras, Nicaragua, Colombia, and El Salvador, along with other Central and Latin American countries. Journalists exposed U.S. involvement in maintaining a climate of state terror through military support. The American public was forced to confront their role in these growing stories of human rights abuses. In many of these countries, theatrical spectacles of terror were used to intimidate citizens into a position of silence and compliance. In *The Conduct of Life* Leticia speaks of naked bodies left in the streets with genitals stuffed into their mouths, which she reads as deliberate messages from the military. Here, women's issues are portrayed as community issues. In these contexts, certain graphic representations of violence (photojournalism, testimonial, storytelling, theater) become extremely important because they challenge the audience to bear witness to what has been unspeakable, to break the silence, to learn from history.

Pedagogical Issues and Suggestions

The greatest concern I have about teaching *The Conduct of Life* regards its scenes of graphic sexual violence. I'm initially concerned with how a survivor of sexual trauma will respond to the play. Will the student have a breakdown in my class? Will the text inadvertently open up old wounds? Will students find the text pornographic? How can I, as a literature professor, prepare myself for such possibilities? One might think about setting up a contact person in counseling and career services and the women's center. I begin by rereading the play and updating my notes to emphasize the importance of presenting a network of historical contexts.

My goal is to take students back in an intellectual time machine that allows them to envision the critical interventions Fornes originally attempted with this play, a work that critics still describe as powerfully relevant. We read reviews and essays, now readily available in Marc Robinson's important sourcebook, *The Theater of Maria Irene Fornes.* I include sections and photographs from Klaus Theweleit's study of fascist culture, *Male Fantasies* (1987); introductory chapters from Susan Jeffords's *Hard Bodies: Hollywood Masculinity in the Reagan Era* (1994); and essays on the pornography debates and violence against women from the anthology *Front Line Feminism, 1975–1995* (1995), along with radical counter-advertisements from ACT UP and Guerilla Girls. (UC Riverside Graduate student Cheryl Edelson recently suggested including clips from the landmark documentary *Killing Us Softly.*) These readings provide students with a potent context for understanding 1980s cultural politics and the theatricality that informs the issues of the play.

In my Latina drama course, I begin teaching with Fornes since all of the dramatists we read in that class studied under her direction at the Hispanic Playwrights' Lab. We start with *The Conduct of Life* and then read Cherríe Moraga's *Giving Up the Ghost* and Migdalia Cruz's *The Have-Little,* all three of which were written at the lab. Students discuss and write about the clear thematic connections between the three plays—each features a young girl in crisis and explores the relationship between state or community violence and domestic violence. They are also quick to note stylistic similarities and shared attention to detail. To further pursue these latter issues, I include in my reader several tribute essays by lab participants available in Maria Delgado and Caridad Svich's *Conducting a Life: Reflections on the Theatre of Maria Irene Fornes.*

Notably, those students who have revealed to me that they are survivors of violence find Nena a powerful reminder of how one negotiates a sense of humanity in the face of inhumanity. The play enables students to develop a vocabulary to talk about violence outside of the discourse provided by the dominant media, which typically portrays an evil perpetrator whose hideous acts of violence are completely inexplicable and leave behind helpless victims forever devastated by his violence. Students know the story is much more complicated, and they are hungry for a language that will enable them to productively and critically talk about violence.

First and foremost, the play must be read in the context of cultural debates and political events of the 1980s. However, there are also strong connections to contemporary social issues. In the scope of my class on U.S. Latina/o drama, we discuss the ways Latinos are asked to carry out state-sanctioned violence in their own communities in the name of democratic freedoms. For example, what about the ways law enforcement provides Latinos with some of the greatest employment opportunities—as police officers, sheriffs, correctional officers, district attorneys—at the same time that Latinos represent the largest growing demographic of the prison population? The play focuses on an extreme situation of fascist violence, yet it also asks us to examine our own roles as witnesses to atrocities in contemporary society. Orlando is a villain and our sympathies clearly lie with Nena. But how do people become like Alejo, Olimpia, or Leticia? Why and when do we choose to look away from everyday situations clearly charged with violence? What are the clear limitations to witnessing violence? How might we become witnesses in a way that might promote personal and social change in a world bombarded by violent images and increasingly violent behaviors? In 2002, students couldn't help but read the play in light of September 11.

Some questions and issues for classroom discussion, quizzes, or papers:

Why does the play open with the image of Orlando doing jumping jacks?

How does this set up our understanding of his character and his behavior in the rest of the play?

What is the reader's first image of Nena? How does Fornes bring her onto the stage? Why is this significant?

The title is taken from Nena's monologue; what is the significance of the word "conduct"—in Nena's monologue, in the title, and for the play generally?

What happens to Orlando at the end? is this justice? What is the final word Leticia utters to close the play?

What are some of the possible meanings here?

What finally motivates her to kill Orlando?

There are two deaths in the play, Orlando's torturous murder of Felo and Leticia's killing of Orlando; is there a difference between the two killings? Why or why not?

What does it mean to feel someone deserves to die?

How is Fornes working throughout the play to complicate notions of justice, punishment, family, and community?

What is important for playwrights, readers, and audiences about stories of violence?

How and, importantly, why does Fornes make violence central to issues
of identity and community?
In what ways does Fornes use individual bodies (i.e., characters) to
promote a redefinition of larger social bodies (i.e., the family and
the state)?

Before they read the text, discuss with students the cultural contexts
for this play and its relevance to current events. Give a plot summary
and provide study questions. Talk about the arch of the play, especially
how Fornes begins with Orlando, places Nena at the center of the play,
and ends with a focus on Leticia. Ask students to think about the
threads that runs between these scenes and characters that ultimately
shapes the entire play. This preplay conversation helps students understand why the rape scene is critically central to the text and not just
some horrific scene of violence without strategic purpose for the
playwright. I find *The Conduct of Life* an important inclusion in my
yearly teaching because it so wonderfully teaches students the importance of thinking and speaking critically about violence.

Literary Contexts

For Fornes, preconceived notions of identity "prevent us from seeing
characters as human beings; we see them rather as party members."
Fornes created the Hispanic Playwrights Lab to increase the number
of Latina/o dramatists in the United States, to enhance diversity
artistically, and to ultimately elevate the richness of the different styles
and voices, as well as personal and literary perspectives, that characterize a distinctly American theater. She views the lab as a necessary
institutional intervention, noting the importance of role models, as
Hispanic playwrights, in her words, "have no one to look to and think
'Oh, I could be a playwright like so-and-so.'" In a recent tribute
volume to her work, nearly all of her students focus on the artistic gifts
they gained studying under her direction. Migdalia Cruz credits
Fornes with teaching her how to have faith in listening to difficult
voices and telling painful truths. Moraga commends Fornes as a
teacher who asks students to "go to the hardest/ugliest truths (the
writer's truths) of what it is to be Latina, hungry of body and sex and
spirit in this pitiful country. She encouraged those journeys into the
forbidden."
The INTAR lab has played a crucial role in the emergence of a
contemporary Latina dramatic arts movement because it brought

together, for the first time, significant numbers of Latina playwrights who otherwise would most likely have never had the opportunity to work with one another. Nearly an entire generation of Latina dramatists has at some time studied under Fornes's direction (Migdalia Cruz, Cherríe Moraga, Dolores Prida, Caridad Svich, Edit Villareal, Kat Avila, Silvia Gonzalez S., Elaine Romero, Josefina Lopez, Milcha Sanchez Scott, Ana Maria Simo, Ela Troyano, among many others). The lab helped to unify and empower these Latina dramatists, who before coming to the workshop felt entirely isolated within both mainstream and Latino arts spaces.

Comparative Literature

Several critics have made comparisons between Fornes and Tina Howe regarding their explorations of feminist issues. Other scholars have compared Fornes with Sam Shepard. In a private conversation Cheryl Edelson suggests teaching Fornes's work with Kate Chopin's *The Awakening* or Charlotte Perkins Gilman's *The Yellow Wallpaper* as part of a unit that explores feminist responses to patriarchal authority and women's ensuing experiences of violence. Within a more specific cultural context, Fornes, Cherríe Moraga, and Migdalia Cruz represent quite different, if not opposing, views about Latina/o identity and a Latina/o dramatic tradition. Yet their plays clearly stand in dialogue with one another around issues of domestic and political violence.

Including Fornes within a discussion of Latina drama raises a number of crucial questions concerning assumptions that often inform the categorization of Latina plays. Is Latina drama distinguished primarily by matters of ethnic/cultural origins? What about issues of aesthetics, genre, language, and form? Are Latina plays only those that most transparently address identifiable and particularized social, political, and critical issues? In contrast to the feelings of culture clash often associated with U.S. Latinos today, Fornes's sense of cultural hybridity is primarily grounded in her position as a pre-1960s immigrant and avant-garde artist. Historically, most conversations about ethnic theater assume a continuity between a writer's personal politics, the politics of a play, and a community-based social movement. Today, ethnic theater is impressively multifaceted with writers increasingly following Fornes's lead in their complication of identity issues and cultural politics.

BIBLIOGRAPHIC RESOURCES

Primary Sources

Individual and Collected Works by Maria Irene Fornes

Fornes, Maria Irene. *Drowning. Orchards: Seven Stories by Anton Chekhov and Seven Plays They Have Inspired.* Anne Cattaneo, ed. New York: Alfred A. Knopf, 1986.

———. *Plays (Mud, The Danube, The Conduct of Life, Sarita).* New York: PAJ Publications, 1986.

———. *Promenade and Other Plays.* New York: PAJ Publications, 1987.

———. *Fefu and Her Friends.* New York: PAJ Publications, 1990.

———. *Terra Incognita. Theater* 24, no. 2 (1993).

———. *What of the Night? Women on the Verge: Seven Avant-Garde American Plays.* Rosette C. Lamont, ed. New York: Applause Theatre Books, 1993.

———. *Enter the Night. Plays for the End of the Century.* Bonnie Marranca, ed. Baltimore: Johns Hopkins University Press, 1996.

———. *Abingdon Square.* Los Angeles: Green Integer, 2000.

Houghton, James, ed. *Signature Theater 1999 Presents Maria Irene Fornes.* Lyme, N.H.: Smith and Kraus, Inc., 2001.

Secondary Sources

Related Works on U.S. Latina Drama

Arrizon, Alicia. *Latina Performance: Traversing the Stage.* Bloomington and Indianapolis: Indiana University Press, 1999.

Arrizon, Alicia and Lillian Manzor, eds. *Latinas on Stage.* Berkeley: Third Woman Press, 2000.

Carillo, Juliette and Jose Cruz Gonzalez, eds. *Latino Plays From South Coast Repertory.* New York: Broadway Play Publishing Inc., 2000.

Feyder, Linda, ed. *Shattering the Myth: Plays by Hispanic Women.* Houston: Arte Público Press, 1992.

Jeffords, Susan. *Hard Bodies: Hollywood Masculinity in the Reagan Era.* New Brunswick: Rutgers University Press, 1994.

Kahn, Karen, ed. *Front Line Feminism, 1975–1995: Essays from Sojourner's First 20 Years.* San Francisco: Aunt Lute Books, 1995.

Osborn, Elizabeth, ed. *On New Ground: Contemporary Hispanic Plays.* New York: Theatre Communications Group, 1987.

Sandoval-Sanchez, Alberto and Nancy Saporta Sternback, eds. *Puro Teatro: A Latina Anthology*. Tucson: University of Arizona Press, 2000.

————. *Stages of Life: Transcultural Performance & Identity in U.S. Latina Theater*. Tucson, University of Arizona Press, 2001.

Svich, Caridad and Maria Teresa Marrero, eds. *Out of the Fringe: Contemporary Latina/Latino Theatre and Performance*. New York: Theatre Communications Group, 2000.

Theater Journal 52, no. 1 (2000). Special issue on Latino Performance. David Roman, ed.

Theweleit, Klaus. *Male Fantasies*. Minneapolis: University of Minnesota Press, 1987.

Yarbro-Bejarano, Yvonne. *The Wounded Heart: Writing on Cherríe Moraga*. Austin: University of Texas Press, 2001.

On Fornes's Drama

Austin, Gayle. "The Madwoman in the Spotlight: Plays of Maria Irene Fornes," *Making a Spectacle: Feminist Essays on Contemporary Women's Theater*. Lynda Hart, ed. Ann Arbor: University of Michigan Press, 1989.

Delgado, Maria M. and Caridad Svich. *Conducting a Life: Reflections of the Theatre of Maria Irene Fornes*. Lyme, N.H.: Smith and Kraus, 1999.

Garner, Stanton B. "(En)gendering Pain: *The Conduct of Life*." *Bodied Spaces: Phenomenology and Performance in Contemporary Drama*. Stanton B. Garner, ed. Ithaca, NY: Cornell University Press, 1994.

Geis, Deborah R. *Postmodern Theatric(k)s: Monologue in Contemporary American Drama*. Ann Arbor: University of Michigan Press, 1993.

Gruber, William E. *Missing Persons: Characters and Characterization in Modern Drama*. Athens: University of Georgia Press, 1994.

Kent, Assunta Bartolomucci. *Maria Irene Fornes and Her Critics*. Westport: Greenwood Press, 1996.

Keyssar, Helene. "Drama and the Dialogic Imagination: *The Heidi Chronicles* and *Fefu and her Friends*" *Feminist Theatre and Theory*. Helene Keyssar, ed. London: Macmillan Press, 1996.

Kintz, Linda. "Permeable Boundaries, Feminism, Fascism, and Violence: Fornes' *The Conduct of Life*." *Gestos* 6, no. 11 (1991).

Lee, Josephine. "Pity and Terror as Public Acts: Reading Feminist Politics in the Plays of Maria Irene Fornes," in *Staging Resistance: Essays on Theatre and Politics*. Jeanne Colleran and Jenny Spencer, eds. Ann Arbor: University of Michigan Press, 1997.

Lopez, Tiffany Ana. "Beyond the Festival Latino: (Re)Defining Latina Drama for the Mainstage." *Woman Playwrights of Diversity*.

Jane T. Peterson and Suzanne Bennett, eds. Westport, CT: Greenwood Press, 1997.

Moroff, Diana Lynn. *Fornes: Theater in the Present Tense.* Ann Arbor: University of Michigan Press, 1996.

Robinson, Marc, ed. *The Other American Drama.* New York: Cambridge University Press, 1994; Johns Hopkins University Press, 1997.

———. "Maria Irene Fornes." *The Other American Drama.* New York: Cambridge University Press, 1994; Johns Hopkins University Press, 1997.

———. *The Theater of Maria Irene Fornes.* Baltimore: Johns Hopkins University Press, 1999.

Schuler, Catherine A. "Gender Perspective and Violence in the Plays of Maria Irene Fornes and Sam Shepard." *Modern American Drama: The Female Canon.* June Schlueter, ed. Rutherford, NJ: Fairleigh Dickinson University Press, 1990.

Wolf, Stacy. "Re/presenting Gender, Re/presenting Violence: Feminism, Form and the Plays of Maria Irene Fornes." *Theatre Studies* 37 (1992).

Worthen, W. B. "'Still playing games': Ideology and Performance in the Theater of Maria Irene Fornes." *The Theater of Maria Irene Fornes.* Marc Robinson, ed. Baltimore: Johns Hopkins University Press, 1997.

Selected Interviews With Fornes

"Maria Irene Fornes." By Kathleen Betsko and Rachel Koening. *Interviews with Contemporary Women Playwrights.* Kathleen Betsko and Rachel Koening, eds. New York: William Morrow, 1987.

"Maria Irene Fornes." By Una Chaudhuri. *Speaking on Stage: Interviews with Contemporary American Playwrights.* Philip C. Kolin and Colby H. Kullman, eds. Tuscaloosa: University of Alabama Press, 1996.

"Maria Irene Fornes." By David Savran. *Their Own Words: Contemporary American Playwrights.* New York: Theatre Communications Group, 1988.

"Maria Irene Fornes." By Rod Wooden. *In Contact with the Gods? Directors Talk Theatre.* Maria M. Delgado and Paul Heritage, eds. Manchester, U.K.: Manchester University Press, 1996.

"The Playwright as Director." By Bonnie Marranca. *Conversations on Art and Performance.* Bonnie Marranca and Gautam Dasgupta, eds. Baltimore: Johns Hopkins University Press, 1999.

Andrea O'Reilly Herrera

Cristina García,
Dreaming in Cuban

New York: Ballantine Books, 1993.

Textual Overview

Taking as its point of departure the 1959 Cuban Revolution, Cristina García's debut novel *Dreaming in Cuban* (1992) directly explores what the author herself characterized as the effects or "costs" of the revolution and the consequent diaspora "on individuals and families." García treats this central theme by chronicling the lives of three generations of a family divided politically and geographically as a result of the revolution.

Historical Context

On January 8, 1959, Fidel Castro marched into Havana with his triumphant guerrilla troops; shortly thereafter, he systematically eliminated his competition and established himself as prime minister of Cuba. In May 1960, Castro reestablished diplomatic relations with the Soviet Union, and in the following year the United States severed its ties to Cuba. According to many diplomatic historians, by 1962 he had solidified Cuba's economic and philosophical ties with the Soviets. Castro's early reforms and proclamations, such as the inauguration of "The Year of Education" (a national campaign to eliminate illiteracy), won him widespread support among diverse sectors of the Cuban population. Nevertheless the increasing appropriation of land under the Agrarian Reform Laws and the confiscation of privately owned businesses on the part of his government, coupled with growing economic and personal restrictions in the name of reform, caused many to begin to question and consequently challenge not only their leader's intentions but also the direction the revolution was taking. As a result, many Cubans abandoned their native land and sought sanctuary in various parts of the world in a gradual exodus that has come to be known as the Cuban Diaspora.

In addition to making direct references to the various waves of the Diaspora, such as the Freedom Flights (which began in 1965 and were essentially conducted until 1973 with a few sporadic flights until 1975) and the 1980 storming of the Peruvian Embassy, which prompted the Mariel Boat-lift, *Dreaming in Cuban* includes significant moments in the characters' lives that correspond to key events in Cuban history, such as the 1962 missile crisis, the Bay of Pigs (or Playa Girón) Invasion (1961), and the participation of Cuban combat troops in the Angolan War (1975). Throughout *Dreaming in Cuban,* Cristina García also alludes to specific reforms that Castro initiated during the early years of the revolution, such as the Agrarian Reform Laws, which mandated the confiscation and redistribution of land; the Family Code (1975), which established a body of law regulating marriage, family and divorce; and the Family Reunification Program (1978), which permitted Cuban exiles briefly to return to the island to visit their families.

Biographical Background

Born July 4, 1958, in Havana, Cuba, Cristina García migrated to the United States with her parents in 1960. Before trying her hand at creative writing, she was a reporter (1983–85), correspondent (1985–90), and Miami bureau chief (1987–88) for *Time* magazine. In 1996 García was the recipient of the Hodder Fellowship, the Cintas Fellowship, she won both the National Book Foundation Award and the Whiting Writers Award, and was a finalist for the National Book Award. In addition to *Dreaming in Cuban,* she is the author the novel *The Aguero Sisters* (1997).

Reception of the Text

Dubbed as a "completely original novel" (Michiko Kakutanu, *New York Times*), Cristina García's *Dreaming in Cuban* (1992) achieved overwhelming critical success and was the first novel by a Cuban American woman to receive widespread national attention. In addition to characterizing García as a gifted storyteller, whose work is "renewing American fiction" (Ilan Stavans, *Nation* (1997); Pico Ayer, *Time* (1992), reviewers lavishly praised her first novel for its complex narrative strategy (Alan West, *Washington Post Book World* 1992), and its "exquisite realism" (Richard Eder, *Los Angeles Times* 1992). In general, the response from the Cuban exile community has been less positive. Among other things, her critics contend that despite the fact that *Dreaming in Cuban* addresses and represents a host of antithetical political issues and perspectives surrounding the revolution, García fails clearly to position herself politically. Moreover, regarding García's work as being in conflict with the conservative arm of the Miami exile community, a small number of critics have questioned her authenticity and criticized her for not having been raised in a Latino community. As one critic observed, García "failed to experience [the] deep sense of loss or nostalgia common to many Cuban-American children" (Joseph Viera, *Poets and Writers Magazine* 1998).

Major Themes and Critical Issues

At its heart, *Dreaming in Cuban* takes up the intertwined themes of exile, loss, and the preservation, perpetuation, and transformation of culture and memory. Although it has been linked to what has hitherto been a predominantly male tradition of historical revisionary writing in the Caribbean, *Dreaming in Cuban* actually offers a feminized account of the events and the outcomes of the Cuban Revolution, and of Cuba's relationship with the various colonial powers that have dominated her since 1492.

Signaling her acute consciousness of women's exclusion from patriarchal exilic historical discourse (history writ large, as opposed to personal or familial history), García once observed in a personal conversation with Iraida López that "Traditional history, the way it has been written, interpreted and recorded, obviates women and the evolution of home, family and society, and basically becomes a recording of battles and wars and dubious accomplishments of men. You learn where politics really lie: at home. That's what I was trying to explore on some level in *Dreaming in Cuban*" (610).

By connecting women's experiences in the private or domestic sphere to broader social and political events, and thereby positioning women as central figures within the Cuban Revolution, García *quarrels* with a traditional paternal discourse that, according to Francine Maciello, reduces women to their "reproductive functions or domestic labor" and thereby renders them a-historical (33). She accomplishes this through a microcosm/macrocosm paradigm that draws a direct parallel between women's personal relationships (both among themselves and with their partners) and their subsequent activities in the home, and events occurring at the national and international levels.

The del Pino family, for example, is split—both emotionally and physically—as a result of their political differences. On the most obvious level, the trope of the divided family directly alludes to the ideological schisms that resulted in the wake of the 1959 revolution. From a purely literary perspective, *Dreaming in Cuban* may be regarded as an in-depth study of human relationships as depicted through a single family. Although politics have literally split the del Pinos apart, the reader soon discovers that infidelity, betrayal, abandonment, and, as a result, psychic and emotional estrangement not only characterize each succeeding generation of women, but also account for the failure of women's personal relationships. In effect, the del Pino family is a disaster, and nearly every female character in the novel experiences some degree of disillusion with love.

When approached from a different perspective, however, García's novel seems to draw on the nationalistic premise that the state of the family can be equated to the national good. Celia's failed relationships, for example, function as metaphors for Cuba's unfulfilled (and unrequited) relationship with Spain (as embodied in her aborted affair with Gustavo, a relationship that she nurtures and keeps alive only in her imagination); the island's subordinate and paternalistic relationship with the United States (as evidenced by Celia's failed marriage with Jorge, a Cuban who works for an American company); and the gradual disillusionment Cubans experienced in the wake of the revolution (as revealed through Celia's disappointment in El Líder—Fidel Castro—and his broken revolutionary promises to establish Cuba as a nation independent of imperialist rule).

The theme of failed romantic love also suggests the disenchantment that generations of immigrants experienced upon their arrival in the United States, as evidenced by Lourdes's disastrous marriage to Rufino. This, along with the not-so-subtle relationship between Lourdes and El Líder (both are dictatorial parental figures) and the constant play on words such as *puentes* and *du pont* (the word for "bridge" in Spanish and French, respectively), are just three examples of the many cross-references in the novel, which serve to draw disturbing parallels between Cuba and the United States. Thus the dysfunction in the del Pino women's relationships, which crosses geographical and generational divides, ultimately serves as a forceful indictment of the failures of communism as well as of the shortcomings of American democracy and capitalism.

The connection between the private and the political is woven like a leitmotif throughout *Dreaming in Cuban*. Thus, important events in the female characters' lives are directly linked to key historical events. For example, Felicia's wedding coincides with the missile crisis. In the same vein, the intertwined themes of exile, loss, and separation reappear throughout the novel and translate into either personal and/or linguistic loss, or psychic and emotional isolation. As Rocio G. Davis notes, "Language functions in *Dreaming in Cuban* as a measuring device for gauging both connection and separation, loyalty and abandonment, between families and land" (64). In addition to separating mothers and daughters, the loss of language prompts characters like Pilar to "turn to other, nontraditional forms of expression" such as telepathy and painting.

García further emphasizes the relationship between the private and the political by establishing a direct link between patriotism and motherhood. The overarching theme of maternal loss—depicted in the novel by geographical or physical separation, as well as by the emotional distance that characterizes the relationships of most of the characters in the novel—subtly alludes to the larger losses and betrayals that Cuba, as mother country and colonial subject, sustained both prior to and in the wake of the revolution.

Finally, in addition to its feminist concerns, *Dreaming in Cuban* engages a constellation of issues, albeit paradoxical ones, regarding ethnicity and diasporic identity. In addition to depicting the new generation of Cubans (though characters such as Ivanito, Milagro, and Luz), the novel is primarily an exploration of the manner in which Cuban-Americans have come to terms with their hyphenated cultural/ethnic identities. Pilar, for example, is an abstract artist who interprets her bifurcated identity through painting and uses her art as a form of expression and resistance. Throughout the novel, Pilar details her conflicted relationship with her mother, who encourages her daughter to follow her extreme political position and assimilate to American culture. Celia, on the other hand, cultivates a telepathic relationship with her granddaughter and regards her (perhaps because they share their birth date) as being the one best fitted to "remember everything." For her part, Pilar refuses to take a political stance, and she recognizes that even though she may be "more New York" than Havana, she straddles both cultures.

Through characters such as Pilar, as well as Celia (who records history through a series of letters written to her former lover), García also examines the manner in which cultural tradition is preserved, perpetuated, and inevitably transformed and thereby investigates the nature of historical memory itself. The inherently contradictory and subjective nature of recollected and recorded history—both private and public—is reinforced and investigated further through the very structure of the novel. Its combination of various generic forms and shifting, "polyphonic" narrative perspectives reflects this central theme.

Pedagogical Issues and Suggestions

When first approaching *Dreaming in Cuban,* it is imperative that instructors provide a historical context or framework that not only focuses upon the 1959 revolution but also introduces students to the various waves of colonial and imperialistic powers that took possession of the island from 1942 forward: Spain, the United States, and the Soviet Union. Once this is established, students can begin to investigate the manner in which the metaphor of the family functions on various levels throughout the novel, as well as explore the parallels García draws between personal experience and larger historical events.

Instructors can then move on to a discussion of cultural identity, which lends itself to an exploration of the manner in which history and cultural memory are recorded and transformed, as well as the various ways that the second generation negotiates what Gustavo Pérez Firmat refers to as "life on the hyphen." Throughout this portion of the discussion it is particularly helpful to encourage students to reflect upon their own ethnic identities and cultural practices. More sophisticated students will grasp immediately the manner in which the narrative form of García's novel bespeaks these central themes. It is also helpful to provide students with background materials regarding Santería, in light of the relatively central role that Felicia plays in the text and the fact that Celia is directly linked (through color-coding) to this religion. Instructors may also wish to supplement their presentations by discussing with students the role that food and music play in regard to culture. Playing a recording that features the work of Beny Moré would be particularly effective not only because García specifically mentions him in the novel but because he has become a kind of cultural icon for Cubans, both on and off the Island, representing a prerevolutionary world.

Literary Contexts

Cristina García's work is particularly significant among Cuban American authors writing in English in that until recently this genre has been dominated by male writers. In addition to exploring women's roles in the revolution, *Dreaming in Cuban* specifically focuses upon the theme of cultural identity formation. Although instructors may want to consider autobiographical and/or testimonial work that has emerged from other exile experiences, they could also focus specifically upon Cuban American authors such as Gustavo Pérez Firmat *(Life on the Hyphen, the Cuban-American Way,* and *Next Year in Cuba, A Cubano Coming of Age in Cuba),* Pablo Medina *(Exiled Memories),* María del Carmen Boza *(Scattering the Ashes),* Virgil Suárez *(Spared Angola, Memories from a Cuban-American Childhood),* and Andrea O'Reilly Herrera *(ReMembering Cuba: Legacy of a Diaspora).*

Instructors may also want to consider pairing García's novel with authors representing other Caribbean exile traditions, such Sam Selvon, Maryse Conde, Jamaica Kincaid, Beryl Gilroy, Olive Senior, and V. S. Naipaul. Were they to design a course that focused exclusively on Cuban American authors, they would want to consider the following novelists and short story writers: Pablo Medina *(The Marks of Birth* and *The Return of Felix Nogara),* Achy Obejas *(We Came All the Way From Cuba So You Could Dress Like This?* and *Memory Mambo),* Elías Miguel Muñoz *(Crazy Love* and *Brand New Memory),* Roberto Fernández *(Raining Backwards),* Virgil Suárez *(Latin Jazz),* Oscar Hijuelos *(The Mambo Kings Play Songs of Love* and *The Fourteen Sisters of Emilio Montez O'Brien),* Hilda Perera *(Kiki),* J. Joaquín Fraxedas *(The Lonely Crossing of Juan Cabrera),* Margarita Engle *(Singing to Cuba* and *Skywriting),* Ivonne Lamazares *(The Sugar Island),* Andrea O'Reilly Herrera *(The Pearl of the Antilles),* and Ana Menéndez *(In Cuba I was a German Shepherd).* Virgil Suárez's and Delia Poey's coedited anthology *Little Havana Blues* is also a very useful text in courses that focuses on Cuban-American, Latino/a or Diasporic writing.

Comparative Literature

Cristina García's *Dreaming in Cuban* lends itself to comparison with the work of other prominent U.S. Latino/a authors who explore the intertwined themes of identity and racial/ethnic/gender formation within specific cultural and historical contexts. See for example Sandra Benítez *(A Place Where the Sea Remembers* and *Bitter Grounds),* the Chicano/a writers Helena María Viramontes *(The Moths and Other Stories* and *Under the Feet of Jesus),* Sandra Cisneros *(The House on Mango*

Street), Denise Chavez *(The Last of the Menu Girls* and *Face of an Angel)*, Ana Castillo *(The Mixquiahuala Letters* and *So Far from God)*, Ron Arias *(The Road to Tamuzanchale)*, Rudolfo Anaya *(Bless Me, Ultima)*, Alfredo Véa, Jr. *(La Maravilla* and *The Silver Cloud Café)*, or Mary Helen Ponce's memoir *Hoyt Street;* Newyorican writers Judith Ortiz Cofer *(Silent Dancing* and *The Line of the Sun)* and Nicholasa Mohr *(Nilda);* and the Dominican American author Julia Alvarez *(How the García Girls Lost Their Accents* and *In the Time of the Butterflies)*.

Dreaming in Cuban can also be paired with works of contemporary American authors of color who treat specific themes such as negotiating cultural identity (with special focus upon parent/child relationships) and the adolescent's coming of age. See especially Maxine Hong Kingston *(The Woman Warrior)*, Amy Tan *(The Joy Luck Club)*, Tony Morrison *(The Bluest Eye* and *Beloved)*, Alice Walker *(The Color Purple)*, Zora Neale Hurston *(Their Eyes Were Watching God)*, Leslie Marmon Silko *(Ceremony)*, Paule Marshall *(Brown Girl, Brownstones)*, N. Scott Momaday *(House Made of Dawn)*, James Welch *(Fools Crow)*, Dori Sander *(Clover)*, Fae Myenne Ng *(Bone)*, Hisaye Yamamoto *(Seventeen Syllables)*, Ntzake Shange *(Betsey Brown)*, John Okada *(No-No Boy)*, Gish Jen *(Mona and the Promised Land)*, Frank Chin *(Donald Duk)*, Joy Kogawa *(Obasan)*, Barbara Kingsolver *(The Bean Trees)*, Louise Erdrich *(Love Medicine)*, and Betty Louise Bell *(Faces in the Moon)*.

BIBLIOGRAPHIC RESOURCES

Primary Sources

Alvarez, Julia. *How the García Girls Lost Their Accents*. New York: Plume, 1991.

———. *In the Time of the Butterflies*. Chapel Hill, NC: Algonquin Books, 1994.

Anaya, Rudolfo. *Bless Me, Ultima*. Berkeley: Tonatiuh, 1972.

Arias, Ron. *The Road to Tamazunchale*. Tempe, AZ: Bilingual/Review Press, 1987.

Bell, Betty Louise. *Faces in the Moon*. Norman, OK: University of Oklahoma Press, 1994.

Benitez, Sandra. *A Place Where the Sea Remembers*. New York: Scribner, 1993.

———. *Bitter Grounds*. New York: Picador, 1998.

Boza, Maria del Carmen. *Scattering the Ashes*. Tempe, AZ: Bilingual/Review Press, 1998.

Castillo, Ana. *The Mixquiahuala Letters*. Tempe, AZ: Bilingual/Review Press, 1986.

———. *So Far From God*. New York: Norton, 1993.

Chavez, Denise. *The Last of the Menu Girls*. Houston, TX: Arte Público Press, 1986.

———. *The Face of an Angel*. New York: Warner Books, 1994.

Chin, Frank. *Donald Duk*. Minneapolis, MN: Coffee House Press, 1991.

Cisneros, Sandra. *The House on Mango Street*. New York: Vintage, 1985.

Cofer, Judith Ortiz. *The Line of the Sun*. Athens, GA: The University of Georgia Press, 1989.

———. *Silent Dancing: A Partial Remembrance of Puerto Rican Childhood*. Houston, TX: Arte Público Press, 1990.

Engle, Margarita. *Singing to Cuba*. Austin, TX: University of Texas Press, 1993.

———. *Skywriting, A Novel of Cuba*. New York: Bantam, 1995.

Erdich, Louise. *Love Medicine*. New York: Bantam, 1984.

Fernandez, Roberto. *Raining Backwards*. Houston, TX: Arte Público Press, 1988.

Fraxedas, J. Joaquin. *The Lonely Crossing of Juan Cabrera*. New York: St. Martin's Press, 1992.

Hijuelos, Oscar. *The Mambo Kings Play Songs of Love*. New York: Farrar, Straus and Giroux, 1989.

———. *The Fourteen Sisters of Emilio Montez O'Brien*. New York: Farrar, Straus and Giroux, 1993.

Hurston, Zora Neale. *Their Eyes Were Watching God*. New York: Lippincott, 1937.

Jen, Gish. *Mona in the Promised Land*. New York: Vintage, 1996.

Kingston, Maxine Hong. *The Woman Warrior: Memoirs of a Girlhood Among Ghosts*. New York: Vintage, 1976.

Kogawa, Joy. *Obasan*. New York: Doubleday, 1981.

Lamazares, Ivonne. *The Sugar Island*. Boston: Houghton Mifflin, 2000.

Marshall, Paule. *Brown Girl, Brownstones*. New York: The Feminist Press, 1981.

Medina, Pablo. *Exiled Memories: A Cuban Childhood*. Austin, TX: University of Texas Press, 1990.

———. *The Marks of Birth*. New York: Farrar, Straus and Giroux, 1994.

———. *The Return of Felix Nogara.* New York, Persea, 2000.

Menendez, Ana. *In Cuba I Was a German Shepherd.* New York: Grove Press, 2001.

Mohr, Nicholasa. *Nilda.* Houston, TX: Arte Público Press, 1986.

Momaday, N. Scott. *House Made of Dawn.* New York: Harper and Row, 1966.

Morrison, Toni. *The Bluest Eye.* New York: Holt, Rinehart and Winston, 1976.

———. *Beloved.* New York: Alfred A. Knopf, 1987.

Munoz, Elias Miguel. *Crazy Love.* Houston, TX: Arte Público Press, 1989.

———. *Brand New Memory.* Houston, TX: Arte Público Press, 1998.

Ng, Fae Myenne. *Bone.* New York: Harper Collins, 1993.

Obejas, Achy. *We Came All the Way From Cuba So You Could Dress Like This?* Pittsburgh, PA: Cleis Press, 1994.

———. *Memory Mambo.* Pittsburgh, PA: Cleis Press, 1996.

Okada, John. *No-No Boy.* Seattle, WA: University of Washington Press, 1976.

Herrera, Andrea O'Reilly. *The Pearl of the Antilles.* Tempe, AZ: Bilingual/Review Press, 2001.

Perera, Hilda. *Kiki.* Coconut Grove, FL: The Pickering Press, 1992.

Perez Firmat, Gustavo. *Next Year in Cuba: A Cubano's Coming-of-Age in America.* New York: Doubleday, 1995.

Ponce, Mary Helen. *Hoyt Street.* New York: Doubleday, 1993.

Sander, Dori. *Clover.* New York: Fawcett Columbine, 1990.

Shange, Ntzake. *Betsey Brown.* New York: St. Martin's Press, 1985.

Silko, Leslie Marmon. *Ceremony.* New York: Penguin, 1977.

Suárez, Virgil. *Latin Jazz.* New York: William Morrow, 1989.

——— and Delia Poey, ed. *Little Havana Blues: A Cuban-American Literature Anthology.* Houston, TX: Arte Público Press, 1996.

———. *Spared Angola: Memories of a Cuban-American Childhood.* Houston, TX: Arte Público Press, 1997.

Tan, Amy. *The Joy Luck Club.* New York: Ivy Books, 1989.

Vea, Alfredo, Jr. *La Maravilla.* New York: Plume, 1993.

———. *The Silver Cloud Café.* New York: Plume, 1996.

Viramontes, Helena Maria. *The Moths and Other Stories.* Houston, TX: Arte Público Press, 1985.

———. *Under the Feet of Jesus.* New York: Dutton, 1995.

Walker, Alice. *The Color Purple.* New York: Pocket Books, 1982.

Welch, James. *Fools Crow.* New York: Penguin, 1986.

Yamamoto, Hisaye. *Seventeen Syllables and Other Stories.* Latham, NY: Kitchen Table Press, 1988.

Secondary Sources

Alvarez-Borland, Isabel. "Displacements and Autobiography in Cuban-American Fiction." *World Literature Today* 68, no. 1 (1994): 43–48.

———. *Cuban-American Literature of Exile: From Person to Persona.* Charlottesville, VA: University of Virginia Press, 1998.

Araujo, Nara. "I Came All the Way from Cuba So I Could Talk Like This? Cuban and Cuban American Literatures in the US." *Comparing Postcolonial Literatures: Dislocations.* Ashok Bery and Patricia Murray, eds. Basingstoke: Palgrave, 2000.

Brameshuber-Ziegler, Irene. "Cristina García, *Dreaming in Cuban* (1992): Collapse of Communication and Kristeva's Semiotic as Possible Remedy." *Language and Literature* 24 (1999): 43–64.

Davis, Rocio G. "Back to the Future: Mothers, Languages, and Homes in Cristina García's *Dreaming in Cuban.*" *World Literature Today* 74, no. 1 (winter 2000): 60–68.

García, María Cristina. *Havana USA.* Berkeley: University of California Press, 1996.

García, Christina. "'And There Is Only Imagination Where Our History Should Be.'" Interview By Iraida H. López. *Michigan Quarterly Review* 33, no. 3 (summer 1994): 605–17.

Gatto, Katherine Gyekenyesi. "Mambo, Merengue, Salsa: The Dynamics of Self-Construction in Latina Autobiographical Narrative." *West Virginia University Philological Papers* 46 (2000): 84–90.

Gomez-Vega, Ibis. "The Journey Home: Defining Identity in Cristina García's *Dreaming in Cuban.*" *A Journal of Chicana/Latina Studies* 1, no. 2 (summer 1997): 71–100.

———. "Metaphors of Entrapment: Caribbean Women Writers Face the Wreckage of History." *Journal of Political and Military Sociology* 25, no. 2 (winter 1997): 231–47.

Herrera, Andrea O'Reilly. "Women and the Revolution in Cristina García's *Dreaming in Cuban,*" *Modern Language Studies* 27, no. 3, 4 (fall-winter 1997): 69–91.

———. *ReMembering Cuba: Legacy of a Diaspora.* Austin, TX: University of Texas Press, 2001.

Karim, Persis Maryam. "Fissured Nations and Exilic States: Displacement, Exile, and Diaspora in Twentieth-Century Writing by

Women." *Dissertation Abstracts International* 59, no. 6 (December 1996): 2009.

Lopez, Kimberley. "Women on the Verge of a Revolution: Madness and Resistance in Cristina García's *Dreaming in Cuban.*" *Letras Femeninas* 22, no.1–2 (spring-fall 1996): 33–49.

Maciello, Francine. "Women, State, and Family in Latin American Literatures of the 1920s." *Women, Culture, and Politics in Latin America.* Emille Bergmann, ed. Berkeley: University of California Press, 1990.

Mitchell, David T. "National Families and Familial Nations: Communista Americans in Cristina García's *Dreaming in Cuban.*" *Tulsa Studies in Women's Literature* 15, no.1 (spring 1996): 51–60.

Núñez, Luis Manuel. *Santería, A Practical Guide to Afro-Caribbean Magic.* Dallas, TX: Spring Publications, 1992.

Ortiz-Marquez, Maribel. "From Third World Politics to First World Practices: Contemporary Latina Writers in the United States." *Interventions: Feminist Dialogues on Third World Women's Literature and Film.* Bishnupriya Ghosh and Brinda Bose, eds. New York: Garland, 1997.

Pérez, Louis A., Jr. *Cuba, Between Reform and Revolution.* New York: Oxford University Press, 1988.

Perez Firmat, Gustavo. *Life on the Hyphen: The Cuban-American Way.* Austin, TX: University of Texas Press, 1994.

Stefanko, Jacqueline. "New Ways of Telling: Latinas' Narratives of Exile and Return." *Frontiers* 17, no. 2 (1996): 50–69.

Socolovsky, Maya. "Unnatural Violences: Counter-Memory and Preservations in Cristina García's *Dreaming in Cuban* and *The Aguero Sisters.*" *Literature Interpretation Theory* 11, no. 2 (August 2000): 143–67.

Vasquez, Mary S. "Cuba as Text and Context in Cristina García's *Dreaming in Cuban.*" *Bilingual Review* 20, no. 1 (January-April 1995): 22–27.

Viera, Joseph M. "Matriarchy and Mayhem: Awakenings in Cristina García's *Dreaming in Cuban.*" *Americas Review* 24, no. 3–4 (fall-winter 1996): 231–42.

———. "Navigating the Straits of Florida: Gender, Politics and Culture in Cristina García's *Dreaming in Cuban.*" *Dissertation Abstracts International* 11 (May 1997).

Juan Felipe Herrera

Diana García, *When Living Was a Labor Camp*

Tucson: University of Arizona Press, 2000.

Textual Overview

Diana García is a fiery *campesina* speaker from the San Joaquin Valley. She is a solar poet who ignites her heart and casts her sparkle-words into the original fields from where she came—the farm worker *campesino* labor camp. Inside the "camp" of her poetry, housing is created from past experiences that have by extension framed the possibilities of her voice, the prisms of her existence. Because the camp also dissolves and disrupts life, García's words and language move and break across regions, producing bordered voices, styles, and textures—her "snake-skins."

In many ways, Diana García's award-winning *When Living Was a Labor Camp* props up a stark set of questions that may illuminate the ways through which we can read Chicana poetry today. These questions have to do with what in large part Chicana critics have elaborated in the last three decades—the formation of a new way of speaking about the Chicana text. What is salient? García's book seems to say, "the serpentine transformations of consciousness."

This is a book of skin-spiral—voices, selves, and awarenesses going back and forth as they progress in forward motion. In the sixty-one poems sectioned into six vineyard-like chapters, we go from familiar observations to inscrutable mediations. We cross one row to the other, smelling, touching, tasting, and pruning local lives, peering into personal day-to-day encounters and the shifting auras of vast landscapes and intimate seasons. In this narrative flare, cultural relationships, familial memoirs, and the intimate flickering of the self blur, fade, and condense. The speaker transforms and channels hybrid figures: a farmworkers' daughter, a *curandera* casting spells, a lover, and a cast of "other Marías." Within the poems themselves we find multiple voices, other lives and other "undocumented and documented workers" at play—Barbie, women's magazines, Mexican radio fifties classics, even old cassette tape speakers—singing, announcing, presenting, blooming.

The voices also cross over as the seasons and *campesinas* flow in between Mexico and "El Norte." At times the poems in the middle section are as formal, careful, and lyrical as most of the pieces in the first and last sections. At other moments, the speaker's tenor loosens and speaks out bilingually and loudly or fractures into itself, as in "The Love Affairs" and "The Girlfriends" in the third section.

Power, connection, discontinuity, hybridity, and borderlessness are key valences in Diana García's first poetry collection. These inner- and outer-directed narratives are also developed through García's line and stanza work. Most of the time, the poet utilizes a medium-length narrative line; the conversation is personal and seems to be attentive to the "listener." What varies is the stanza, its breath size and architecture. This is how García makes room for stories, how she casts moments and twines the sin templates of time, self, and consciousness.

Historical Context

During and particularly after the male-centered "*Floricanto* Generation" of the late sixties and early seventies, Chicana writers and poets produced, performed, and powered a woman text and a new paradigm of Latina literary practices. These new creative charters of feminist and social concerns are surveyed in groundbreaking critical works such as *Chicana Poetry, Beyond Stereotypes, Borderlands, Women Singing in the Snow, Infinite Divisions,* and *Homegirls: Chicana Literary Voices.* Diana García's new volume reinvigorates these feminist investigations within the position of a California Chicana poetics.

To begin with, García's work is from an "interior" California—from the inner spaces of a woman from the San Joaquín Valley. Naturally, we miss the point to say that *el valle* is well represented by male writers such as José Montoya, Omar Salinas, and Gary Soto. *When Living Was a Labor Camp* is not only one of the most recent collections by a poet from this region but, more significantly, it may be one of only two written by a Latina; the other is Margarita Luna Robles's *Typtich: Dreams, Lust and Other Performances.*

García's California Chicana literary mentors as seen through her work seem to be Gloria Anzaldúa, Lorna Dee Cervantes, and Bernice

Zamora. Although, Anzaldúa and Zamora are not native to the state, they both have spent many years writing major works and establishing a complex and enduring project in the area. It is possible that García is calling out from and into this site. However, to cast García's poems as merely regional is to discard her various contributions.

In a sense García's poetry is double skinned; it crosses nations, selves, women's lives and yet remains oscillating and displaced en *el valle*. And when she does leave *el Valle de San Joaquín*, she migrates to another "valley"—Brawley, Salinas, or deserts-of-sorts in the inner zones of New York, San Diego, and Kansas.

Biographical Background

As her book states, "A native of California's San Joaquín Valley, Diana García was born in Camp CPC, a migrant farmworker labor camp owned by the California Packing Corporation. "During a visit to my Chicano Artistic Expression Class at Cal State Fresno, a few years ago, Diana made it a point to let the students know about her roots, that she had been a "single mother on welfare" while she attended the very same university from 1968 to 1973. She dismantled tired notions regarding "welfare mothers" when she spoke of participating in student protests that demanded the formation of a La Raza studies program on campus, holding a series of odd jobs and spending considerable time as a sentencing consultant to criminal defense attorneys. Years later, she received both her B.A. and her M.F.A. from San Diego State University and went on to teach creative writing at Central Connecticut State University. García currently teaches at California State University, Monterey Bay, where she coordinates the Institute for Human Communication's Reading, Writing and Critical Thinking Program.

Reception of the Text

Since *When Living Was a Labor Camp* is García's first collection (2000), it is not surprising to note that there has been little time to produce a body of critical response to her offerings. Nevertheless, it is important to note that the book won the 2001 Before Columbus American Book Award. It also became one of the California Council

of the Humanities recommended books for its state-wide John Steinbeck Commemoration campaign in 2002. Given the unique "rural"
and mid-California position of the book as well as its multiple
recastings of previous Chicana and Latina concerns, ways of seeing,
and investigations, this material will no doubt be well reviewed and
discussed for years to come. On the road, in terms of community and
audience reception, Diana is invited frequently to visit campuses in
states like Ohio and North Carolina, where Mexicano working-class
populations are on the rise. As these demographic figures increase so
does the thirst for the socially powered poem and García's migrant
illuminations.

Major Themes and Critical Issues

At first glance, reading through García's book and also noting the
concatenation of themes in her vineyard of chapters, a key set of
concerns appears to be encapsulated in the phrase "Woman Observer
of the Senses and the Local." This can be seen as merging a trinity of
clustered themes: feminist concerns, daily life/work, and space.

The speakers in the poems chart their moments, minds, personas,
and environments as Chicanas, women, girlfriends, Marías, daughters,
healer women, and partners with husbands and lovers to evoke a
number of feminist questions:

Who are the Marías?
Why are these gendered speakers so careful with detail?
Why are they so busy documenting voices, locations, stories, families,
    and even "how best to clean tomatoes from twice-picked fields?"
How do gender and cultural identity and class converge?
Which is more central to García's poetic—gender, class, color, or
    culture?
Where, when, and why do these gender figures change?

These questions are all encouraged by the gender perspective of the
work. García's *campesina* camp is thus not as pastoral, static, and
monolithic as seemingly portrayed by the image on the cover. The
shifting and fluid flux of gender positioning is a major key to García's
project.

García's feminist vision also focuses on the issue of the body. This
focus begins with her corporeal frame within a variety of poems that

address the physical aspect. This body lens also gives us the opportunity to talk about the interests in permeating landscapes and relationships as well as the body of women's voices in each chapter. We can also talk of the cultural body, the herstories within the collective text of ninety-seven pieces. These may include issues of language, dialect, and the use of Caló. And perhaps more significant and radically subtle is the body-in-between. This is the speaker that wants to "return" to camp, to remember it, to feverishly document it with a "practical" air that conveys the smell, touch, and sounds of the site. Despite this insider perspective the speaker remains locked outside, in the "wild zone" as Chicana critics say, in the "Nepantla" space, in between two time spaces and time places. No matter how hard she tries to sense the "camp," the speaker is elsewhere. One of the primary activities in this in between zone is the myriad of photographic documentary operations and intimate relationships of daily life, power relations, and work.

From the initial poem, almost as a camp birthing ritual, the collection begins with "we cradled hoes." And in an ironic gesture, after we labor through the complexities and shifts of the progressive chapters, the last page ends with the migrant family "claiming the floor," an act somewhere in between work and pleasure, showing the young Diana (as narrator) how to dance. Indeed, labor is one of the central macrothemes throughout the book, whether it is by hand, the mind at work, or performed by the various agents that animate García's writing. However, there is another kind of "work" represented by García's book, something we might call *curandera* practice even though García seems to categorize it as "Serpentine."

In the third chapter, García opens with "Serpentine Voices," a poem that asks the question that indirectly and directly flows throughout the entire book and consequently may be Diana's Ars Poetica: "How many voices can I plum in this poem?" Readers thus move from hoeing cotton to crafting voices. It is this literary shaman behavior, the extracting of selves, the words of other Marías, taken from the writing body of these poems, that suggests the conjurer poet working as a healer-woman, a poetry *curandera.*

The next major thematic element of woman as observer of the senses and the local has to do with "migrant space"—the ways time and place shift, intermingle, and change frames. The "camp" that Diana yearns for and seeks to map has a seemingly fixed location—Montgomery, California—and to further contain its boundaries we can imagine, almost by occupational definition, that it is a dwelling place for a loose-knit collective of migrant farm worker families. García's text moves beyond a single locale, representing the camp as more of a blurred foreground that loses its lines of demarcation as soon as the poem begins to spiral between that distant place in the past and the speaker's present space. This interplay of time, space, and voice creatively portrays the significant "camp," the one that is inhabited by numerous counterpoints, conflicts, wavy memory fragments. And because of its migratory and peripheral nature, it is brimming with power, creativity, and the possibility for transformation—"serpentine" consciousness.

Pedagogical Issues and Suggestions

A lethal pitfall in working with Diana García's text, as with other Chicana and Latina writers, is to disconnect the examination of the text from its sociopolitical and cultural contexts and from the prismatic explosion of artistic literary materials, influences, and networks that Chicanas have recently detonated.

Chicana and Latina creative writing plays with, refers to, and is associated with an interdisciplinary field of feminist research and literary outputs. It makes good sense to prepare the way for García's work by introducing students to developments from various disciplines such as anthropology, women's studies, history, Latin American literature, art, music, film, media, performance, queer studies, Chicano and Latin American studies and American studies.

A good starting point for a discussion of García's work is to look at the recent work of Tey Diana Rebolledo, Eliana S. Rivero, and Alvina E. Quintana. In *Infinite Divisions: An Anthology of Chicana Literature,* Rebolledo and Rivero cover a incisive critical review of the literature, a new historical overview of Chicana "Foremothers," as well as a generous thematic anthology of Chicana poets. Quintana charges ahead in *Home Girls: Chicana Literary Voices* with a brilliant cultural and literary analysis of the thematic positions of Chicana poetry, envisioning a musical form, a fugue—as a new way of looking at and hearing the work.

A more immediate way to prepare the way for García's work might include the work of her mentors, her poetic "girlfriends"—Lorna Dee Cervantes, Bernice Zamora, and Gloria Anzaldúa. Cervantes's groundbreaking poetry collection, *Emplumada,* lays out much of what García takes on as her poetic charge: the personal and lyrical voice, the out-loud speaker, the role of documentary scribe, the "birdwoman," and even the sequential chapter-work of poetry made of careful mid-length stanzas. Zamora offers similar concerns in *Restless Serpents,* as well as powerful short-form poems that seem to operate as Latina poetry parables—things that must be deciphered among women about women. With *Borderlands/La Frontera: The New Mestiza,* Anzaldúa acts as Chicana thought woman, offering a magnetic set of brown feminist investigations interlacing the shamanic art of "border" writing with a pantheon of "border" goddess deities. García has studied these forerunners and taken them into her own campground.

Diana García's chapters can be further explored with some of her own mentors and favorite writers, Pat Mora, Sandra Cisneros, Czeslaw Milosz, and Elva Treviño Hart—those that pushed her into literary bravery, talking about the bigger political, personal, and global picture. Sandra Cisneros's *Loose Woman* has played a major role in encouraging a stark and open poetics about sexuality. Mora's *Chants* and other texts have delved into the powers of healing and of the voice. Milosz's *Separate Notebooks* provides the profound social convictions that poetry can embrace. Treviño-Hart, in *Barefoot Heart: Stories of a Migrant Child,* echoes and nourishes the migrant camp poetics and memoir poetry that García knows by heart.

At a more geopoetic layer, we can simply examine Mexican and immigration history in the Southwest and note how the subjects of immigration and migration are imbedded in García's verse. We can also take on an agriliterary level and review the history of the United Farm Workers' Union, one of the major catalysts for Chicana and Chicano poetry, fiction, *teatro,* music, and film. On a more contemporary dimension, discussion on world trade systems and policies will enrich the reading of Diana García's collection—global, day-to-day work by women, men, and families within the orbs of power and powerlessness.

Since García uses various poetic strategies, teaching her book creates the space for teacherly experimentation. One might begin the interpretive process by drawing a map of the places mentioned in the book and follow with a casting of family, friends, and lovers, then adding on female media icons from magazines, film posters, and toy departments. This experimental reading process might culminate by gathering these charts and using them to create a visual poetry camp García. Finally students can record some of García's poems and some of their own in order to put everything into a play that will allow them to migrate through the new camp and document their observations: the smells, the race, the gender and power relationships among the materials, the voices, and the Marías.

Literary Contexts

Published at the beginning of the new millennium in the Camino del
Sol series of the University of Arizona Press in Tucson, García's
volume is ushered in by a larger set of circumstances. To begin with,
Garíca completed her manuscript after a decade of intense movement
and work as an MFA student at California State University, San
Diego and as a professor at Central Connecticut State University.
Second, the book's publication was encouraged by Camino del Sol, a
successful and new Chicana and Chicano imprint, established in the
early nineties at the University of Arizona Press. This support materi-
alized after a decade when mid-size to large publishers had begun to
accept text produced by Chicanas and other women of color. And
finally, in the eighties and nineties the fruitful innovations, dialogue,
and volcano-like eruption of autobiographies, poetry, fiction, and
memoirs by Chicanas and Latinas had taken hold and to a degree
helped establish a Chicana way of writing and speaking about poetry.
Also, by this time much national attention and global visions had
been garnered for Chicana writers with the successes and media
coverage of writers such as Sandra Cisneros, Ana Castillo, Julia
Alvarez, Isabel Allende, and Laura Esquivel. Diana García's first title
enters the world of Latina Letters in this moment of excitement and
renewal.

Comparative Literature

Alison Hawthorne Deming's anthology, *Poetry of the American West*
provides a potent view for the placement of Diana García's work within
a North American context. Here García finds kinship with poets who
combine cultural and feminist sensibilities to highlight issues revolving
race, class, and gender. From nineteenth-century writers Gwendolen
Haste and Janet Lewis to twentieth-century writers Denise Levertov,
Adrienne Rich, Lucille Clifton, Pat Mora, Tess Gallagher, and Ofelia
Zapeda to Latin American writers María Luisa Bombal, Luisa Valenzuela,
Rosario Castellanos, Elena Poniatowska, García develops a literary
spectrum with shared interests such as the idea of a documentary
poetics, tracing the day-to-day lives of women and also releasing
women's empowered *gritos*—"no-holds-barred" voices. García builds
upon a Latin American surreal style of imagistic leaps into the subcon-
sciousness in order to fathom the abyss between the "familiar woman"

of daily affairs and the primordial and "spectral women" of absurd flight and luminous bliss.

BIBLIOGRAPHIC RESOURCES

In the area of recent Chicana literary criticism there are three books that point to Diana García's literary practice. Already mentioned is *Infinite Divisions: Anthology of Chicana Literature,* edited by Tey Diana Rebolledo and Eliana S. Rivero, and Alvina E. Quintana's *Home Girls: Chicana Literary Voices,* and lastly *Feminism on the Border: Chicana Gender Politics and Literature* by Sonia Saldívar-Hull. Of particular interest regarding the notions of writing as a healer-woman *curandera* practice and the idea of in-betweenness and hybridity are the books *Borderlands/La Frontera: The New Mestiza* by Gloria Anzaldúa and *Nepantla: Essays from the Land of the Middle* by Pat Mora. For a more general overview of Latina and Latino writers there are various collections: *The Prentice Hall Anthology of Latino Literature,* edited by Eduardo L. del Río, *Herencia: The Anthology of Hispanic Literature in the United States,* edited by Nicolás Kanellos, and *Touching the Fire: Fifteen Poets of the Latino Renaissance,* edited by Ray Gonzalez.

Finally, looking at the larger debate having to do with the intersections between culture, writing, poetics and the attempt to describe the "Other" there are three landmark books: *Culture and Truth* by Renato Rosaldo, *The Predicament of Culture in Twentieth Century Ethnography* by James Clifford, and *Writing Culture: The Poetics and Practice of Ethnography,* edited by James Clifford and George B. Marcus. These materials, written by men and centered primarily upon the debates of social anthropology, may contribute fresh insights for Chicana literary criticism, specifically the work of Diana García, since they focus on the subjects of ethnographic surrealism, cultural translation, and postmodern ethnography—keys to the ways in which Diana García picks at and harvests new snakeskins, a poetics of empowered consciousness.

Primary

Cervantes, Lorna Dee. *Emplumada.* Pittsburg: University of Pittsburgh Press, 1981.

    Cisneros, Sandra. *Loose Woman.* New York: Vintage, 1994; 1995).

    del Río, Eduardo L., ed. *The Prentice Hall Anthology of Latino Literature.* New York: Prentice Hall, 2001

Deming, Alison Hawthorne. *Poetry of the American West*. New York: Columbia University Press, 1996.

Gonzalez, Ray, ed. *Touching Fire: Fifteen Poets of Today's Latino Renaissance*. New York: Doubleday, 1998.

Kanellos, Nicolás, ed. *Herencia: The Anthology of Latino Literature*. London: Oxford University Press, 2001.

Milosz, Czeslaw. *Separate Notebooks*. New York: Ecco Press, 1984.

Mora, Pat. *Nepantla: Essays from the Land in the Middle*. Albuquerque: University of New Mexico Press, 1993.

———. *Chants*. Houston: Arte Público Press, 1994.

Rebolledo, Tey Diana and Eliana S. Rivero, eds. *Infinite Divisions: Anthology of Chicana Literature*. Tucson: University of Arizona Press, 1993.

Robles, Margarita Luna. *Typtich: Dreams, Lust and Other Performances*. Santa Monica, CA: Santa Monica College Press, 1993.

Treviño-Hart, Elva. *Barefoot Heart: Stories of a Migrant Child*. Tempe: Bilingual/Review Press, 1999.

Secondary

Clifford, James. *The Predicament of Culture in Twentieth Century Ethnography*. Cambridge: Harvard University Press, 1988.

———. and George B. Marcus, eds. *Writing Culture: The Poetics and Practice of Ethnography*. Berkeley: University of California Press, 1986.

Quintana, Alvina E. *Home Girls: Chicana Literary Voices*. Philadelphia: Temple University Press, 1996.

Rosaldo, Renato. *Culture and Truth: The Remaking of Social Analysis*. Boston: Beacon Press, 1993.

Rosa Morillas-Sánchez

Alicia Gaspar de Alba, "The Mystery of Survival"

In *The Mystery of Survival and Other Stories,* Tempe,
AZ: Bilingual/Review Press, 1993.

Textual Overview

Alicia Gaspar de Alba's short story "The Mystery of Survival" in *The Mystery of Survival and Other Stories* tells the story of a ten-year-old girl who is taken to live with Lucía, a cousin of her mother's, in the *colonia* La Gran María in Ciudad Juárez. Abused by her stepfather, the protagonist is taken by her mother on this trip. The story is told from the point of view of the protagonist, which forces the reader to approach the text through the naive filter of the protagonist's innocence. What is clear is that both mother and daughter are escaping from an abusive male figure, and they are in search of a better life.

The leitmotif of the story is the trip. It is the link between the nameless protagonist's past and the promise of a better future. During the trip, the girl and her mother talk (the girl mainly complains). During the silences between the conversation, we have access to the girl's memories, and these shed light on previous events. The reader gets information about what the girl has had to go through and realizes that the protagonist is going to learn many things that will not to make any sense to her, particularly the teachings that her mother instills in her that challenge logic (at least the logic of a ten year old). They are the kind of things that she will understand when she grows older, the mysteries of survival.

The young protagonist is half scared, half resigned about moving to Lucía's house. When she arrives she is tired; her memories are so painful and her fear so intense that she loses consciousness for a moment. When she wakes up, she is being taken care of by women, and she becomes conscious in a twofold sense, conscious after her previous state of shock and conscious of the reality that awaits her: She will be abandoned by her mother (this is the second time this happens, because she was left with her mother's sister two years before), and life will not be as easy as her mother promised. Fear of men is common in her thoughts because of a memory of her stepfather that haunts her. When the girl discovers that Lucía's father is simply a harmless old man with cataracts in his eyes, she is somehow relieved.

From then on, the protagonist will live with her mother's cousin (we don't know for how long) with the promise that her mother will return when she has a job in "*el otro lado*" (the other side), a better life for them in the United States, and the prospect of education for the girl. Symbolically, the story ends with the vision of a wooden sign that says: "*ESCUELA LA GRAN MARÍA*" (The Grand Maria School).

Historical Context

Critic Mary Helen Ponce (1995, 105) attributes the scarcity of creative works by Mexican-American women prior to World War II to several factors: lack of time, lack of models that could influence them, and the difficulty of publication (105). It is important to point out that there was a group of women from Texas that, although they did not have the time to publish, were activists in the Chicano workers movement during the 1930s. Though this fact seemingly has little to do with literature, it is significant because literature offered a way to fight for *la causa*.

Ponce refers to a group of women folklorists that wrote theses at the University of Texas as "*las precursoras*." Their writings have been criticized because they often presented a romanticized vision of a situation that in reality was incredibly hard work. But the importance of this kind of sentimental fiction should not be denied for several reasons. First, it constitutes a valid document of the folklore of the region. Second, through the romantic vision of Hispanic life on the border, we are familiarized with facts and events that are relevant to the understanding of literary works that were to be written later. Finally, despite the fact that the perspective is not overly critical, the depiction of the characters and the society remains accurate enough to be able to show "a repressive patriarchal society" (Ponce 1995, 107, my translation) between the lines. From the point of view of tradition, these women are important because they reflect the customs, folklore, and way of life of the Chicanos

During the 1950s, Mexican American women were not known outside their own North American society. This does not suggest that they did not write, as they were certainly writing about their experiences, but merely that their writings were simply unknown. It was after 1960, the year in which Mexican Americans began to be referred to as Chicanos (Rebolledo and Rivero 1993, 1), and especially during the Chicano Movement (1968–74) that Chicana writers began publishing, primarily poetry. This poetry, generally published both in English and Spanish, offered a reflection of the new Chicano nationalism (denouncing racism, searching for identity, reclaiming the mythical Aztlán, etc). With the mid-1970s came a number of narrative works that began to parallel the poetic endeavors. Although novels were being produced, the primary narrative form employed by Chicana writers in the 1970s and 80s was the short story. The current success of Chicano literature is undeniable, and one almost feels tempted to say that it will soon be incorporated into the American canon, since it has been "anthologized" greatly since the 1990s. The great proliferation of anthologies on Chicano literature has a very clear purpose: The compilation of works by Chicano authors, the presentation of new writing, the emphasis on works written by Chicanas, etc. not only celebrate and demarcate the "admission" of Chicano literature into the literary market (creating a Chicano canon) but also contribute to the integration of Chicano literature within the mainstream. As a proof of this, I refer to *The Heath Anthology of American Literature* and *The Norton Anthology of American Literature* and point out that the inclusion of Chicano works has increased incrementally in the past decade.

One of the essential themes of Chicano literature is the search for identity. Identity is of paramount importance for recreating one's own history. In the United States this identity quest necessitates at least two things: memory and struggle. I will refer to this process as "re-membering," involving "memory" and "putting pieces back together." This process is absolutely necessary for Chicanos, both in the political and historical context and also in the literary one.

Out of the panorama of Chicana writers, I have selected the voice of Alicia Gaspar de Alba, a writer who, although not included in "mainstream" anthologies as of yet, skillfully represents Chicana identity and the process of re-membering. In different terms Gaspar de Alba successfully completes the twofold process of memory and putting back together. In her personal essay "Literary Wetback" (2000), she recalls her childhood, putting forth memories that prove essential to reconstructing her adult identity as a Chicana, a lesbian, and a writer.

Biographical Background

Alicia Gaspar de Alba (1958-) describes herself as "the first Chicana fruit . . . from a two-headed tree of mexicanos" (Gaspar de Alba et al. 1989, 3), "that treasured, above everything else all of its ties to el Méjico real: customs, values, religion, and language" (Gaspar de Alba 1989: 10). Her childhood was spent in El Paso, Texas, very near the Córdoba bridge—a bridge that connects the United States and Mexico. She recalls her neighbors having Mexican names and her education being, somehow, different from theirs. She attended Loretto Academy, a private Catholic girls' school ruled by strict nuns who gave her an education closer to Anglo ideals than the environment she was immersed in would probably suggest.

When she was in seventh grade, Alicia and her family moved to the east side of town, a more Anglo neighborhood. She was constantly switching between Mexican and American environments, producing what she calls "cultural schizophrenia" (which for her constitutes the basis of Chicana identity): "Ser de origen mexicano en los estados unidos significa crecer con una esquizofrenia cultural que para mi es la base de la identidad chicana" (Gaspar de Alba 2000, 9). She was, then, either American or Mexican, depending on the cultural context, but never Mexican American or Pocho, as her parents referred to themselves, implying that they were a kind of inferior breed that could not speak properly either Spanish or English. In addition, the passage from elementary school to high school made the writer conscious of a more adult reality. Her attraction to women's liberation struggles also inadvertently fostered her interest in journalism. Sex also became more important to her in high school. At the age of sixteen, she met the man she married at nineteen. Here she "took [her] first bite out of Eve's apple" (Gaspar de Alba 1989, 3), which would greatly influence her young writings.

Gaspar de Alba later became a student at the University of Texas at El Paso, where she took some classes in writing fiction. Her interest in poetry did not emerge until her last year in college, when she took a class with James Ragan, to whom she owes "a deep respect for the imagery of [her] Mexican-American heritage" (Gaspar de Alba 1989, 3). It was through a Chicano literature class, the only one she took in college, that she discovered her own Chicana identity. After obtaining her B.A. in English (1980), she decided to pursue an M.A. in English with a concentration in creative writing, from the same university. Her Master's thesis, a first version of what later would be her book of poems *Beggar on the Córdoba Bridge,* was completed in 1983. Two years later she received a Minorities Fellowship to the University of Iowa, where she planned to earn a Ph.D. in American studies. She completed her doctoral work in American studies at the University of New Mexico (1990–94) with her dissertation: "Mi Casa [No] Es Su Casa": The Cultural Politics of the Chicano Art: Resistance and Affirmation, 1965–1985, Exhibit," (1994). The dissertation was awarded the Ralph Henry Gabriel Award for Best Dissertation in American studies of the same year.

She has taught English as a second language (ESL) in Mexico, transcribed children's books into Braille, taught composition and ESL at the University of Massachusetts in Boston, and worked as a teaching assistant in English and American studies at the University of New Mexico, a visiting lecturer in the Chicano/Latino studies program at the University of California, Irvine, and a minority scholar-in-residence at Pomona College in Claremont, CA, among other positions. During her tenure as a teacher/scholar she has never ceased to produce critical essays on Chicano culture. It was during her stay at Boston that she decided to "trade[d] American Studies for poetry" (Gaspar de Alba 1989, 3).

Her poetry, short fiction, personal essays, and some excerpts of her novel on Sor Juana Inés de la Cruz have appeared in many journals and anthologies. She has published a full-length collection of poetry, *Beggar on the Córdoba Bridge,* her first book of poetry, in the volume *Three Times a Woman: Chicana Poetry,* which appeared in 1989. Her first collection of short stories, *The Mystery of Survival and Other Stories,* was published in 1993 and awarded the Premio Aztlán in 1994. Her interest in cultural studies culminated with the publication of the "bicultural" book *Chicano Art Inside/Outside the Master's House: Cultural Politics and the CARA Exhibition,* that appeared in 1998. Her latest novel, *Sor Juana's Second Dream: A Novel,* was published in 1999 and awarded "Best Historical Fiction" in the Latino Literary Hall of Fame in 2000. The novel has been translated and published in Spain. Since 1994 she has been a professor, the first one promoted to tenure (in July 1999), at the César E. Chávez Center for Chicano/Chicana Studies at UCLA.

She is also the recipient of other awards and honors, which include but are not limited to the Massachusetts Artists Foundation Fellowship

Award for Poetry (1989), the Shirley Collier Prize for Literature (UCLA English Department Award, 1998), the Border-Ford/Pellicer-Frost Award for Poetry (1998), and Distinguished Visiting Professor at the University of Texas, El Paso (1999).

Reception of the Text

Clearly, Gaspar de Alba's artistic career has been varied. Though her more recent novel, *Sor Juana's Second Dream: A Novel,* has been reviewed quite positively, as have her many art installations, *The Mystery of Survival and Other Short Stories* has received limited critical attention. In contrast, her essays on cultural and autobiographical topics have received critical acclaim, and Susana Chavez-Silverman has written extensively on her poetry. *The Mystery of Survival and Other Stories* has been reviewed by sources such as the *Library Journal* and *Publisher's Weekly,* leaving room for much more critical attention responding to the complexity of this volume. Even though Florence Moorhead-Rosenberg has fruitfully examined the intersections between memory, identity, and culture in the collection, the volume warrants further critical consideration.

Major Themes and Critical Issues

"The Mystery of Survival" is the chronicle of a trip toward the border. Told from the perspective of a ten-year-old girl, the reasons her mother has to start the trip constitute a mystery for the protagonist. The numerous questions the girl poses either remain unanswered or are given an abstract and unsatisfactory answer by her mother. This is the way the author directs the reader's attention to the girl's innocence. The protagonist experiences a gradual loss of innocence that will not be completed by the end of the story. The girl is just awakening to life (for her a matter of surviving), and she does not have the keys for it; she is too young to understand "the mystery." When the story begins, the girl is already at her destination, that is, the events are told retrospectively, and this technique helps the narrator create a feeling of "mystery," of not quite understanding why things are the way they are.

The journey can be considered both in a literal and a metaphorical sense. In the former, we will focus on the getting away from one place to another (in the story we have enough information to know that they are escaping from an oppressive male authority); and in the metaphorical sense the journey can be taken simply as a way of rejecting that authority and finding a better way to live. The journey, this need for change, symbolizes the need for liberation from the old patterns, from the domestic ruling of men. This explains why in Lucía's house there is only an old and harmless man as a symbol of tradition. Obviously, this man is no longer the authority of the house and should only be considered as symbolically reminiscence of the past. Once the desired future is reached, women can have lives of their own. I find it interesting to approach with the journey motif from a double perspective, addressing the following questions: What are they escaping from? What are they going to find? The information in the text comes through the girl's memories, and she does not quite understand the reasons for a second trip (she was left with her aunt two years before). The very first sentence provides important information that is relevant for the understanding of the events that will take place later: one, that the girl has been "left" by her mother; and two, that at the early age of ten the girl hates men, and she is conscious of that (it is a choice forced by abuse, but a conscious choice). These two facts introduce the second big theme of the story, that the girl has been a victim of sexual abuse.

Significantly, abuse is the first thought that comes to the girl's mind when thinking about their getaway. Her life with her stepfather corresponds to his conception of life: Men have the upper hand and women exist merely to serve them and give them pleasure. The simile used by the girl's stepfather to refer to women explains it all. For him "women were like the earth, and . . . men could mine them and take anything they wanted" (9). The image of a man "mining" a woman provokes in the girl the denial of her own sexuality. Admitting that she is a woman would be accepting that she had to be "mined" by the male tool that terrifies her: "'I am not a woman,' I cried, terrified, staring down at the thing sticking out of his pants" (9). It is clear that they are escaping from abusive male authority, and the example given by the author is the worst of all the possible offences: The man is abusing the girl sexually. Literally, rape represents a sexual abuse, which explains why the girl hates men. Metaphorically, rape acts as a metaphor of men's way of acting in a patriarchal society. As María Herrera-Sobek explains: "Chicana writers . . . have utilized the rape-as-metaphor construct to critique the patriarchal system that oppresses them" (1996, 245).

Both of these interpretations help us introduce the theme of lesbianism. A lesbian identity in this work can be seen simply as a hypothesis, since there is no evidence in the text that the girl's rejection of men is due to an incipient lesbianism. However, given that the author is a lesbian herself and deals with this issue in her writing, it should be addressed. The reader can consider the metaphorical lesbianism of the protagonist as demonstrated in her obvious rejection (both sexual and emotional) of men. We can apply what Elena Poniatowska says when talking about Ana Castillo's lesbianism in relation to the hypothetical or incipient lesbianism of the protagonist: "su lesbianismo podría ser una contraparte del machismo, aquel que sometió a su madre, a su abuela, e hizo de la condición femenina una función subalterna" (Her lesbianism could be a counterpart of the machismo that subordinated her mother, her grandmother, making the feminine condition a subaltern occupation) (1995, 46).

Following the connecting threads encountered in the textual journey, we find another theme that is important in the text: the border, the contrast between Mexico and United States. Mother and daughter travel toward the border, and when they get to their destination, they will be closer to the United States, just separated by a river. The connotations suggested by this fact are clear. In order to get a better life the protagonist's mother has to "cross the river," has to go to *el otro lado,* and her intention is to bring her daughter with her once she has gotten a job.

This theme is intimately related with another very important one that has also appeared in other works by Chicana writers: education, getting independence and freedom through education, education as a way to escape from submission to the male. Gaspar de Alba suggests the theme of education in a very open way. In the last sentence that appears in the story, she uses capital letters—probably because she refers to a sign that appears nailed a wall—to refer to the name of the school where the girl is going to learn "English, too" (18). It is meaningful that the story ends with the name of the school in capital letters, because it is an undeniable sign that the girl has to get an education in order to become independent. But this need for education is also expressed in a more subliminal way, because the protagonist's mother goes to *el otro lado* with the hope of getting a job at a university. The university, and with it, education, appears as a symbol of the promise for a better future. Both mother and daughter, one on each side of the border, are going to have contact with education: Education and cultural knowledge is the way to become independent and free.

The next important theme in the text is memory, which constitutes a very important topic in Chicano/a literature. In fact, is a central theme in all the stories that make up the volume. Memory appears as a leitmotif that structures the protagonist's life, as well as the author's. Memory is related to tradition and in this sense, there is an explicit allusion to it in the story, when the girl asks her mother about the proverb that appears painted on a wall (again in capital letters): "EL PUEBLO QUE PIERDE SU MEMORIA PIERDE SU DESTINO" (A people that loses its memory loses its destiny). The girl asks her mother about the meaning of that sentence, and the mother says that she does not know, that "Mexican proverbs don't mean anything anymore." The use of "anymore" suggests that in the mother's opinion that proverb was once true, but now, because of things that have happened and their intention to leave the country, she is changing her opinion about the traditional Mexican values simply because she wants to change their destiny. The term "memory" should also be taken from a more personal perspective: the girl's. We have to take into consideration that the girl's memories are basically bad ones, or, at least, that the most haunting one is something that she wants to forget very badly: being sexually abused by her stepfather. She is affected not only by the moments of physical abuse but by the consequences of them, such as the feeling of guilt the man instilled in her and the idea that she deserves the abuse as a punishment. Her stepfather told her, "You're a bad girl! Men have to punish bad girls. Get the devil out of them. Clean the devil out with this. Swallow it! Swallow it!" (14). So there is a slight difference between the loss of memory in both characters: The mother is forced to lose her memory, she is resigned to it, while the daughter really wants to lose it but has to fight very hard to do so because those memories haunt her. She has to be more active in the process of forgetting, which is a characteristic more typical of all of Gaspar de Alba's young characters, in contrast to the passivity of old ones.

Pedagogical Issues and Suggestions

The first suggestion for approaching this text, given that it is short enough, is that it be read in class. Once this task is completed, a good way to enter the text is through a reader-response strategy. I find it useful to make the students think about any similar experiences they may have had: if they have moved; if they were happy or unhappy about that fact; how they felt about the things/people they left behind; what expectations they had about the new place they were going to, etc. This conversation helps establish the two perspectives about the journey motif that I have exposed in the previous section. The theme of sexual abuse can be raised, and students should be encouraged to give their opinions about the topic. In order to approach this theme in the story, it is useful to explore the image of men mining women and taking anything they want from them. Ask students to think or write about what the term "mine" suggests. Direct their attention toward the word "obedience." Ask them to think about the sentence "the mystery of survival is obedience" and examine why the protagonist's mother advises her daughter: "If we can obey even the most terrible thing, we will survive it. If we disobey, we will always lose. Remember that. Obey and you will survive. Disobey and you will suffer" (9). Obviously, it is very difficult to separate this sentence from the context that precedes it. Her stepfather has also told the girl that "girls . . . who talked back and disobeyed had to be dealt with in a special way" (9). Traditional Chicano culture ingrains obedience in women. Girls are commonly advised to be obedient by their mothers and fathers. In "Los derechos de la Malinche" obedience also plays a central role: "Dad, tú a mi me escribiste dos veces. La primera fue una carta para cuando cumplí seis años. Me decías que no me cortara el pelo. Que obedeciera a mi abuela." (Dad, you wrote to me on two occasions. The first was a letter when I celebrated by sixth birthday. You told me not to cut my hair and to obey my grandmother) (49).

Students can then explore the connections between obedience and survival in the stories. Survival refers to the process of endurance, things one has to bear in order to continue living. The equation is not obedience = life, but obedience = survival, and this makes all the difference. If the protagonist's mother says that "the mystery of survival is obedience," why does she "disobey" and leave? This is the line of reasoning that the girl is supposed to follow. Her mother's behavior seems contradictory, and during the whole story we know that there is something that the girl has to learn. She will learn it in an abrupt way: by having to escape and being left by her mom. The girl will receive no explanation about what is happening, she will have to discover it on her own, little by little.

Most students are familiar with these elements, and from them they will deduce that we are dealing with an initiation story. Encourage them to point out the different "rites of passage" the protagonist experiences in the story (sexual abuse, a journey, being left alone, etc.). It will also be useful to tell the students that Alicia Gaspar de Alba refers to some events in her life (such as moving, having sex, etc.) as "rites of passage" (1989, 3). A rite of passage involves a process of growth, and it implies either rebellion or painful acceptance. This will help students understand what is hinted at at the end of the story. I ask students to point out the narrative elements that show that the girl is also rebelling against the established order, tradition, or customs. This rebellion hints that the girl will fight in the future to be independent. Ask students how the protagonist will achieve this independence and lead them to have a discussion on the theme of education for Chicanas. Here I find it helpful to refer to Sandra Cisneros's *The House on Mango Street* (1983), and introduce students to Cisneros's proposal for Chicanas to get out of the oppressive *machista* Chicano environment (see Morillas Sánchez 2000) through education rather than a marriage based on confining cultural traditions. Finally, if the students have not noticed it before, point out the fact that readers are ignorant of the protagonist's name but know Lucia's. The class can then discuss the connotations of her name: It can be connected with light and with knowledge and it is also the name of the patron saint of the blind. These meanings, together with the fact that the only man that could constitute a threat for the girl is blind, give symbolic clues to the future of these women.

Literary Contexts

As it has been already commented, the search for identity is one of the most fruitful themes in Chicano literature. Chicano writers have created infinities of heroes who share a similar search for their roots, for their identity as a people. This common quest evokes a "remembering" process that involves memory, recovering the past, and putting the pieces of a dismembered identity back together again. This is a general process that takes place in Chicano authors, both men and women, a difficult but necessary search to find a literary identity, to find themselves a place in the literary panorama of the United States. This process is especially difficult and painful for women writers because their position is between feminism (generally represented by Anglo authors/ activists) and "chicanismo" (initially represented by male writers), which translates into a twofold fight, simply because they are "trapped" between two minority, often-opposed groups. They are "a marginal group within a marginal group" (Herrera-Sobek 1985, 10). Chicana writers have to fight their male oppressors in the feminist sense, but they want to share with them traditions, the search for identity, and other factors that comprise Chicano literature and culture, their own culture. At the same time, Chicana writers share feminist theories but not completely. So, more than creating their own literature and feminism from scratch, they translate the existing ones into more palatable models.

Another important fact to consider is the development of academic writings by Chicanas on Chicana literature. This has been a consequence of the need of Chicana writers to be admitted into the contemporary literary canon or canon debates. For example, one of the big achievements of Chicanas in the literary context is female characterization. The creation of female characters more in concordance with real Chicanas is a popular strategy in Chicana fictional narratives, although we can also easily translate this to the poetic personas created by Chicanas. Chicana authors no longer apply the stereotype of the *hispano* to these characters, and instead, readers can discuss the masterful depiction of strong and individual women that live in the real world. This is one of the most important differences between the female characters created by Chicano authors and those created by Chicana writers.

Gaspar de Alba rises from this literary context, which is marked by the difficulty of being a Chicana writer, a context in which, quoting Tey Diana Rebolledo, "[t]he Chicana writer . . . is an anomaly by definition" because when she becomes a writer she is ready "to take control, to express [her] environment and to break away from acceptance" (1985, 95). When Rebolledo refers to the Chicana she agrees with other authors when she says that "[she] is thrice oppressed by virtue of being a woman in a male-dominated culture, a minority in the white/Anglo culture, and because of her own ambivalence of place and state in society. She is struggling to find who she is and now to define herself within two cultures and two value systems" (1985, 94). Gaspar de Alba is four times oppressed because of her lesbianism, another flag she has hoisted that creates another "handicap" for her from the perspective of the majority.

Comparative Literature

One of the most outstanding characteristics of American short stories is precisely the theme of initiation literature, the exploration of the "rite of passage." In a literal or figurative way humans have to go through experiences that mark them and make them achieve a certain degree of maturity in a painful or abrupt way. It is precisely here that "The Mystery of Survival" fits perfectly in the American literary tradition, since this short story follows the pattern of an initiation story. A fruitful way to approach the story in question would be to juxtapose it with other traditional short stories (traditional here meaning canonical, traditionally included in syllabi) that fit under the heading of "initiation stories." I would draw, then, parallels between the short story object of our study and one that I traditionally include in my American fiction class syllabus: "My Kinsman, Major Molineaux" (1832) by Nathaniel Hawthorne. In this story, a young man travels from his village to the city in search of a better life. In order to do this, he counts on his kinsman Major Molineaux's help. The parallels with Gaspar de Alba's story are easy to draw: the journey motif, the search for a better life, and the innocence of both protagonists are worth mentioning. The resolutions of both stories differ; although the family links are present in both stories, they also trigger these differences. Family links appear as something stronger in Chicano literature (and society), especially among women, as exemplified in Gaspar de Alba's work.

Another initiation story that I find useful to compare is "I Want to Know Why" (1921). In this story by Sherwood Anderson the idea of the journey as a motif that pushes the young protagonist to achieve maturity in an abrupt way is also present. The protagonist escapes from home (a functional, happy household in this case) without his parents' permission to go to a horse race. As in "The Mystery of Survival," the protagonist discovers sex in an abrupt and traumatic way. He is confused and does not understand the implications of the experience but begins realizing his homosexuality. This tentative discovery, together with another painful one, his discovery of his capability to feel hatred for someone he had previously loved in an idealized way, forces the young protagonist to abandon the innocent world of childhood.

Other comparisons may be established so that the students understand initiation stories and the significance of the journey motif in literature. For example, we could refer to Huck Finn and Jim escaping from different oppressive impositions of society. In a similar light, our protagonist and her mother are also escaping from the machismo present in society, from the male oppressive abuse. Finally, I relate "The Mystery of Survival" with the short story "Good Country People" (1955) by Flannery O'Connor. I find it interesting to compare these two stories for several reasons: Both protagonists are female, they are both sexually violated and robbed of their innocence, and they both live in environments in which religion is vital. The settings of both stories are similar in the sense that they are marginal. "Good Country People" takes place in a Southern environment ((marginal," compared to the North), and in "The Mystery of Survival" a trip north takes place in order to get out of a "marginal" environment, closer to the border, with the hope to getting to the United States.

BIBLIOGRAPHIC RESOURCES

Primary Sources

Anderson, Sherwood. "I Want to Know Why." *American Literature: The Makers and the Making,* vol. 2. New York: St. Martin's Press, 1973. 1934–38.

Cisneros, Sandra. *The House On Mango Street.* Houston: Arte Público, 1983.

Gaspar de Alba, Alicia. "Abstract of a Life in Progress." *Three Times a Woman: Chicana Poetry.* Tempe, AZ: Bilingual Press: 1989. 3.

———. "Beggar on the Cordoba Bridge." *Three Times a Woman: Chicana Poetry.* Tempe, AZ: Bilingual Press, 1989. 5–50.

———. "Los Derechos de la Malinche." *The Mystery of Survival and Other Stories.* Tempe, AZ: Bilingual Press, 1993. 47–52.

———. "The Mystery of Survival." *The Mystery of Survival and other Stories.* Tempe, AZ: Bilingual Press: 1993. 9–18.

———. *"Mi Casa [No] Es Su Casa:" Cultural Politics of the Chicano Art: Resistance and Affirmation, 1965–1985 Exhibition.* Ph.D. diss. Albuquerque, NM: University of New Mexico, 1994.

———. *Chicano Art—Inside/Outside the Master's House: Cultural Politics and the CARA Exhibition.* Austin: University of Texas Press, 1998.

———. *Sor Juana's Second Dream: A Novel.* Albuquerque, NM: University of New Mexico Press, 1999.

———. "Literary Wetback." *Literatura Chicana: Reflexiones y Ensayos Críticos.* Rosa Morillas Sánchez and Manuel Villar Raso, eds. Granada: Comares: 2000. 9–17.

Hawthorne, Nathaniel. "My Kinsman, Major Molineaux." *The Complete Novels and Selected Tales of Nathaniel Hawthorne.* Norman Holmes Pearson, ed. New York: The Modern Library, 1209–1223.

Lauter, Paul, ed. *Heath Anthology of American Literature.* Boston: Houghton Mifflin, 2002.

The Norton Anthology of American Literature. Nina Baym, ed. New York: Norton, 1999.

O'Connor, Flannery. "Good Country People." *The Complete Stories of Flannery O'Connor.* New York: Farrar, Straus and Giroux, 1979. 271–291.

Secondary Sources

Herrera-Sobek, María. "Introduction." Beyond Stereotypes. *The Critical Analysis of Chicana Literature*. Maria Herrera-Sobek, ed. Binghamton, NY: Bilingual Press: 1985. 9–28.

———. "The Politics of Rape: Sexual Transgression in Chicana Fiction." *Chicana Creativity and Criticism. New Frontiers in American Literature*. María Herrera Sobek and Helena María Viramontes, eds. Albuquerque: University of New Mexico Press: 1996. 245–256.

Lomelí, Francisco A. "Chicana Novelists in the Process of Creating Fictive Voices." *Beyond Stereotypes. The Critical Analysis of Chicana Literature*. Maria Herrera-Sobek, ed. Binghamton, NY: Bilingual Press: 1985. 29–46.

Moorhead-Rosenberg, Florence. "Another Bridge to Cross: Memory, Identity and Cultural Syncretism in *The Mystery of Survival and Other Stories* by Alicia Gaspar de Alba." Paper presented at the Asociación de literatura femenina hispánica, Arizona State University, Tempe, AZ, September 1998.

Morillas Sánchez, Rosa. "Out of the 'Barrio': Breaking the Myth of Chicana Women in Cisneros' *The House of Mango Street*." *Literatura Chicana: Reflexiones y Ensayos Críticos*. Rosa Morillas Sánchez and Manuel Villar Raso, eds. Granada, Spain: Comares: 2000. 273–282.

Ponce, Mary Helen. "Escritoras Chicanas: Una Perspectiva Histórico-Literaria (1936–1993)." *Las Formas de Nuestras Voces: Chicana and Mexicana Writers in Mexico*. Claire Joysmith, ed. Mexico, D.F.: Third Woman Press: 1995. 105–123.

Poniatowska, Elena. "Escritoras Chicanas y Mexicanas." *Las Formas de Nuestras Voces: Chicana and Mexicana Writers in Mexico*. Claire Joysmith, ed. Mexico, D.F.: Third Woman Press: 1995. 45–49.

Rebolledo, Tey Diana. "Walking the Thin Line: Humor in Chicana Literature." *Beyond Stereotypes. The Critical Analysis of Chicana Literature*. Maria Herrera-Sobek, ed. Binghamton, NY: Bilingual Press. 1985. 91–107.

———, and Eliana S. Rivero. "Introduction." *Infinite Divisions: An Anthology of Chicana Literature*. Tey Diana Rebolledo and Eliana S. Rivero, eds. Tucson: University of Arizona Press, 1993. 1–33.

———. "The Politics of Poetics: Or What Am I, a Critic, Doing in This Text Anyhow?" *Chicana Creativity and Criticism. New Frontiers in American Literature*. María Herrera-Sobek and Helena María Viramontes, eds. Albuquerque: University of New Mexico Press, 1996. 203–212.

Salazar Parr, Carmen, and Genevieve M. Ramirez. "The Female Hero in Chicano Literature." *Beyond Stereotypes. The Critical Analysis of Chicana Literature.* Maria Herrera-Sobek, ed. Binghamton, NY: Bilingual Press, 1985. 61–70.

Sánchez, Rosaura. "Chicana Prose Writers: The Case of Gina Valdés and Sylvia Lizárraga." *Beyond Stereotypes. The Critical Analysis of Chicana Literature.* Maria Herrera-Sobek, ed. Binghamton, NY: Bilingual Press. 1985. 61–70.

Silverman, Susana Chávez. "Memory Tricks: Re-Calling and Testimony in the Poetry of Alicia Gaspar de Alba." *Rocky Mountain Modern Review* (spring 1999): 67–81.

Claudia Sadowski-Smith

Andrea O'Reilly Herrera, *The Pearl of the Antilles*

Tempe, AZ: Bilingual/Review Press, 2001.

Textual Overview

The Pearl of the Antilles tells the story of five generations of Cuban women in a narrative that moves from prerevolutionary Cuba (part one) to the 1980s United States (part two). Alluding to its allegorical treatment of Cuban history, the novel's title refers both to the island itself and to a term of endearment for one of its main characters, Rosa, who is married to a domineering and unfaithful husband. In interwoven narratives, anecdotes, and dream sequences, we also learn of the marital difficulties in the lives of Rosa's mother and grandmother, and we are introduced to Tata, a black servant of the family. The second part of the novel focuses on Rosa's daughter, Margarita, who has chosen exile in the United States, and, once there, needs to come to terms with her divided identity and her failure to communicate her past to her daughter Lilly. The novels' two parts are bridged by a collection of sometimes fragmentary or repeated letters, which span nearly twenty years and represent the only tangible connection between the two worlds and time periods depicted in *The Pearl of the Antilles*.

The novel thus touches on several major themes of twentieth- and twenty-first-century Latina and, more specifically, Cuban American women's writing. This work attempts to represent the emergence of a diasporic culture replete with intergenerational conflict and critique tenets of white, paternalistic Cuban culture, characterized by assumptions of male superiority. *The Pearl of the Antilles* highlights the plight of women in Cuba before the 1959 revolution and also censures the harsh treatment of blacks stemming from times of slavery. As Andrew Gorgey has observed in his review of the novel, *The Pearl of the Antilles* provides "a solid glimpse of life among the wealthy, landholding gentry, who were later targeted for obliteration in Castro's pursuit of a classless society" (34). In its central focus on the relationship between Margarita and her daughter Lilly, the novel also emphasizes issues of Cuban exile, immigration, and acculturation that have become staples of Cuban American writing.

Historical Context

The Spanish colonial rule of Cuba began in 1492 when Columbus claimed the island for the Spanish crown, and it lasted for four centuries. Spanish settlement led to the extermination of most of Cuba's indigenous population by the early 1500s. In the first decades of the sixteenth century, African slaves arrived to work in the gold mines, and ever-larger numbers were later employed on tobacco farms, coffee plantations, and in sugar mills. Starting in the 1840s, Yacatecan Indians from Mexico and Chinese contract workers also entered the island in considerable numbers. At the same time, racial segregation became enforced in public places. Slavery was abolished in 1886, and in 1897 Cuban rebels declared the island's independence from Spain—an event that helped incite the Spanish-American War. While the 1898 Treaty of Paris granted Cuba independence from Spain, it also gave the United States control of the island. The 1933 uprising, known as the "Revolt of the Sergeants," ultimately led to the installation of a Cuban government under Fulgencio Batista, which was officially recognized by the United States. In 1959, Fidel Castro's revolutionary forces overthrew Batista and established a socialist state, nationalizing companies, expropriating large farmlands, and eliminating land ownership by foreign parties. The ensuing largest out-migration in the island's history proceeded in a number of diverse waves and culminated in the official proclamation of Cuba as a socialist country in 1965.

Since Cuban American literature is the product of this relatively recent immigration, it is currently undergoing a process of transition from émigré or immigrant to ethnic literature. As the third largest group of Latinos, Cuban American writers have just begun to establish themselves on the scene of U.S. multiethnic and Latina writing. While Mexican Americans were the first group to unearth a literary heritage largely tied to the U.S. Southwest, they were soon followed by Puerto Rican authors, whose writing often reflects on the migration and immigration experiences of rural and working-class Puerto Ricans to the areas of New York and the northeastern United States.

Similar efforts to establish a Cuban American tradition of writing are currently under way as well. These attempts also focus on the continuities among Cuban literary productions in and off the island. As Pamela Smorkaloff has shown, Cuba's most famous writers in the eighteenth and nineteenth centuries, including Esteban Borrero, Cirilo Villaverde, and José Martí, lived, wrote, and published outside of Cuba. José Martí's writings in the late nineteenth century can even be said to exemplify the birth of the Cuban American literary tradition. As a result of immigration and the emergence of a second generation, a larger body of Cuban American literature appeared in the late 1980s and early 1990s. It includes works such as Roberto G. Fernández's *Raining Backwards* (1988), Cristina García's *Dreaming in Cuban* (1992), Oscar Hijuelos's *The Mambo Kings Play Songs of Love* (1989) as well as the poetry of Gustavo Pérez Firmat, Ricardo Pau-Llosa, and Carolina Hospital. The recent growth in literature by Cuban American women also coincided with a general surge in Latina writing in the 1980s. Katherine Gyekenyesi Gatto refers to these Latina writers as "a new breed of bilingual, bicultural, mestiza writers, who are political, *tercermundista, feminista,* and familial, and who suffer from the insecurities of straddling two cultures" (84). It is significant that the first novel in English by a Cuban American woman, Cristina García's *Dreaming in Cuban,* has attracted a broader audience than other Cuban American texts in recent years.

Latino writing has been generally divided along generational lines into work by artists who emigrated to the United States as adults and treat themes relevant to their homeland, on the one hand, and into the writings of those who were born in the United States and focus on representing issues of cultural identity in this country, on the other. Even though it is important to recognize that Cuban American writing has similarly been produced by a variety of generational and linguistic groups, O'Reilly Herrera's work shows that any categorization of intergenerational differences can only remain an approximation. Like Cristina García, O'Reilly Herrera is part of a generation of writers who left Cuba as infants or were born in the United States to Cuban parents. Sometimes also divided into "American-raised Cubans" or "American-born Cubans," this generation has been described by Gustavo Pérez Firmat as leading a "life on the hyphen" (1994). Like much other second-generation Cuban American writing, O'Reilly Herrera's novel incorporates distinctly drawn Cuban American characters and uses the United States as a central setting. At the same time, however, the novel also employs representations of prerevolutionary Cuba and engages aspects of the Cuban American relationship with the island, including the Miami community of Cuban exiles, in ways that resemble the thematic preoccupations of many first generation Cuban American authors who left the island as adults.

Biographical Background

Andrea O'Reilly Herrera is Professor of Literature and the Director of the Ethnic Studies Program at the University of Colorado, Colorado Springs. She was born in Philadelphia, Pennsylvania in 1959 of a Cuban mother and a second-generation Irish American father. O'Reilly Herrera is the editor of a collection of testimonials, *ReMembering Cuba: Legacy of a Diaspora,* and she has published fiction and poetry in such anthologies as *Little Havana Blues: A Cuban-American Literature Anthology* (edited by Dalia Poey and Virgil Suárez) as well as in a number of literary journals.

In her contribution to *Contemporary Authors,* she has said that *The Pearl of the Antilles* may be regarded as a creative counterpart to *ReMembering Cuba: Legacy of a Diaspora,* even though it predates the volume by many years. In her own creative contribution to the collection, O'Reilly Herrera writes that it "wasn't until adulthood that I came to the realization that my social and political consciousness was displaced, as it were, for it had been shaped not nearly as much by the Civil Rights Movement as by the historical events in Cuba, which were discussed every Sunday at my grandparents' house." She continues: "I . . . grew up longing for and dreaming about a world that no longer exists and a physical place I have never seen, except in photographs, but somehow know. As a result, I am confronted with a sense of deep personal loss, which is at once ephemeral and haunting" (317–8). Her sense of what she calls a "second-hand exile condition" is derived, in part, by inexplicable ancestral forces that, as she describes, lie apart from the conscious self.

Reception of the Text

Though at the time of this writing the novel has not yet been widely reviewed, Cuban American critic and poet Lourdes Gil has observed that *The Pearl of the Antilles* represents "a quest for origin and legitimacy, exquisitely written in a language that draws on the mysterious forces of continuity and renewal." She has described the novel as "a luminous celebration of [Cuba's] contrapuntal facets: its sensuous, ever-present physical beauty, alongside the cruelty and the violence that resulted in the shattering of an old order" (335). In its central focus on the lives of Cuban women on and off the island, *The Pearl of the Antilles* is potentially of interest to those pursuing topics in feminist, Cuban American, Latina, and, more generally, ethnic American and diasporic literature. O'Reilly Herrera's skill in weaving specific immigrant and ethnic cultural material into broad concerns about spirituality, inter-generational dialogue, and questions related to women's health, child-birth, and child rearing give the novel wide appeal.

Major Themes and Critical Issues

The novel's first part is filled with recovered stories and anecdotes that suggest ways in which middle- to upper-class girls like Rosa and Margarita were socialized in Cuba. The second part explores the meaning of "diaspora" for Cubans living in exile both inside and outside Miami, as well as for their children, who have never been to the island. Margarita, who is in many respects the central character of the novel, embodies the fragmentation and the deep sense of dislocation felt by Cubans in diaspora. Focusing on the lack of communication be-tween Margarita and her U.S.-born daughter Lilly, the second portion of the novel explores how elements of Cuban culture and tradition nevertheless continue to be passed down to members of Lilly's generation.

Drawing on the richness of Cuban culture, *The Pearl of the Antilles* asks readers to participate in culturally specific modes of knowing and perceiving the world. The novel employs dream-like visions, communi-cations with spirits, and telepathic conversations as ways to recreate a lost past and prophesy a future. These practices are most clearly embodied in Tata, a former slave and *santera* with fundamental links to a land that is also claimed by the Cuban descendants of Spanish colonizers. Several moving passages in the novel draw attention to the revolting treatment of Africans in Cuba—first by the Spaniards, then by colonial Cuban plantation owners, and finally by aristocratic families in prerevolutionary Cuba who continue to subordinate former slaves as farmhands and servants.

Tata's pursuit of spiritual practices eventually comes to be shared by Rosa and Margarita in ways that suggest a certain convergence of generations and races, as well as a more general affirmation of elements of Cuban culture within an emerging U.S. ethnic identity. At the end of the novel, Lilly begins the work of establishing a more meaningful bond with Margarita through the discovery of her grandmother's diary, which is filled with newspaper clippings, dream meditations, essay compositions, and photographs, as well as with Margarita's inscriptions. Although Lilly is unable to read the Spanish-language diary, its discovery prompts her to imaginatively reconstruct both her mother's and grandmother's lives. Lilly's appropriation of her matriarchal heritage and ancestry is reminiscent of the ways in which Margarita had earlier attempted to reconstruct parts of her own mother's life through the memory of her great-grandmother Mariela Ocampo (Abuela Azul). The novel thus suggests the possibility of pangenerational connection and women's solidarity through the recovery of grandmothers and through the help of spiritually powerful women like Tata.

In depicting several generations of marital conflict, the novel also critiques paternalistic elements within Cuban and American culture. After conversing with the spirit of her deceased mother, Rosa, for example, realizes that under the influence of her domineering father, Rafaela had merely become an ornament in the house, "a curio case, a vase of cut flowers" (174). Nevertheless, the next two generations of women end up marrying men that are like their fathers; and despite being shunned and abandoned by her own father, Margarita prefers her son Peter to her daughter. Only Lilly's efforts of connecting with her mother finally open Margarita's eyes to the importance of her own matriarchal heritage.

The many intergenerational and marital conflicts represented in *The Pearl of the Antilles,* coupled with its overarching and multilayered theme of loss and exile, suggest the cyclic nature of a history that Tata envisions in the opening sequence of the novel. In effect, O'Reilly Herrera depicts a Cuba that, to borrow Antonio Benítez-Rojo's concept, is caught in a cycle of endless "repetition," which is tied to Cuba's colonial history. In its focus on the relationship between Margarita and her daughter, *The Pearl of the Antilles* proposes that some elements of that history and culture continue to shape the outlines of the Cuban diaspora in the United States.

Pedagogical Issues and Suggestions

The Pearl of the Antilles can be taught in classes on Cuban American, Latina, ethnic, diasporic, and women's writing. As a parable of Cuban colonial history and as a fictional representation of the central role that memory plays within the Cuban diaspora, the novel may be integrated into courses that emphasize similar themes in Cuban American writing. The novel also echoes many of the thematic and formal preoccupations of writing by Latina authors. On the one hand, *The Pearl of the Antilles* is involved in efforts to explore the diasporic condition of émigrés/ immigrants and to trace the contours of an emerging ethnic American identity that has its roots in Cuban culture. On the other hand, the novel emphasizes non-Western forms of perception and spirituality, incorporates culturally specific materials into an otherwise English-dominant work, blurs various genres and art forms, and employs storytelling by a community of women.

The dream-like visions and conversations with the sprits of deceased kin represented in the novel can be associated with the tradition of *abuela* (grandmother) and *curandera* (healer, seer) writing that has become characteristic of much Latino/a fiction. These women figures usually combine strength and independence with the wisdom and ability to heal. In addition, the novel's integration of Cuban cultural material into an otherwise English-dominant work ensures that these elements can continue to function as reservoirs of cultural identity and as bridges across generations and geographical locations. Like other Latina writing, *The Pearl of the Antilles* blurs generic borders by integrating poems, folktales, diary entries, newspaper clippings, and letters into its narrative. Addressed to Margarita after her emigration to the United States, the letters performatively enact the very stories they tell as they recreate the ways in which Cuban émigrés tended to receive news about the island after the 1959 revolution. Several of the letters are repeated or presented as fragments to indicate how Cuban censors curtailed communication with relatives on the island. In addition, the scattered references to paintings and sculpture throughout the novel suggest a close relationship to other art forms. In *Contemporary Authors*, O'Reilly Herrera has stated that *The Pearl of the Antilles* was inspired by a watercolor painting, reproduced on the cover of the novel, which she began after her grandmother's death. The painting is a composite of several photographs of her grandmother as a young girl, and it is also described at various points in the novel as a photograph of Rosa.

Placed in the more general context of U.S. ethnic women's writing, *The Pearl of the Antilles* opens up discussions about the ways in which depictions of intergenerational differences take on a specific significance for racialized women, allowing them to think through their connections and disconnections to the cultures of their countries or regions of origin. Like other women authors, including Louise Erdrich, Amy Tan, and Barbara Kingsolver, O'Reilly Herrera employs multiple narrators to give voice to several generations of immigrants or exiles, rejecting traditional assumptions that a unitary, synthesizing narrator is capable of telling the stories they have to disclose and instead opting for multiple voicings. Because of its diasporic lens, *The Pearl of the Antilles* could also be paired with writings by Cuban, Caribbean, or Latin American authors.

Besides discussing the novel in these culturally specific contexts, it can also be usefully analyzed from several other critical angles. Thematically, it could, for example, be integrated into courses that deal with the cold war, issues of U.S. immigration, U.S.-Caribbean relations, or a more general hemispheric framework. Because *The Pearl of the Antilles* recreates prerevolutionary Cuba by engaging various forms of memory, nostalgia, and longing, the novel could be analyzed in classes stressing the narrative genres of autobiography and memoir, and their often complex ways of expressing cultural notions of selfhood and gender.

When assigned to younger readers, the novel's blending of different historical time periods and narrative voices may need to be contextualized. Instructors may want to emphasize the family tree at the beginning of the novel, highlight the dates that introduce major book chapters, and provide students with a timeline of Cuban history. An excellent timeline is available at http://www.historyofcuba.com.

Literary Contexts

Besides its Caribbean orientation, *The Pearl of the Antilles* is also in direct dialogue with the work of authors like Virginia Woolf, William Blake, William Faulkner, Emily Bronte, Toni Morrison, and Marguerite Duras. It opens with quotations from *The Odyssey* and *Agamemnon* and incorporates allusions to various Western myths. But the novel also represents an important contribution to the tradition of Cuban American writing in the United States. *The Pearl of the Antilles* creatively broaches questions of ethnicity and gender from a minority perspective, giving voice to a less well-known émigré and immigrant community. The integration of Spanish lexicon into the English-dominant novel raises interesting questions about the intended audience of contemporary Latina cultural production. O'Reilly Herrera employs Spanish, which she does not always translate into English, as a language of emotion and everyday life that is associated with food, religion, family, terms of endearment, and political events. This bilingual mode communicates elements of a culture and history that are not easily translatable, points to some of the difficulties in the relationship between members of different generations of immigrant women, and significantly complicates tendencies to uncritically appropriate Latina writing.

Comparative Literature

In its thematic preoccupations, O'Reilly Herrera's writing resembles Cristina García's *Dreaming in Cuban,* which gives voice to three generations of Cuban American women divided by relocation and exile. Moreover, *The Pearl of the Antilles* alludes to some of the same issues pursued in Achy Obejas's *Memory Mambo,* which was one of the first novels in Cuban American women's literature to explore the importance of memory for the Cuban diaspora. Even though it employs a different approach to these questions, *The Pearl of the Antilles* similarly focuses on intergenerational conflict and examines the interlinked themes of history, memory, and culture. Together, these three novels by Cuban American women writers project interesting and varied portrayals of extended Cuban families in exile or immigration. They also attest to the growth of a vibrant and diverse Cuban American community and of writing by and about Cuban Americans throughout the last few decades.

In its emphasis on the Cuban diasporic condition, *The Pearl of the Antilles* resembles work by authors such as Gustavo Pérez Firmat *(Next Year in Cuba),* Virgil Suárez *(Spared Angola* and *Latin Jazz),* Oscar Hijuelos *(The Mambo Kings Play Songs of Love* and *The Fourteen Sisters of Emilio Montez O'Brien),* and Pablo Medina *(Exiled Memories).* As it focuses on issues of cultural identity and employs certain aesthetic elements that have become characteristic of Latina writing, *The Pearl of the Antilles* could also be fruitfully juxtaposed with authors such as Helena María Viramontes, Ana Castillo, Denise Chavez, and Judith Ortiz Cofer. The depiction of Tata and Abuela Azul in *The Pearl of the Antilles,* in particular, draws on and contributes to the extensive tradition of *abuela* figures in Latino writing, exemplified, among others, in Rudolfo Anaya's novel *Bless Me, Ultima* and Ana Castillo's *So Far From God.* Similar to the *curandera* practices represented in Anaya's and Castillo's works, Tata's communication with deceased family members, her belief in the power of dreams, and her premonitions allow her to function as a bridge between past and future generations. Instructors may also consider pairing *The Pearl of the Antilles* with the work of female Cuban authors like Dora Alonso. Her 1969 novel *Tierra Inerme* condemns insurmountable differences between the working and *campesino* class and rich landowners in prerevolutionary Cuba, while also censuring racism against Afro-Cubans and critiquing the discrimination of women.

Moreover, *The Pearl of the Antilles* would lend itself well to discussion within a more general diasporic framework. It could be juxtaposed with the work of Latin American women authors like Elena Poniatowski (Mexico) and Isabel Allende (Chile). Finally, the novel's emphasis on mother-daughter relationships is reminiscent of literature by U.S. ethnic women authors, including Chinese American writer Amy Tan's *The Joy Luck Club,* Dominican writer Julia Alvarez's *In the Name of Salome,* and African American author Toni Morrison's *Beloved.*

BIBLIOGRAPHIC RESOURCES

Primary Sources

Alvarez, Julia. *How the García Girls Lost their Accents.* New York: Plume, 1992.

———. *¡Yo!* Chapel Hill, NC: Algonquin Books, 1997.

———. *In the Name of Salome.* Chapel Hill, NC: Algonquin Books, 2000.

Alvarez-Borland, Isabel. *Cuban American Literature of Exile.* Charlottesville, VA: University Press of Virginia, 1998.

———. "Narrativa escrita fuera de Cuba a partir de 1959." *Anales Literarios Narradores* 3, no. 3 (2001): 9–19.

Anaya, Rudolfo. *Bless Me, Ultima.* Berkeley, CA: Tonatiuh International, 1972.

Castillo, Ana. *The Mixquiahuala Letters.* Binghamton, NY: Bilingual Press, 1986.

———. *So Far From God.* New York: W. W. Norton, 1993.

Fernández, Roberto G. *Raining Backwards.* Houston, TX: Arte Público Press, 1988.

García, Cristina. *Dreaming in Cuban.* New York: Ballantine Books, 1992.

———. *The Agüero Sisters.* New York: Knopf, 1997.

Hijuelos, Oscar. *The Mambo Kings Play Songs of Love.* New York: Farrar, Straus, Giroux, 1989.

———. *The Fourteen Sisters of Emilio Montez O'Brien.* New York: Farrar, Straus and Giroux, 1993.

Kingsolver, Barbara. *The Poisonwood Bible.* New York: Harper Perennial, 1998.

Morrison, Toni. *Beloved*. New York: Knopf, 1987.

Obejas, Achy. *Memory Mambo*. Pittsburg, PA: Cleis Press, 1996.

Pérez Firmat, Gustavo. *Next Year in Cuba: A Cubano's Coming-of-Age in America*. New York: Doubleday, 1995.

Suárez, Virgil. *Latin Jazz*. New York: W. Morrow, 1989.

———. *Spared Angola*. Houston, TX: Arte Público Press, 1997.

Tan, Amy. *The Joy Luck Club*. New York: Putnam, 1989.

Secondary Sources

Behar, Ruth, ed. *Bridges to Cuba/Puentes a Cuba*. Ann Arbor, MI: University of Michigan Press, 1995.

———. "Foreword." *Cubana: Contemporary Fiction by Cuban Women*. Mirta Yánez, Dick Cluster, and Cindy Schuster, eds., trans. Boston, MA: Beacon Press, 1998.

Benítez-Rojo, Antonio. *The Repeating Island*. Durham, NC: Duke University Press, 1992.

Brameshuber-Ziegler, Irene. "Cristina García, *Dreaming in Cuban* (1992): Collapse of Communication and Kristeva's Semiotic as Possible Remedy." *Language and Literature* 25 (1999): 43–64.

Castillo-Speed, Lillian. *Latina: Women's Voices from the Borderlands*. New York: Simon & Schuster, 1995.

Christie, John S. *Latino Fiction and the Modernist Imagination*. New York: Garland, 1998.

"Class Struggle, World War." Review of *Pearl of the Antilles*. *Publishers Weekly* 248, no. 4 (January 22, 2001): 305.

Connor, Olga. "La diáspora cubana." *El Nuevo Herald* 4 July 2001.

Duany, Jorge. "Reconstructing Cubanness: Changing Discourses of National Identity on the Island and in the Diaspora during the Twentieth Century." *Cuba, the Elusive Nation*. Damian J. Fernandez and Madeline Camara Betancourt, eds. Gainesville, FL: University Press of Florida, 2000.

Fernández Olmos, Margarite and Lizabeth Paravisini-Gebert, eds. *Healing Cultures: Art and Religion as Curative Practices in the Caribbean and Its Diaspora*. New York: Palgrave, 2001.

Gatto, Katherine Gyekenyesi. "Mambo, Merengue, Salsa: The Dynamics of Self-Construction in Latina Autobiographical Narrative." *West Virginia University Philological Papers* 46 (2000): 84–90.

Gil, Lourdes. "Lo cubano como vocación." *Encuentro* 20 (2001): 335–37.

Gorgey, Andrew. "Cuban Then and Now." *Independent* 10, no. 16 (2002): 43.

"Herrera, (C.) Andrea O'Reilly." *Contemporary Authors* vol. 193. Farmington Hills, MI: Gale Group, 2001. 190–192, 200.

———, ed. *ReMembering Cuba: Legacy of a Diaspora*. Austin, TX: University of Texas Press, 2001.

Medina, Pablo. *Exiled Memories*. Austin, TX: University of Texas Press, 1990.

Nara, Araujo. "I Came all the Way from Cuba so I Could Speak like This?: Cuban and Cubanamerican Literatures in the US." *Comparing Postcolonial Literatures: Dislocations*. Ashok Bery and Patricia Murray, eds. New York: St. Martin's Press, 2000.

Pardiñas, Patricia. "La dialéctica del plantado: ¿cubanía o hibridez?" *Encuentro* 19 (2000–2001): 184–86.

Pérez Firmat, Gustavo. *Life on the Hyphen: The Cuban-American Way*. Austin, TX: University of Texas Press, 1994.

Poey, Delia and Virgil Suárez. "Introduction." *Little Havana Blues: a Cuban-American Literature Anthology*. Ed. Delia Poey and Virgil Suárez. Houston, TX: Arte Público Press, 1996.

Rivero, Eliana. "From Immigrants to Ethnics: Cuban Women Writers in the U.S." *Breaking Boundaries: Latina Writing and Critical Readings*. Asuncion Horno-Delgado, Eliana Ortega, Nina M. Scott, and Nancy Saporta Sternbach, eds. Amherst, MA: University of Massachusetts Press, 1989.

Smorkaloff, Pamela Maria. *Cuban Writers On and Off the Island*. New York: Twayne, 1999.

"The Timetable of the History of Cuba." Compiled by J.A. Sierra. Available at http://www.historyofcuba.com. Accessed May 19, 2002.

Stefanko, Jacqueline. "New Ways of Telling: Latinas' Narratives of Exile and Return," *Frontiers: A Journal of Women Studies* 17, no. 2 (1996): 50–69.

Weddell, Leslie. "A New Wave of Cubans," *The Gazette*. 21 April 2002.

Lisa Sánchez González

Nicholasa Mohr, *A Matter of Pride and Other Stories*

Houston: Arte Publico Press, 1997.

Textual overview

The seven stories in *A Matter of Pride and Other Stories* focus on the daily lives and desires of women of color in the urban United States. Each story in this collection deals with how Boricua women confront, analyze, and resolve the paradoxes of their daily lives in ways that affirm their basic humanity. Mohr deftly and often humorously explores the complications and strategies that women devise in transgressing the limits imposed on their lives by others. Her work touches on all of the major themes found in late-twentieth-century Latina fiction, including poverty, domestic violence, internalized racism, class and racial stereotyping, the rise of crime and gentrification in urban communities, competition between women for male attention and affection, the politics of bilingualism, Latina self-esteem, Anglocentric standards of beauty, homosexuality, and homophobia. *A Matter of Pride and Other Stories* provides a rich set of issues for class discussions, reading groups, and private reflection.

Together, the stories suggest that unexamined desire is often a dangerous force in women's lives, and that women of color must, in critical ways, self-consciously take control over and responsibility for their desire. The ethical message underlying Mohr's stories is that when a woman understands and reclaims this control over and responsibility for her desires, she can accomplish anything. For each of the central characters, understanding her desires requires careful deliberation over what, precisely, she wants from life, what she is willing to sacrifice in its attainment, and what she must do in order to mobilize her actual resources (no matter how slim) to satisfy her needs. In Mohr's fiction, the longing for a home, a career, an education, a family, or even a man transforms into a journey of self-authorship and self-ownership. Ultimately, this journey is a "matter of pride," because it entails an arduous process of maintaining self-respect and self-love in a national and communal context that otherwise socializes low-income women of color to disrespect and despise themselves and others.

Historical Context

U.S. colonialism, the relocation and internal migration of U.S. communities of color, and changes affecting New York City's low-income neighborhoods are the most immediate historical contexts for Nicholasa Mohr's fiction. Most of Mohr's characters live within the *Boricua*—or stateside Puerto Rican—community. *Boricuas* have a unique history among Latina/o groups because the nation to which they have intergenerational cultural and familial ties—Puerto Rico—has been a colony of the United States since the Spanish-American War of 1898. *Boricuas* are thus the only U.S. Latina/o community that cannot properly be described as an immigrant community. *Boricuas* share this colonial diasporic condition with some Asian American communities, such as native Hawaiians, Guamanians, and Pacific Islanders. And like African Americans and American Indians, Puerto Ricans have become citizens of the United States perforce (without their explicit consent) as an Act of Congress (the Jones Act of 1917). Since *Boricuas* are citizens by birth, their settlement in the continental United States is not an immigrant experience but rather a migrant experience. Nicholasa Mohr has described *Boricuas*'s relationship to the U.S. national community via the metaphor of adoption; like adopted children, *Boricuas* are generally considered helpless outsiders who have been taken in as an act of charity. The result is that *Boricuas* are merely tolerated as members of the nation's family, are usually unloved, and are considered ungrateful wards when they express resentment toward their guardians.

Boricuas also share with African Americans and American Indians a history of collective relocation and internal migration in the United States; large segments of all three communities were jettisoned en masse from rural to urban areas during and immediately after the turn of the twentieth century, and to and from various urban centers during the second half of the twentieth century. *Boricuas* have built important communities in many cities. Nicholasa Mohr's fiction highlights two of the oldest *Boricua* communities, East Harlem (Spanish Harlem or "El Barrio") and the South Bronx.

Biographical Background

Nicholasa Mohr was born in Spanish Harlem in 1935 and raised in the Bronx. She attributes her evolution as a writer to her experiences as a child in one of New York City's "urban villages" during the 1930s and 1940s. The Great Depression and the prewar period form an important chapter in *Boricua* history, and most of Mohr's fiction concentrates on what it was like growing up in that environment. In the past twenty years, Mohr has earned international acclaim as an author, scholar, and artist. She studied art at New York City's Art Students League, the Brooklyn Museum of Art, and the Pratt Center for Contemporary Printmaking, and her artwork has been exhibited throughout the Americas. During the 1980s and 90s she was a writer and scholar in residence at Columbia University, the National Book Foundation, the Smithsonian Institute, and the Bronx Museum of Arts, among other universities and institutes. Her awards and distinctions for her writing and service to the Latina/o community include an American Book Award, a Hispanic Heritage Award, a lifetime achievement award from the National Conference of Puerto Rican Women, and an honorary doctorate from the State University of New York at Albany. She is currently living in New York City and continues to write, lecture, and publish in a variety of venues. Her recent projects include the preparation of a musical libretto based in her novel, *Nilda,* and a number of one-act plays. Her dramatic work merges her early training as a visual artist with her writing. Within the coming year, a number of these dramatic works are projected for off-Broadway production.

Reception of the Text

Nicholasa Mohr's fiction has often been categorized as autobiographical and "juvenile" literature. Yet her complete corpus assumes much broader audiences. The author also regards the bulk of her creative writing as fiction rather than autobiography. Academic literary critics have only recently begun to recognize her as an important twentieth-century American author, and she has been duly included in a number of major American literature anthologies.

Her work appeals to those pursuing interests in feminist, working-class, and ethnic American literatures. Many scholars have difficulties dealing with the hard-hitting critiques that Nicholasa Mohr's texts assert. They are also hard-pressed to understand her appropriation of certain genres of writing, especially her use of the "coming of age" bildungsroman story. Literary scholars have devoted little critical attention to the artwork included in some of her fiction.

A Matter of Pride and Other Stories, like most of Mohr's fiction, seems to send different messages to different audiences. Latina readers tend to find her fiction vindicating, primarily because they enjoy seeing aspects of their personal lives interpreted from a feminist perspective. Readers from different cultural or class backgrounds sometimes find her work vexing, because of the overlapping edges of class, racial, gender, linguistic, sexual, and colonial oppressions that she represents. Because Mohr's work is provocative rather than merely evocative of the Latina condition, her fiction elicits critical and emotional response. She does not rely on the stereotypical representations of Latinas, nor does she employ the usual nostalgic or otherwise conventional tropes and characterizations—such as the *sufrida* (all-suffering woman), Latin spitfire, *abuelita* (saintly grandmother), *curanderismo* (racialized mysticism), *cocina maravillosa* (cultural food fetishization), and derivative "magical" realist devices—now common to immigrant Hispanic women's writing. Her writing therefore requires critical consideration of the relationship of various audiences' life experiences to the experiences presented in her work, as well as a close consideration of the conventions and audience expectations of Hispanic women's writing.

Major Themes and Critical Issues

Virtually all of Mohr's short stories explore how young adult women, adolescents, and children in the *Boricua* community manage to survive and even thrive despite the manifold forces of oppression that assault their minds, bodies, and souls. Her fiction addresses how poverty, physical and emotional abuse, racial prejudice, employment discrimination, and other hostile life conditions are expressed, internalized, and contested in the most intimate aspects of daily life. Mohr's characters negotiate these oppressions and try to transgress the limits imposed on their lives in creative ways, sometimes with mixed success. Yet her protagonists tend to win this struggle for self-respect and self-love, and in detailing their successes Mohr offers a pedagogical lesson on female self-sovereignty.

Self-sovereignty—the challenge of taking responsibility for and control over one's destiny—is a major theme in twentieth-century ethnic American literature. This theme addresses an important, basic, and urgent question for all Americans: How can women of color live autonomous and fulfilling lives when their lived environments generally bar them from access to material resources (money and property), to institutional resources (education, legal rights, and jobs), and to social connections (influential networks), all of which are necessary resources for success in the United States? These issues are extremely relevant to *Boricua* women, who collectively experience one of the highest poverty rates and one of the lowest employment and educational attainment rates in the United States.

Pedagogical Issues and Suggestions

Her main characters' wit, persistence, and intelligence in the face of seemingly insurmountable obstacles imply a certain pedagogical function in Mohr's stories. Her narrators are especially important to this method; they tend to present a specific dilemma with feminist acumen and work it through to a just resolution. Instructors can make this hermeneutic process explicit to their students and thus open discussions about how women of color successfully take control of their lives by critically examining, reshaping, and then acting upon their own desire. This lends an opportunity for students to evaluate both the characters' and the narrators' assessments of women's traditional roles and possible reasons for accepting, redefining, or rejecting these roles. Whether students agree with the narrators' feminist interpretations or not, these stories tend to open a series of fascinating and usually polemical discussions in the classroom. These stories also evince aesthetic innovations and thus provide interesting material for both college seminars and creative writing workshops. Mohr's innovations on the American short story—her succinct presentation of emblematic paradoxes in daily life, her intransigent insistence upon centering and valuing female desire, her skill in defining social context in miniature, her engagement of the reader in her plot structure, her attention to broad ethical concerns such as social justice, and her skill at weaving first person narration, first person indirect discourse, and dialogue—provide a wealth of topics for discussion of craft and literary innovation.

Literary Contexts

Nicholasa Mohr belongs to the generation of *Boricua* writers who began publishing fiction in the wake of the U.S. civil rights movement.

Across ethnic lines, writers of this era appropriated and reinvented many literary genres and conventions. Her work is especially relevant to the evolution of twentieth-century ethnic American social realism.

Critics of Mohr's fiction often and erroneously assume a Latin American literary influence in her work. She herself has asserted that there is no tacit link between her writing and insular Puerto Rican literature. In fact, where women writers are concerned, the rift between American and Latin American writing is wide. Latina writing of the post-war period evolved in the discursive context of civil rights and social protest. Whether composed in English, Spanish, or Spanglish, Latina writers creatively broach questions of race, ethnicity, class, and gender from a minority standpoint. Their work voices the experience of abjectly disempowered constituencies—or subaltern communities—in the United States through genres relevant to U.S. literary history, while Latin American women writers tend to voice perspectives of more privileged constituencies through genres that have evolved in distinct national and regional literary historical contexts.

It makes sense that, given more privilege—actual material resources and access to influential networks and institutions, such as flagship national universities and political parties—women writers from Latin America have a very different world view and set of experiences informing their work. Subaltern feminine perspectives in Latin American writing are usually represented by elites via highly problematic characterizations. Likewise, since Latin American literary critics have yet to identify and analyze any distinct bodies of ethnic women's literature in national and regional contexts, the representation of subaltern voices is usually comprehended by nonfictional and more anthropological genres, such as the testimonial writing and ethnography.

Yet one might convincingly argue that the literary influence is currently working in reverse of the standard assumption, or that Latina writers have had an impact on Latin American women writers. For example, there is evidence of a strong and positive influence of Latina short story writing on the work of Ana Lydia Vega as well as the Latina reinvention of the bildungsroman—especially the mode of representing the narrator's coming to consciousness as a sexualized process—on the novels of Magali García Ramis and Mayra Santos. Another interesting inquiry of late has been the economic motives behind marketing translations of elite Latin American women writers, such as Rosario Ferré and Isabel Allende, as Latina writers by U.S. publishers. Critical and somewhat political questions have arisen about this insertion of elite perspectives into a corpus of writing that has been largely proletarian in the United States.

Comparative Literature

Some of the allusions in *A Matter of Pride and Other Stories* are to important feminist figures in American history, such Sojourner Truth, Jane Addams, and Margaret Sanger. One of her characters in this text also alludes to Simone de Beauvoir's feminist manifesto, *The Second Sex.*

There is a strong literary historical and thematic link between African American, Afro Caribbean, and *Boricua* trajectories in Mohr's work, especially writing of the trans-Latino and pan-American New York City experience. Comparisons with novelists such as Piri Thomas, Paule Marshall, Jamaica Kincaid, Claude Brown, and Edwidge Danticat, and short story writers such as Ed Vega, Nella Larsen, and Jack Agueros, are especially pertinent. The work of Luisa Capetillo, Pura Belpré, and Sandra María Esteves is also relevant to understanding and contextualizing Nicholasa Mohr's fiction.

BIBLIOGRAPHICAL RESOURCES

Primary Sources

Mohr, Nicholasa. *El Bronx Remembered: A Novella and Stories.* New York: Harper and Row, 1975.

———. *In Nueva York.* New York: Dial, 1977.

———. *Felita.* New York: Dial, 1979.

———. *Rituals of Survival: A Woman's Portfolio.* Houston: Arte Público Press, 1985.

———. *Going Home.* New York: Dial, 1986.

———. *Nilda.* New York: Bantam, 1974. Rpt. Houston: Arte Público Press, 1986.

———. "The Journey toward a Common Ground: Struggle and Identity of Hispanics in the U.S.A." *Americas Review* 18, no. 1 (spring 1990): 81–85.

———. *All for the Better: A Story of El Barrio.* New York: Steck Vaughn, 1993.

———. *Growing Up Inside the Sanctuary of My Imagination.* New York: J. Messner, 1994.

———. *La canción del coquí y otros cuentos.* New York: Viking, 1995.

―――. *The Magic Shell.* New York: Scholastic. 1995.

―――. *Old Letivia and the Mountain of Sorrows.* New York: Viking, 1996.

―――. *A Matter of Pride and Other Stories.* Houston: Arte Público Press, 1997.

Secondary Sources

Cooney, Rosemary Santana and Alice Colón. "Work and Family: The Recent Struggles of Puerto Rican Females." *Historical Perspectives on Puerto Rican Survival in the United States,* 2d ed. Clara E. Rodríguez and Virginia Sánchez Korrol, ed. Princeton, NJ: Marcus Wiener, 1996. 69–85.

De Jesús, Joy L. *Growing Up Puerto Rican: An Anthology.* New York: Morrow, 1997.

Dwyer, June. "The Wretched Refuse at the Golden Door: Nicholasa Mohr's 'The English Lesson' and America's Persistent Patronizing of Immigrants." *Proteus* 11, no. 2 (fall 1994): 45–48.

Fernández Olmos, Margarite. "Growing Up Puertorriqueña: The Feminist Bildungsroman and the Novels of Nicholasa Mohr and Magali García Ramis." *Centro II,* no. 7 (1989–90): 56–73

―――. *Sobre la literatura puertorriqueña de aquí y de allá: Approximaciones feministas.* Santo Domingo. Ed. Alfa y Omega, 1989.

Gregory, Lucille H. "The Puerto Rican 'Rainbow': Distortions vs. Complexities." *Children's Literature Association Quarterly* 18, no. 1 (spring 1993): 29–35.

Heredia, Juanita. "Down These City Streets: Exploring Urban Space in *El Bronx Remembered* and *The House on Mango Street.*" *Mester* 22–23, no. 2–1 (fall/spring 1993/4): 93–105.

Hernández, Carmen Dolores. *Puerto Rican Voices in English: Interviews with Writers.* Westport, CT: Praeger, 1997.

McCracken, Ellen. "Latina Narrative and Politics of Signification: Articulation, Antagonism, and Populist Rupture." *Critica: A Journal of Critical Essays* 2, no. 2 (fall 1990): 202–07.

Mohr, Nicholasa. "Puerto Rican Writers in the U.S., Puerto Rican Writers in Puerto Rico: A Separation beyond Language: Testimonio." *Breaking Boundaries: Latina Writing and Critical Readings.* Asunción Horno-Delgado, et al., eds. Amherst: University of Massachusetts Press, 1989. 111–116.

Rodriguez-Luis, Julio. "De Puerto Rico a Nueva York: Protagonistas femeninas en busca de un espacio propio." *La Torre: Revista de la Universidad de Puerto Rico* 7, no. 2 (July-December 1993): 577–94.

Sánchez Korrol, Virginia. *From Colonia to Community: The History of Puerto Ricans in New York City.* 2d ed. Berkeley: University of California Press, 1994.

Dionne Espinoza

Cherríe Moraga, *Loving in the War Years: Lo Que Nunca Pasó Por Sus Labios*

Boston: South End Press, 1983.

Textual Overview

Loving in the War Years, a semi-autobiographical text, documents the political and personal journey of the author, a mixed-race Chicana lesbian feminist. In poetry, journal entries, short prose pieces, and essays, Moraga explores the issues of family socialization; mother-daughter relationships; internalized ideas about race, class, gender, and sexuality; the intersections of cultural identity and sexuality, especially as these impact Chicana lesbians; the complexities of women loving women in a homophobic society; the limitations of liberation movements that do not adequately address the intersection of oppressions; and the need for coalition politics in projects of social change.

The essays "It Is You, Sister, Who Must Be Protected," "Pesadilla," "La Güera," and "A Long Line of Vendidas" in particular unravel the intersections of family, gender, race, and cultural identity as these influence her capacity to articulate sexual self-determination. In "La Güera" and "A Long Line of Vendidas" (both of which have been reprinted in numerous anthologies), Moraga explores the intimate space of her family sphere, where expectations about race, class, gender, and sexuality are manifested in cultural practices and belief systems about what it means to be a man or a woman in Chicana/o culture. Within this intimate space, Moraga internalizes racism, sexism, and homophobia, which impede her ability to acknowledge her identity as a lesbian.

In "A Long Line of Vendidas," the capstone essay of the text, Moraga not only considers her childhood socialization but goes on to examine how the sexual politics of Chicano culture are manifested in the Chicano movement. Observing that social movements claiming to seek social justice for a group have the potential for reproducing sexism, homophobia, and racism among their own constituencies, she criticizes racism in the women's movement and the lesbian separatist movement. Arguing that we must move beyond these exclusionary practices, Moraga embraces and advances the concept of Third World feminism and calls upon oppressed groups to challenge their internal contradictions and to create agendas that truly seek the flourishing of all of their members.

Historical Context

Closely following the publication of *This Bridge Called My Back: Writing By Radical Women of Color* (1981)—the landmark anthology that challenged racism in the women's movement and that she coedited with writer Gloria Anzaldúa—Moraga's *Loving in the War Years* (1983) appeared within the following contexts: a surge in independent, progressive, and lesbian feminist small presses after the crystallization of a lesbian feminist movement from within the women's movement; the rise of a "women of color" and "Third World feminist" political identity after women's challenges to sexism in the male-dominated race-based social movements of the sixties and seventies; the disappointments experienced by women of color who encountered racism in the women's movement; a boom in Chicana literary production; and the conservative politics of the Reagan presidency.

During the rise in independent feminist and lesbian publishing with the latter part of the women's movement, Persephone Press opened and produced several pivotal texts speaking to lesbian and feminist movements, including *The Coming Out Stories* (edited by Susan Wolfe and Julia Penelope), in which young lesbian writers, including Cherríe Moraga, who contributed "La Güera," offered their testimonies. Additionally, Persephone Press originally published *This Bridge Called My Back,* but after they closed in 1983, the founders of Kitchen Table: Women of Color Press negotiated to publish a second edition of the manuscript.

Moraga's first book-length manuscript, *Loving in the War Years: Lo Que Nunca Pasó Por Sus Labios,* was published by South End Press, an independent publishing collective committed to producing books that address issues of social justice. The text explicitly identifies with Third World feminism, a concept emerging from the disappointments experienced by women of color in the male-dominated, race-based social movements of the 1960s and 70s, especially the Black Power and Chicano Power movements, and from the lack of attention to race, as well as outright racism, in the women's movement of the 1970s, where women of color were often ignored in the political agenda put forward by white women. For this reason, within the publishing establishment, a group of lesbians of color, including Cherríe Moraga, founded the Kitchen Table: Women of Color Press Collective, in which Moraga was the first non-black member.

During the 1970s, there was a literary and cultural renaissance of the Chicano movement, which fostered poetry readings, writing workshops, visual arts, and theatre performances. Many Chicana and Latina writers participated in this literary and cultural renaissance, where they not only read their poetry and short fiction at political and arts gatherings but also began to publish in literary magazines and journals. By the 1980s, along with *This Bridge Called My Back* (1981) and *Loving in the War Years* (1983), a "boom" in Chicana and Latina writing appeared to be taking place, with the appearance of Lorna Dee Cervantes's collection of poetry *Emplumada* (1981), Sandra Cisneros's award-winning *House on Mango Street* (1983), and Helena María Viramontes's *The Moths and Other Stories* (1985). Moraga contributed to this boom with her coediting of the groundbreaking collection *Cuentos: Stories by Latinas* (with Alma Gómez and Mariana Romo-Carmona, 1983) and *The Sexuality of Latinas* (with Norma Alarcón and Ana Castillo, 1983).

In addition to participating in the "boom" in Chicana/Latina literary production in the 1980s, *Loving in the War Years* represented a "first" in writing by Chicana and Latina lesbians. By the 1990s, Latina lesbians had produced an impressive body of work, including Terri De La Peña, *Margins* (1992), Carla Trujillo, *Chicana Lesbians: The Girls Our Mother Warned Us About* (1993), Emma Pérez, *Gulf Dreams* (1996), Achy Obejas, *We Came All the Way from Cuba So You Could Dress Like This?* (1994) and *Memory Mambo* (1996). Although the 1980s represented a decade of conservative public and foreign policies, including a backlash against the feminist and gay rights movements, U.S. intervention in the self-determination process of Latin American countries, and Reagonomics, which increased the gap between the upper class and working class, Moraga's work and that of other lesbians of color continued to raise the issues of social justice as lived by working-class women of color in the United States.

Biographical Background

Born in 1952 and raised in California's San Gabriel Valley, Cherríe Moraga is the daughter of a Mexican mother and a white (Irish) father. She attended Immaculate Heart College in Los Angeles, where she received her B.A. Reflecting upon that experience Moraga stated, in an interview with Rosi Reyes, "It wasn't like a regular Catholic school—it was very radical." After she came out, in 1974, she began writing regularly and, after encountering classism and racism in the lesbian feminist movement, developed writing circles for working-class women and women of color. In 1980, she received an M.A. in literature at San Francisco State University and has taught courses at Stanford University, San Francisco State University, and UC Berkeley.

Moraga has won several awards for her work, including the Before Columbus Foundation American Book Award (1986) for *This Bridge Called My Back: Writings by Radical Women of Color;* The Fund for New American Plays Award for "Shadow of a Man" (1990) and "Watsonville: Some Place Not Here" (1995); and the Pen West Award for Drama, the Critics Circle Award, and the Will Glickman Prize for the Best Play of 1992 for "Heroes and Saints." She has been a recipient of the National Endowment for the Arts' Theatre Playwrights' Fellowship (1993). In 2001, she was honored as a National Association for Chicana and Chicano Studies Scholar for her literary accomplishments, her commitment to Chicana/o communities, and her history of teaching excellence.

In 2000 *Loving in the War Years* was reissued as an expanded edition with a new preface and additional material (South End Press Classics). Moraga's other publications include *The Hungry Woman: A Mexican Medea* (2001), *Waiting in the Wings: Portrait of a Queer Motherhood* (1997); *Heroes and Saints & Other Plays* (1994); *The Last Generation: Prose & Poetry* (1993); *Giving Up the Ghost: Teatro in Two Acts* (1986). In addition to *This Bridge Called My Back,* she coedited several important volumes of Chicana/Latina writing, including *Cuentos: Stories by Latinas* (with Alma Gómez and Mariana Romo-Carmona, 1983); *The Sexuality of Latinas* (with Norma Alarcón and Ana Castillo, 1983); and the Spanish translation of *This Bridge Called My Back, Esta Puente, Mi Espalda: Voces de Mujeres Tercermundistas en Los Estados Unidos* (with Ana Castillo, translated by Ana Castillo and Norma Alarcón, 1988).

Reception of the Text

At the time of its publication, *Loving* broke silences around sexuality and lesbian identity within Chicana/o communities and challenged the homophobia of the Chicano Movement of the 1960s and 70s. As Terri de la Peña stated in a reflection on Chicana lesbian writing, "In those unflinching poems and essays, Cherríe seemed to speak directly to me with her candid depiction of the intense dynamics between a lesbian daughter and her Mexican American family." These dynamics not only spoke to Chicana lesbian feminists, who had, to that time, few publications that openly spoke of homophobia and heterosexism, but also to heterosexual Chicana feminists, who welcomed Moraga's honest exposé concerning the perpetuation of cultural norms that subordinate women and maintain male sexual privilege by representing women as potential sexual traitors, as embodied in the story of the indigenous woman, *La Malinche,* who served as Hernan Cortéz's translator.

Major Themes and Critical Issues

A major theme in *Loving in the War Years* speaks to the dynamics of the family sphere, and in particular, women's complicity in the reproduction of gender roles within Chicano families. In the first section of "A Long Line of Vendidas," Moraga declares, "My Brother's Sex Was White. Mine, Brown," and relates the expectation that she and her sister meet her brother's demands, including serving refreshments to his friends, making his bed, cleaning his room, shining his shoes, and ironing his shirts. While she locates this expectation in her mother's own socialization within her own family, she does not blame her mother for participating in the process of reproducing gender limitation. Rather, she comes to a clearer understanding of the dynamics of oppression and of her subordination as a woman and to a stronger identification with her mother (90–94).

The baggage of internalized racism, sexism, and homophobia and the intersection of race, gender, sexuality, and culture also occupy a prominent place in Moraga's text. In "La Güera" and "A Long Line of Vendidas," Moraga admits that she is encouraged to pass as "white" by her mother. Given her increasing awareness of her sexual preference for women and her sense that she would be "sexually stigmatized" in Chicano culture, which held a "personal power" over her, Moraga

passes in order gain sexual mobility and self-determination: "I gradually became anglocized because I thought it was the only option
available to me toward gaining autonomy as a person without being
sexually stigmatized . . . I instinctively made choices which I thought
would allow me greater freedom of movement in the future" (98).
When Moraga comes out as a lesbian, she also comes to a deeper
awareness of her deep cultural ties and connections to her mother's
ethnicity.

Moraga also goes beyond her family sphere to launch an analysis of
how the cultural and sexual politics of the Chicano Movement of the
1960s and 70s, while advancing a social change agenda, nevertheless
undermined women's sexual freedom. In a searing analysis of sexism
and homophobia in the Chicano movement, she identifies the factors
contributing to a hostile environment for gay and lesbian Chicanos,
including male dominance and sexual control of woman through
regulating myths such as that of *La Malinche;* the alongside-our-men
knee-jerk reaction of women who refused to challenge male privilege;
and the limitations of early Chicana feminist rhetoric, which named the
harassment and labeling of feminists as "lesbians" but did not critique it
(105–113).

Finally, coalition politics are also a central preoccupation in *Loving
in the War Years.* In an often-quoted and difficult passage from "La
Güera," Moraga declares, "In this country, lesbianism is a poverty—as
is being brown, as is being a woman, as is being just plain poor. The
danger lies in ranking the oppressions. The danger lies in failing to
acknowledge the specificity of the oppression. The danger lies in
attempting to deal with oppression purely from a theoretical base.
Without an emotional, heartfelt grappling with the source of our own
oppression, without naming the enemy within ourselves and outside of
us, no authentic, non-hierarchical connection among oppressed groups
can take place" (53). Moraga draws a connection between "oppressions"
through the metaphor of poverty. But Moraga does not simply collapse
oppressions into each other or claim that everyone is "oppressed."
Instead, she calls for a recognition of the different ways that individuals
are oppressed, as necessary to a more inclusive coalition politics.

Pedagogical Issues and Suggestions

This text has proven to generate a high level of student interest in
discussing the topics of Chicano family dynamics, Chicana lesbian

identity, women's sexual agency in Chicana/o culture, and coalition politics. Students are less likely to consider the narrator's analysis of class differences within the Chicano community or how class intersects with race and gender. In a revealing account of how class intersects with racism and sexism in the educational system, Moraga describes the racialization of her Chicana friends by her mother, who warns her against them for their darker skin, and by the educational system, where, despite their abilities, they are placed in the vocational track.

Because the figure of *La Malinche* in "A Long Line of Vendidas," is so central to the analysis, supplementary reading on the history of *Malintzin Tenepal,* or *La Malinche,* the indigenous woman who translated for Hernan Cortéz, would enhance students' understanding of Moraga's argument. Two key references for considering the complexities of this figure as the origin of beliefs about Chicana/Mexicana womanhood and sexual agency are Adelaida Del Castillo's landmark essay, "*Malintzin Tenepal:* A Preliminary Look into a New Perspective," and Norma Alarcón's "Chicana's Feminist Literature: A Revision through *Malintzin* or *Malintzin:* Putting Flesh Back on the Object."

Moraga's internal critique of Chicana/o culture requires careful consideration of her declaration that "To be critical of one's culture is not to betray that culture" (108). Students who lack a larger understanding of sexism and heterosexism in U.S. society may be inclined to simplistically see in Moraga's account proof that Chicano men are excessively "macho" and sexist. They may also perceive Chicana/o culture as "more" homophobic in relation to mainstream U.S. society. To work students through the complexities of Moraga's analysis, one can draw attention to sexism and heterosexism in U.S. society and to the significance of the Catholic church in Mexican culture and its regulation of sexuality. Additionally, students should be asked to consider, based on Moraga's account, how gender and sexuality are lived by individuals based on one's cultural identity, which can include race and ethnicity, religion, nation of origin, linguistic choice, and class identity.

The following list of discussion topics can aid in drawing out the central ideas of the text:

Describe the dynamics of the narrator's relationships with her mother and her father.
How does class intersect with race and gender in Moraga's educational and family experiences?
What are Moraga's reasons for "passing" as "white"?

How does the narrator claim *La Malinche* and apply it to her own life?
What does the phrase, "We Fight Back With Our Families" mean? What
   is Moraga's criticism of the Chicano Movement? How does Moraga
   redefine family?
According to Moraga, what are some of the issues impeding Chicana
   sexual freedom? Analyze the following quote from "La Güera": "In
   this country, lesbianism is a poverty—as is being brown, as is being a
   woman, as is being just plain poor. The danger lies in ranking the
   oppressions. The danger lies in failing to acknowledge the specificity
   of the oppression" (52). How can this statement contribute to a
   productive coalition politics?

Literary Contexts

A common theme in the 1980s "boom" literature by Chicanas and
Latinas was an increasing attention to the experiences of young
women in Chicano/Latino culture, especially the dynamics of gender
socialization through family, the church, male-female relationships,
and the imposition of regulating taboos and myths about sexuality.
Contributing to this dialogue, *Loving in the War Years* served as a
forum in which Moraga addressed these issues as they occurred
within the spheres of the family, church, and educational system, but
went further to question how sexism—and, more personally and
painfully, heterosexism—have been reproduced within political communities. She specifically engages in a critique of the Chicano Movement of the 1960s and early 70s for its perpetuation of cultural-
gender roles—exemplified by the ideology of *la familia* as the unit of
political resistance—and advocates for a Third World feminist coalition politics.

In addition to advancing political theory through a literary text,
Loving in the War Years introduced the technique of bridging more
than one genre—including poetry, short prose pieces, journal entries,
and essays—a technique that is now identified strongly with writing by
Chicanas/Latinas. As exemplified in the later publication of Gloria
Anzaldúa's *Borderlands/La Frontera: The New Mestiza* (1987), the
choice of multiple genres invites a consideration of the most effective
ways to represent silenced stories in literary form. In addition to mixing
genres, Moraga also mixed languages, choosing to move between
Spanish and English in selected pieces.

In an interview with Norma Alarcón, Moraga identified several
literary influences. She has described her sense of connection with the

writings of Rudolfo Anaya and James Baldwin as conveying a sense of "*familia*" and the "feminine." She cites Adrienne Rich's "Diving into the Wreck" and Judy Grahn's "A Woman Is Talking to Death" as poetry that "had a great effect on me. "Rich's work showed her that poetry can be used to "make sense of her life" while Grahn's demonstrated that one can use "a very simple, ordinary language to talk about very complex ills in our world." This emphasis on naming personal experience and articulating larger social issues speaks directly to Moraga's sense of the role of the educated, working-class intellectual.

Comparative Literature

Loving in the War Years participates in the tradition of ethnic autobiography in which the narrator recounts his or her experience as an ethnic minority within dominant U.S. society and culture as a series of encounters with racism and as a set of conflicts between cultures. But *Loving in the War Years* goes further than this in two ways: 1) by calling for attention to sexism and heterosexism within ethnic minority and dominant U.S. society and culture, and 2) by claiming a bilingual and bicultural identity in a society that requires monolingual and monocultural identity.

In contrast to *Loving in the War Years*, Richard Rodriguez argues in his autobiography *Hunger of Memory: The Education of Richard Rodriguez* that it is necessary to privatize cultural experience and suppress differences of race, class, gender, sexuality, and language in order to become an effective citizen in American society's "public" realm. Alternatively, *Loving in the War Years* adds to an understanding of lesbian history when taught alongside Audre Lorde's *Zami: A New Spelling of My Name,* identified by Lorde as a "lesbian biomythography," in which she explores her coming of age in the lesbian bar culture of the 1950s.

In a course that addresses the politics of race and feminism in the U.S. women's movement, additional complementary texts include Audre Lorde's *Sister/Outsider: Essays and Speeches* (1984) and Adrienne Rich's essay "Disloyal to Civilization: Feminism, Racism, Gynophobia" (1978) in *On Lies, Secrets, and Silence: Selected Prose 1966–1978.* Gloria Anzaldúa's *Borderlands/La Frontera: The New Mestiza* (1987) can also be taught alongside *Loving in the War Years* as a way to discuss not only similarities in the writers' strategies but

also how regional histories inform differences between Chicana
writers.

BIBLIOGRAPHIC RESOURCES

Primary Sources

Alarcón, Norma and Ana Castillo, eds. *Sexuality of Latinas*. Berkeley: Third Woman Press, 1983.

Anzaldúa, Gloria. *Borderlands/La Frontera: The New Mestiza*. San
Francisco: Spinsters/Aunt Lute, 1987.

———— and Cherríe Moraga, eds. *This Bridge Called My Back:
Radical Writings By Women of Color*. Watertown, MA: Persephone
Press, 1981; 2d. ed. New York: Kitchen Table Press, 1983.

Cervantes, Lorna Dee. *Emplumada*. Pittsburg: University of Pittsburgh Press, 1981.

Cisneros, Sandra. *The House on Mango Street*. Houston: Arte
Público, 1983.

De La Peña, Terri. *Margins*. Seattle: Seal Press, 1992.

Gómez, Alma and Mariana Romo-Carmona, eds. *Cuentos: Stories
by Latinas*. New York: Kitchen Table Press, 1983.

Grahn, Judy. *The Work of A Common Woman: The Collected
Poetry of Judy Grahn*. New York: St. Martin's Press, 1978.

Lorde, Audre. *Zami: A New Spelling of My Name*. Freedom, CA:
Crossing Peers Press, 1982.

————. *Sister/Outsider: Essays and Speeches*. Trumansburg, NY:
Crossing Peers Press, 1984.

Cherríe Moraga. *Giving Up the Ghost: Teatro in Two Acts*. Berkeley: Small Press Distribution, 1986.

————. *Esta Puente, Mi Espalda: Voces de Mujeres Tercermundistas
en los Estados Unidos*. Norma Alarcon and Ana Castillo, eds. and
trans. Berkeley: Third Woman Press, 1988.

————. *The Last Generation: Prose and Poetry*. Boston: South End
Press, 1993.

————. *Waiting in the Wings: Portrait of a Queer Motherhood*.
Ithaca, NY: Firebrand Books, 1997.

————. *The Hungry Woman: A Mexican Medea*. Albuquerque:
University of New Mexico Press, 2001.

———. *Heroes and Saints & Other Plays.* Albuquerque: University of New Mexico Press, 2001.

Obejas, Achy. *We Came All the Way from Cuba So You Could Dress Like This?* Pittsburg, PA: Cleis Press, 1994.

———. *Memory Mambo.* Pittsburg, PA: Cleis Press, 1996

Pérez, Emma. *Gulf Dreams.* Berkeley: Third Woman Press, 1996.

Rich, Andrienne. "Disloyal to Civilization: Feminism, Racism, Gynophobia." *On Lies, Secrets, and Silence: Selected Prose 1966–1978.* New York: Norton, 1979.

Rodriguez, Richard. *Hunger of Memory: The Education of Richard Rodriguez.* Boston: D. R. Godine, 1982.

Trujillo, Carla, ed. *Chicana Lesbians: The Girls Our Mother Warned Us About.* Berkeley: Third Woman Press, 1993.

Viramontes, Helena María. *The Moths and Other Stories.* Houston: Arte Público, 1985.

Secondary Sources

Alarcón, Norma. "Chicana's Feminist Literature: A Re-vision through *Malintzin* or *Malintzin:* Putting Flesh Back on the Object." *This Bridge Called My Back: Writings by Radical Women of Color.* Gloria Anzaldúa and Cherríe Moraga, eds. Watertown, MA: Persephone Press, 1981. 182–190.

———. "'What Kind of Lover Have You Made Me, Mother?'" *Women of Color: Perspectives on Feminism and Identity.* Audrey T. McCluskey, ed. Bloomington: Women's Studies Program. Indiana University, 1985. 85–110.

———. "Interview with Cherríe Moraga." *Third Woman* 3, nos. 1 & 2 (1986): 127–134.

De la Peña, Terri. "The Latina Legacy: A Personal Overview of Latina Lesbian Literature." *Lambda Book Report,* 7, no. 11 (1999): 12.

del Castillo, Adelaida. "*Malintzin Tenepal:* A Preliminary Look into a New Perspective." *Essays on la Mujer.* Rosaura Sanchez and Rosa Martinez Cruz, eds. Los Angeles: University of California, Chicano Studies Center Publications, 1977. 124–149.

Espinoza, Dionne. "Women of Color and Identity Politics: Translating Theory, Haciendo Teoría." *Other Sisterhoods: Literary Theory and U.S. Women of Color.* Sandra Kumamoto Stanley, ed. Urbana and Chicago: University of Illinois Press, 1998. 44–62.

García, Alma. "The Development of Chicana Feminist Discourse, 1970–1980." *Gender & Society* 5, no. 2 (1989): 217–238.

Moya, Paula M. L. "Realism, Postmodernism, and Identity Politics: Cherríe Moraga and Chicana Feminism." *Feminist Genealogies, Colonial Legacies, Democratic Futures.* Jacqui Alexander and Chandra Talpade Mohanty, eds. New York: Routledge Press, 1998. 125–150.

Quintanales, Mirtha N. "Loving in the War Years: An Interview with Cherríe Moraga." *Off Our Backs* 14, no. 12 (1985): 13–14.

Reyes, Rosi. "After the War Years." *Color Lines* 4, no. 2 (summer 2001): 33–35.

Romero, Lora. "'When Something Goes Queer': Familiarity, Formalism, and Minority Intellectuals in the 1980s." *The Yale Journal of Criticism* 6, no. 1 (1993): 121–141.

Sharpe, Christina. "Learning to Live Without Black Familia: Cherríe Moraga's Nationalist Articulations." *Tortilleras: Hispanic and Latina Lesbian Expression.* Lourdes Torres, ed. Philadelphia: Temple University Press, forthcoming.

Short, Kayann "Coming to the Table: The Differential Politics of *This Bridge Called My Back*" *Genders* 3 (1994).

Umpierre, Luz Maria. "With Cherríe Moraga." *The Americas Review* 14, no. 2 (summer 1986): 54–67.

Wolfe, Susan and Julia Penelope, eds. *The Coming Out Stories.* Watertown, MA: Persephone Press, 1980.

Yarbro-Bejarano, Yvonne. "Cherríe Moraga." *Dictionary of Literary Biography.* Francisco A. Lomelí, Carl R. Shirley, eds. Volume 82: Chicano Writers. First Series. Detroit, MI: Gale Research, 1989. 165–177.

———. *The Wounded Heart: Writing on Cherríe Moraga.* Austin: University of Texas, 2001.

Michelle Habell-Pallán

Marisela Norte, *NORTE/word*

New Alliance Records, NAR CD 062, 1991,
compact disk.

Textual Overview

Zooming across the geography of the southwest borderlands, Marisela
Norte's 1991 compact disc *NORTE/word* projects a transnational
imaginary that humanizes the daily trials and triumphs of a transnational
female work force caught in the web of economic exploitation and
dysfunctional personal relationships. Envisioned as an "alternative to a
book" (Snowdon 1991) *NORTE/word* consists of nine tracks of lucid,
hypnotic spoken-word narratives. Taken as a whole, *NORTE/word* is
structured like a film, composed of a series of fade-in and fade-out
vignettes. *NORTE/word*, eloquently bilingual, is about women and
girls on the "outside"—women and girls outside of the home, outside of
loving relationships, outside of adequate education and health care
systems, and outside of the mass media. Moreover, *NORTE/word* is at
once a subtle and eloquent critique of power relations that attempt to
limit the possibilities of Latinas and a loving homage to the city of Los
Angeles and the Latinas themselves who keep the city running even as
their "stockings lay defeated after hours of crossing and double crossing" ("El Club Sufrimiento 2000"). *NORTE/word*'s opening track,
"Peeping Tom Tom Girl"—a wry meditation on the place of Latina
women and girls in the public urban borderland spaces of greater Los
Angeles—provides the location, sets the tone for the entire compact
disk, and introduces a voluminous cast of characters rarely seen in
Hollywood films. The protagonists of *NORTE/word* are many—from
a girl in a too-tight pink dress who is forced to listen to her parents fight,
to Silent, who can't find childcare, a stable male, or a job, to Rosemary,
who doesn't know what to do with her future, to a homeless woman
who "sleeps in doorways, Hefty bag wardrobe, broken tiara and too

much rouge" to finally, the first-person "narratrix" who records the lives of these women.

Historical Context

Norte's writing emerges in late-twentieth-century Los Angeles, California, the U.S. city second only to Mexico City in its population of people of Mexican descent. Her writings and spoken word chronicle the daily life of "Nuestra Señora de Los Angeles" a city who from its very establishment in the 1700s has been a cauldron of mixing and clashing cultures, forever shaped by the presence of indigenous communities, Spanish and Mexican colonization, as well as by Asian and African American labor force and U.S. invasion.

Norte's writing, however, documents a great demographic shift in California's current population. Norte's late-twentieth century Eastside emerges from the white population's flight from post—World War II suburban neighborhoods and the influx of new immigration from Mexico, Central America, and Asia. Although the official U.S. border begins in San Ysidro, California, Norte shows us that culture flows through the border and transforms Southern California on its way through. She documents a landscape where fifth-generation U.S.- born Chicanas encounter immigrant seamstresses, "at bus stops or standing all the way home after ten hours shifts with red, white, green, and black strings all over their clothes" (Norte, "Spoken Word" remix, 2000) returning from Asian immigrant—owned downtown garment factories.

In addition, Norte's accounts for the way Hollywood—with its close proximity to East Los Angeles—casts its long entertainment industry shadow over the cultural life of the Eastside community, making it unlike any other Chicano community in the southwest. Her writing dances to the competing rhythms of ever-present radio stations competing for Spanish ballad and *banda* listeners, oldie-but-goodie lovers, old-school freestylers, as well as rock and urban hip hop fans. Her words flicker against the backdrop of 1950s black and white television, film noir, and gangster films.

Biographical Background

Born in 1955 and fondly embraced as the "the cultural ambassador of East L.A," Norte began writing because it "enabled me to speak out when keeping silent was the only choice" (Norte 2001). Norte grew up and attended public schools in an East Los Angeles suburb during the politically and socially turbulent sixties and seventies. Despite the era's general push for Mexican Americans to become monolingual, her Chihuahuan father's strict enforcement of "Spanish only" at home guaranteed her bilingual fluency, while her mother, born in Vera Cruz, bequeathed Norte her sharp wit. Childhood drives through East Los Angeles on the way to view Hollywood B-movies with her father animated her love of cinematic images so infused in her writing and evident in the following passage, "we'd get into a car / with little gas / and coast / the dark curves /of Little Valley / the black and blue houses / cut out against / a cemetery backdrop / through *Tercera* to Rowan down East Sixth Street / where he would roll his window down / point at the landscape / and tell me / 'this belongs to you'" ("Dance in the Shadows," Norte, *NORTE/word,* 1991). Norte claims this landscape through her writing.

After graduating in 1973 from George M. Shurr High school in Montebello, California , Norte began life-transforming visits to Mexico. Upon returning from her first trip, she enrolled in East Los Angeles City College and then studied at California State University, Los Angeles from 1976 to 1978, but abandoned formal education after an "English professor returned a paper I wrote, asking what was I doing in his class and if I was 'illiterate.' It was about this time that I rediscovered public transportation and downtown Los Angeles, taking refuge inside such childhood haunts as Clifton's Cafeteria on 7th and Broadway, Grand Central Market, the counter at J. J. Newberry, and the tea room in Bullock's department store, where I began to write" (Norte 1999).

Yet the place that impacted her writing most heavily is her "mobile office," the number 18 bus to downtown. Norte explains, "As a writer, the bus has been my transportation and my inspiration for the past 30 years. It has become my 'mobile office,' the space where I write about the daily lives of Angelenos that ride the bus to and from work. My writing circulates as I do through economically marginalized parts of the city in spoken word form . . . My work is an ethnography of post-industrial Los Angeles culture viewed through a bus window" (Norte 1997). After years of writing on the bus, Norte's essays circulated in over 2,000 Los Angeles buses when in 1997 the MTA selected Norte and photographer Willie García to develop a series of photos and essays, posted as placards in bus interiors, that honored metro system operators.

Throughout the 1980s, Norte developed her writing in the well-respected Latino Writers Workshop and Asco's performance collectives and honed her craft by performing "at universities, over the radio on

KPFK's morning readings, at cultural centers, and at the California Rehabilitation Center for Women at Norco, California . . . In 1983 she was recognized for her poetry by Eastern Michigan University at Ypsilanti, Michigan at the National Association of Chicano Studies Conference" (Southern California Women Writers and Artists 1984, 162).

As the "bad girl poet" of Asco's performance collective, Norte began important collaborations with María Elena Gaítan (*La Condicíon Feminina* play), Diane Gamboa (whose painting "Mistress" graces the cover of *NORTE/word*) and with Glugio "Gronk" Nicandro (whose 1995 Hammer Museum painting for the "Four Directions" installation was inspired by *NORTE/word*'s "Baby Sitter Girl"). Norte's most recent collaboration, the Ovation-nominated play *Black Butterfly, Jaguar Girl, Piñata Women and Other Superhero Girls Like Me* was performed at the Kennedy Center in 2000 and combines the poetry of Norte, Sandra C. Muñoz, and Alma Cervantes under the direction of Luis Alfaro.

Reception of the Text

Reviewers in the United States and the United Kingdom bestowed accolades upon *NORTE/word*. It is considered by scholars the best of its genre to capture the cinematic beauty and brutality of daily life in Los Angeles. The fact that *NORTE/word* was reviewed in *Rolling Stone, Wired,* and *Face* magazines, instead of literary journals, can be attributed to the compact disc format of her collection. Reviews are often found in the music section of magazines and she is considered to be part of a group of creators who have produced some "of the most dynamic and innovative forms of youth culture in the postindustrial era" (Lipsitz 1994, 20).

Her reviewers persistently note that her perspective as a woman dramatically informs her work. Ed Morales, in the *San Francisco Weekly* (16 January 1992) writes that, "Although Norte's work is . . . accomplished enough to stand up in print, it is a special treat to the sardonic sweetness of her delivery as she feels for the girls and holds off the boys with a wise-ass flirtiness." He commended "Dance in the Shadows" (Norte 1991) for being "at once angry, defiant ('So many of us are getting pregnant, getting gray hairs, and being lied to') and soothing, seductive ('I keep a full moon in a glass by my bed')." More recently, he notes that her "fluid Spanglish captures the speech rhythms of her native East Los Angeles" (Morales 2002, 116–117). Cynthia Rose praised her work as "something to behold, her low, sweet voice shifting from English to a passionate, rhythmic Español her words capturing contemporary moments as brilliantly as Kodachrome snapshots . . ." (Rose, 1991, 23). Cultural critic George Lipsitz notes her "devoted, indeed . . . fanatical, following among young women who purchase compact discs and cassettes of her spoken word art at underground raves and at Norte's performances and readings. Her art reaches its listeners through conduits every bit as circuitous as the Los Angeles city bus routes that inspired it in the first place. Norte's devoted female fans . . . regularly secure invitations for her to read her work before community and school groups, and her work is assigned often in college classrooms" (Lipsitz, 226).

Major Themes and Critical Issues

NORTE/word reflects themes consistent in her writing for the past twenty years: girls' and womens' subjection to and survival of sexual, ethnic/racial, and economic violence. In looking at her body of work over the last twenty-plus years, Norte has illuminated social context that continues to disempower Mexican American and immigrant women. That is, Norte's eloquent spoken word captures the effects of global economic shifts on the personal lives of women who are forced to cross national borders to work or forced to work within self-contained barrios in the United States. As a self-defined chronicler of *"las vidas de ellas,"* Norte chronicles the poetry and humor in the cultural landscape of what others less tuned-in might find just bleak. For example, *Black Butterfly, Jaguar Girl, Piñata Women and Other Superhero Girls Like Me* thematizes the promises, perils, and models of survival for adolescent girls in East Los Angeles. A butterfly tattoo Norte spied on a young woman bus rider that said " . . . 'I'll remember you' under it in that swirling, gorgeous East L.A. writing," (Norte, *L.A. Weekly* 2000) inspired the play's final act. Norte explains, "to me it was more than a tattoo—it was ink." In the play, a girl bus rider witnesses a mother "talking real mean to her daughter . . . 'You're just so stupid.'" No one stops the abuse, so the witnessing girl takes action. Moved by the tattoo of a "homegirl on the bus" she sprouts "big, soft black, velvety butterfly wings . . . I see that little girl through the bus window, I want her to open her eyes, look up, and see me. When she finally does, she makes a big old smile when she sees her wings, and then she's outside and I see her lifting her sister up in the air. All of a sudden there's thousands of black butterflies in the sky, flying together and we spell out, 'I'll Remember You.'"

Illuminating the social context that continues to disempower Mexican American and immigrant women, Norte's eloquent spoken word captures the effects of global economic shifts on the personal lives of working women subject to the violence and vicissitudes of immigration policy, local politics, and patriarchy. Chronicling the harsh realities of and paying tribute to working women, Norte—as a "Revlon revolutionary"—seeks to "mobilize every immobile woman I see at the bus stops" (Norte, "Spoken Word" remix, 2000).

Pedagogical Issues and Suggestions

NORTE/word is a joy to teach because of the inherent flexibility of the compact disc format. The format allows for options of assigning the compact disc as a whole or of assigning single tracks. Because the pieces are either in English or Spanish, single tracks can be used in English- or Spanish-dominant courses. Also, it is not difficult to locate the text version of most of the *NORTE/word* tracks. The compact disc works well in a variety of courses, from introduction to Chicano studies, writing by women of color, Latino popular culture, and Latina/o theater. A brief web search identified *NORTE/word* as a text on "Generation X in Literature and Culture" and "Religion and Chicana Writing" course syllabi. Students at all levels are intrigued by the innovative form and compelling content of Norte's compact disc.

Because Norte's pieces are organized around images, she tends, "to deal first with an image, rather than an experience . . . if you're walking somewhere and you see something . . . that makes a bad or good impression on you, you build your story around that particular incident" (Norte 1983). I highlight excerpts that are full of visual detail. I find these best for generating discussion.

You may want to generate discussion of Norte's text by first explaining the overarching theme of the following quotes, critiquing the social practices that force working-class women to live on the edge of society, on the street, and/or with out a job, or on the border. These women survive without the protection sanctioned by patriarchal culture for "proper" women only. These are women without basic necessities, from shelter to childcare. I then ask students to reflect on the following: How does analysis of Norte's *NORTE/word* make visible the lives of women marginalized in U.S. society? How do these women negotiate double standards imposed on women?

The narrator of "Peeping Tom Tom Girl" observes through the window the women of Los Angeles while riding the downtown bus. As an anxious teenager listening to her parents argue, she studies and empathizes with a widow carrying flowers and her counterpart, a homeless woman counting down the days in English and Spanish: "She sleeps in doorways, Hefty bag wardrobe, broken tiara and too much rouge." Norte's narrator exalts her with the title ". . . the Countess, Nuestra Señora, la Reina Perdida que cayo en Los [Our Lady of the Lost Queen who fell/landed in Los Angeles]" (Norte 1999).

Use the questions below to help unpack Norte's language to understand her use of images.

> Use examples of Norte's language to explain what sensory aspects (sight or sound) are highlighted in the text.
> Who is the narrator? What does she call herself? What does her name suggest?
> Who is the narrator describing? What is her attitude toward them?
> What part of town are they driving through? How do we know?

Literary Contexts

NORTE/word emerged with the "do-it-yourself" aesthetics of punk that permeated the world of spoken-word poetry in the 1980s. Advancements in compact disc technology make the production of spoken work relatively inexpensive, especially when compared to book production. This medium is ideal for creative writers who are drawn to experimentation and challenging conventional literary form.

The Los Angeles Latino Writers Workshop, Chismearte, and Asco are artist forums that have played important roles in what critics refer to as the Chicano Cultural Renaissance of the 1970s. The groups include a number of writers and artists such as Ron Arias, Alejandro Morales, Luis Rodriguez, Helena María Viramontes, Naomi Quiñones, Harry Gamboa, Gronk, Willie Herron, and Patssi Valdez. Many of these writers recognized the importance of the Chicano movement and participated in it, but in time felt confined by the limitations of nationalist aesthetic practices and more interested in considering broader issues that could also incorporate aesthetic cultural critiques about gender roles, sexuality, state violence, and postmodern alienation.

Forging a space betwixt and between Chicano and mainstream art, these groups often incorporated members like Norte, who shared their precarious position within and outside of the art world.

Comparative Literature

George Lipsitz asserts that Norte is part of a cohort of writers and artists that, "In a city where low-wages, mass migration, racism, sexism, and homophobia compound the alienations and indignities of everyday life for millions of people, face up to the things that are killing them and their communities" (2001, 227). As such, *NORTE/word* compliments Luis Alfaro's *Downtown* compact disc (which Norte coproduced), Wanda Coleman, Michele Serros (whom she influences greatly), Ruben Martinez, Harry Gamboa, Jose Montoya, and even L.A. punk stars/poets Exene Cervanka and Henry Rollins. Mainstream American literature that comes to mind when listening to or reading Norte's work is writing by John Rechy, Joan Didion, and Dorothy Allison.

Since her early narratives focused in part on survival in the face of sexual, racial, and economic violence, the sophisticated and compelling form and content tend to continue challenging literary conventions of both American and Latino writings. Fortunately, the context of literary studies does not limit *NORTE/word,* and it can be affectively taught alongside Diane Gamboa's provocative visual art and as well juxtaposed with the lyrics and soundings of Chicana punk music by the East L.A. group The Brat.

BIBLIOGRAPHIC RESOURCES

Primary Sources

Alfaro, Luis. *Down Town*. Lawndale, CA: New Alliance Records, [1993]. Sound recording (65 min.): digital; 4 3/4 in.

Burnham, Linda. "Marisela Norte." *High Performance* 35 (1986): 56.

Norte, Marisela. "Se Habra Inglés." *Southern California Women Writers & Artists*. Los Angeles: Books of a Feather, 1984. 89–93. Also recorded on *NORTE/word*.

———. "Lost in Los." *Black and Tan Club*. Lawndale, CA: New Alliance Records, NAR CD 060, 1991. Compact disk.

————. *NORTE/word*. Lawndale, CA: New Alliance Records, NARC CD 062, 1991. Compact disk.

————. "Dolores Fuertes: A Short Story." *Alchemy* 1 (1992): 14–16.

————. "Three Little Words." *DisClosure: Voice of Women.* Lawndale, CA: New Alliance Records, NAR CD 067, 1992. Compact disk.

————. "Wind Cries Mari." *Alchemy* 1 (1992): 32–33.

————. "Angel." *L.A. Photo Journal.* Voyager, 1992. Video laser disk.

————. "Misfortune in Woman's Eyes." Untitled: A Literary Art Journal 2, no. 1 (fall 1993): 29–32.

————. "976-LOCA." *Recent Chicano Poetry/Neueste Chicano-Lyrik.* Heiner Bus and Ana Castillo, eds. Bamberg: Edition Band 8, 1994. 15–30.

————. "Peeping Tom Girl." *The Geography of Home: California's Poetry of Place.* Christopher Buckley and Gary Young, eds. Berkeley: Heydey Books, 1999. 271–273. Also recorded on *Norte/word.*

————. "Peeping Tom Tom Girl," online audio download. Available at http://www.salon.com/audio/2000/10/05/norte/

Secondary Sources

Buckley, Christopher and Gary Young, eds. *The Geography of Home: California's Poetry of Place.* Berkeley: Heyday Books, 1999.

Burnham, Linda. "Viewpoint: Life: The ASCO Version. *High Performance* 8 (1985): 66–67.

Camacho-Schmit, Alicia. *Migrant Subjects: Race, Labor and Insurgency in the Mexico-U.S. Borderlands.* Ph. D. diss. Stanford University, 2000.

Cruz, Adam. "Latin Lookers." *Elle Magazine* 3, no. 12 (1988): 38–45.

Gamboa, Jr., Harry. "Marisela Norte." *La Opinion (La Comunidad Section)* 117 (October 17, 1982): 10–11.

————."ASCO," *Imagine: International Chicano Poets Journal* (summer-winter 1986): 64–66.

George-Warren, Holly. "New Faces." *Rolling Stone* 656 (May 13, 1993): 27.

González, Jennifer and Michelle Habell-Pallán. "Heterotopias: Navigating Social Spaces and Spaces of Identity." *Inscriptions: Enunciating Our Terms* 7 (1994): 80–104.

Habell-Pallan, Michelle. "No Cultural Icon: Marisela Norte." *Women Transforming Politics.* Kathy Jones, Cathy Cohen, and Joan Tronto, eds. New York: New York University Press, 1997. 256–268.

Hicks, Emily D. *Border Writing: The Multidimensional Text.* Minneapolis: University of Minnesota Press, 1991. 112, 117.

Kosiba-Vargas, S. Zaneta. *Harry Gamboa and ASCO: The Emergence and Development of a Chicano Art Group.* Ph. D. diss. Ann Arbor: University of Michigan, 1989.

Lipsitz, George. "We Know What Time It Is: Race, Class, and Youth Culture in the Nineties." *Microphone Fiends: Youth Music and Youth Culture.* Andrew Ross and Tricia Rose, eds. New York: Routledge, 1994.

————. *American Studies in a Moment of Danger.* Minneapolis: Minnesota University Press, 2001.

Morales, Ed. *Living in Spanglish.* New York: St. Martin's Press, 2002.

Norte, Marisela. Transcipts from *Califas: Chicano Art and Culture in California conference.* Santa Cruz, CA. April 16–18, 1983.

————. Metropolitan Transit Authority (MTA) Art web site, accessed November 1997. *http://www.mta.net/other_info/metroart/temp/ma_pep1.htm.*

————. *L.A. Weekly,* 16–22 June 2000. "To Be Young, Female and Living in East L.A." Interview by Judith Lewis.

————.Oral presentation with transcription of "Spoken Word" remix. Transforming Public and Academic Cultures Symposium. Seattle, University of Washington, May 2000.

————. "The Road to Aztlan: Art from a Mythic Homeland." *Writers in Focus.* Program biographical notes. Los Angeles County Museum of Art, June 22, 2001.

Rosado, Wilfredo. "Our Latin Thang." *Interview* 18, no. 2 (February 1988): 101.

Rose, Cynthia. "Word UP!" *Face* 51 (December 1991): 23.

Snowden, Don. "A New Spin of Words and Music" *Los Angeles Times* 3 December 1991. Calendar Section. F1 and F6.

Southern California Women Writers and Artists. Los Angeles: Books of a Feather, 1984. Series title: Rara avis; 6–7.

Varney, Ginger. "Faces in the Crowd." *L.A. Style* (November 1985): 77.

Weizman, Alan. "Born in East L.A." *L.A. Times Sunday Magazine.* 27 March 1988: 11–25.

Alvina E. Quintana

Loida Maritza Pérez, *Geographies of Home*

New York: Plume/Penguin Press, 1999.

Textual Overview

Loida Maritza Pérez's *Geographies of Home* weaves a vivid, gripping story about a family in crisis. The novel is significant in that it enhances many of the issues brought forth by the work of other, more well-known Latina writers like Julia Alvarez and Sandra Cisneros. Exploring issues of cultural dislocation, familial responsibility, sexual abuse, spirituality, and mental health, *Geographies of Home* raises a number of critical questions that are pertinent to race, class, and gender analysis. This first novel thus provides an important contribution to the literature, offering readers the opportunity to consider its connection to other African diaspora narratives. The novel's powerful prose is skill-fully balanced with intense imagery that contrasts the family's island life with the urban Brooklyn environment that shapes their immigrant experience in America. At the center of the narrative is Illiana, who is forced by a variety of family crises to withdraw from college in order to help her parents and thirteen siblings, who live in a dilapidated, Brooklyn barrio townhouse. The story is told through a series of flashbacks that reflect Pérez's transnational sensibility and her Caribbean and Latin American literary influences.

Marketed as a teacher-friendly tool, *Geographies of Home* includes a reader's guide that features a useful introduction, an interview with the author, and questions for discussion. The final paragraph of the introduction sums up Pérez's novel stating:

> Pérez portrays an immigrant experience that few writers have chronicled and many readers might find unimaginable. In her graphic depiction of the troubles of one family, she exposes lives untouched by the promises of

the American Dream. Writing from the perspective of a generation brought up in America and seeking to reconnect with and understand their roots in places they know only through the stories of their parents, she explores how cultural heritage—including traditional rules of right and wrong and long-held assumptions about the roles of men and women in society—profoundly affects individual perceptions and expectations. As she delves into the contradictions faced by those caught between cultures and superstitions, joys, and pains that bind families together, Pérez shows that survival ultimately depends on creating a home for oneself-"not a geographical site but . . . a frame of mind able to accommodate any place as home." (4)

Historical Context

Although the narrative action is set in a contemporary American context, it employs a magical realist approach that effectively juxtaposes memories of a Dominican Republic history marked by the rule of dictator Trujillo, where "the horror of nightmares appeared full-blown in life," with the family's new reality of struggle brought on by the dislocation, poverty, alienation, and racism that characterizes their "minority status" in the United States.

Biographical Background

Loida Maritza Pérez was born in the Dominican Republic in 1963 and raised, from an early age, in Brooklyn, New York. She began her novel as an undergraduate at Cornell in an autographical writing course taught by Henry Louis Gates. She is a winner of several fellowships including Djerassi's Pauline and Henry Louis Gates Sr. Fellowship in 1996, the 1994 Ragdale Foundation's U.S.-Africa Writers Project, and a 1992 New York Foundation for the Arts grant for writing. Currently, she teaches creative writing in New Mexico.

Reception of the Text

Geographies of Home has been reviewed in a number of important venues. Commenting on the power of her prose, Robin Taylor states "The pleasures of *Geographies of Home* are like those of memoir: The characters are complex and real, and their memories are vivid and full of emotional detail ... Pérez writes boldly and precisely of love, bitterness, desire, sin, madness, fear, and forgiveness." In *World Literature Today,* Jim Hannan credits Pérez's potential as an emergent writer, suggesting that the novel "merits reading for the way it demonstrates how individuals and families endure the tribulations of displacement, but it is not the accomplished, compelling novel that Peréz's best qualities suggest she is poised to write." Similarly Erica Sanders, in a *New York Times Book Review,* notes "Pérez relates much of this story in eerie flashback. Memories of a plentiful island life in the Dominican Republic collide with Brooklyn's alienating landscapes. The result is a deluge of intense imagery where the magical and the real occupy the same awful and sometimes sensual space ... This is not a flawless book, but one suspects Pérez's next one could be." Caribbean writer Edwidge Danticat has welcomed the writer into the fold, stating "Loida Maritza Pérez is a bold and graceful novelist. She uses her magnificent narrative powers to shed light on the darkest and most glorious aspects of family, migration, kinship, passion, death, and the human heart. *Geographies of Home* will leave you feeling both amazingly breathless and wonderfully redeemed."

Major Themes and Critical Issues

The novel's themes and experimental form necessitate a detailed discussion concerning the history of the Dominican Republic as well as an introduction to the interconnections between Caribbean and Latin American literary traditions. The first line of chapter one raises one of the novel's reoccurring themes that prompts an awareness of issues related to the African diaspora. This reference also initiates the novel's powerful tone, challenging readers to reassess their understanding of "Hispanic" culture(s). "The ghostly trace of "NIGGER" on a message board hanging from Iliana's door failed to assault her as it had the first time she returned to her dorm room to find it" (1).

Geographies of Home offers an important contribution to U.S. Latina literature because it forces readers to move beyond simplistic notions of so-called typicality or the idea that U.S. Latinos can be marked by their racial invisibility. Pérez's response to how she would describe the representation in her novel as typical of the Dominican experience in this country illustrates my point.

There is no "typical experience" either for Dominicans living in this country or for those remaining in the Dominican Republic, just as there is

none for Americans who have lived in the United States since their
ancestors arrived on the *Mayflower*. We live our lives in myriad different
ways. Therefore, when I set out to write *Geographies of Home,* I had no
intention of writing a definitive text of any sort. Instead, my intention
was to write a narrative wherein I explore the lives of a particular family
or specific means living under specific circumstances. Any attempt to do
otherwise would have resulted in stereotypes. (5)

Pérez's response is invaluable because it explicates many of the narrative choices she has made in this text. These choices, like the magical
and real elements she employs, force readers to become active participants as they consider the complexity brought on by difference, heterogeneity, and multiplicity (to quote Lisa Lowe, 60) found in U.S. Latino
culture(s). She is a bold writer who challenges convention by avoiding
the predictable and the tame. Her representation of sexual abuse,
mental illness, and the Seventh-Day Adventist religion can thus hold the
potential to create a sense of discomfort for many students.

Pedagogical Issues and Suggestions

This novel works remarkably well in small seminar as well as large
lecture women's studies and literature courses. In general terms the
novel facilitates a deeper understanding about the misconceptions
created by the government and mainstream press's "Hispanic" categorization, while on a deeper level it also allows teachers to demonstrate
the interconnections between African American, Chicano, Puerto Rican,
Cuban, Dominican, and Panamanian literature. I often begin by asking
students to consider how Pérez combines race, class, gender, language,
and *Latinidad* in her novel.

In addition, Pérez's novel raises the issue of gender violence in the
domestic sphere. In this context, students can be motivated to research a
variety of topics that include: date rape, domestic abuse, child abuse,
and women's madness. The reader's guide included in the novel offers a
variety of discussion questions, some of which are:

> *Geographies of Home* focuses on the schisms among members of a
> Dominican family. Are the conflicts Pérez discusses unique to a
> particular culture and family structure? What parallels are there to
> your own life and your relationships with other family members? To
> what extent are they influenced by your own cultural heritage?
> Does Iliana's recognition of her father's doubts and fears help her face her
> own life more realistically?

How much does understanding who we are depend on understanding the cultural heritage of our parents?

Does the search for roots liberate people or does it lock them into outdated images of themselves and what they accomplish?

Compare the immigrant experience Pérez describes to other narratives you may have read. How does it differ from Julia Alvarez's *How the Garcia Girls Lost Their Accents*, another tale about Dominican émigrés?

From accounts about Asians, the Irish, Jews, as well as other Latinos who have settle in America?

What impact do race, language, and economic status have on a group's ability to fit in? Do government policies and public opinion about immigration influence the immigrant's experience, and if so, in what ways? (11–12)

Literary Contexts

Pérez's writing synthesizes the practices of several literary traditions, which include Latin American, African American, Caribbean, and mainstream American. Her emphasis on cultural and linguistic difference is reminiscent of Julia Alvarez's *How the García Girls Lost Their Accents;* Veronica Chambers's *Mama's Girl,* and Sandra Cisneros's *The House on Mango Street.* In addition the issues she raises concerning the tension between mothers and daughters, between old cultural traditions and those of the new world influences, are also reoccurring themes in Caribbean-American literature as well. Edwidge Danticat's *Breath, Eyes, Memory,* Paul Marshall's *Brown Girl, Brownstones,* Jamaica Kincaid's *Annie John* and *Autobiography of My Mother,* Zora Neal Hurston's *Their Eyes Were Watching God,* for example, tell stories about young women struggling to develop an autonomous self-identity within a transnational and confining social context.

Comparative Literature

Pérez's novel adds another voice to canonical renderings of the American Dream and would thus work beautifully if taught along side Benjamin Franklin's *The Autobiography,* Mark Twain's *Adventures of Huckleberry Finn,* or Henry David Thoreau's *Resistance to Civil Government.* Reminiscent of mainstream American women's literature, *Geographies of Home* builds upon the feminist issues represented in Kate Chopin's *The Awakening,* and Charlotte Perkins Gilman's *The*

Yellow Wall-paper. The narrative also makes a solid contribution to ethnic-American writing such as Coco Fusco's *English Is Broken Here,* Maxine Hong Kingston's *The Woman Warrior,* Tomás Rivera's *Y no se lo Tragó la Tierra / And the Earth Did Not Devour Him;* Amy Tan's *The Joy Luck Club,* Lois Ann Yamanaka's *Wild Meat and the Bully Burgers,* and Karen Tei Yamashita's *Through the Arc of the Rain Forest.* Obviously, Pérez's *Geographies of Home* would make a wonderful addition to any course featuring African American writers in that the issues it relates correspond nicely with the writing of Gwendolyn Brooks, Charles Wadell Chesnutt, W. E. B. Dubois, Paul Laurence Dunbar, Ralph Ellison, Langston Hughes, Nella Larsen, Toni Morrison, and Alice Walker, to name only a few.

BIBLIOGRAPHIC RESOURCES

Primary Sources

Chopin, Kate. *The Awakening.* New York: Knopf, 1992.

Danticat, Edwidge. *Breath, Eyes, Memory.* New York: Random House, 1998.

Franklin, Benjamin. *The Autobiography of Benjamin Franklin.* New York: Bedford, 1993.

Gilman, Charlotte Perkins. *Herland, The Yellow Wall-paper and Selected Writings.* New York: Penguin, 1999.

Hurston, Zora Neale. *There Eyes Were Watching God.* New York: Lippincott, 1937.

Kincaid, Jamaica. *The Autobiography of My Mother.* New York: Farrar, Straus and Giroux, 1996.

———. *Annie John.* New York: Farrar Straus and Giroux, 1997.

Kingston, Maxine Hong. *The Woman Warrior: Memoirs of a Girlhood Among Ghosts.* New York: Vintage, 1976.

Marshall, Paule. *Brown Girl, Brownstones.* New York: The Feminist Press, 1981.

Rivera, Tomás. *Y no se lo Tragó la Tierra / And the Earth Did Not Devour Him.* Houston, TX: Arte Público Press, 1992.

Tan, Amy. *The Joy Luck Club.* New York: Ivy Books, 1989.

Thoreau, Henry David. *Walden and Resistance to Civil Government: Authoritative Texts, Thoreau's Journal Reviews and Essays in Criticism.* Owen Thomas, ed. New York: Norton, 1992.

Twain, Mark. *The Adventures of Huckleberry Finn.* New York: Oxford University Press, 1999.

Yamanaka, Lois Ann. *Wild Meat and the Bully Burgers*. New York: Harcourt Brace, 1996.

Yamashita, Karen Tei. *Through the Arc of the Rain Forest*. Minneapolis, MN: Coffee House Press, (1990).

Secondary Sources

Bonilla, Frank, Edwin Meléndez, Rebecca Morales, and María de los Angeles Torres, eds. *Borderless Borders: U.S. Latinos, Latin Americans, and the Paradox of Interdependence*. Philadelphia: Temple University Press, 1998.

Fusco, Coco. *English Is Broken Here: Notes on Cultural Fusion in the Americas*. New York: The New Press, 1995.

Gómez-Peña, Guillermo. *Warrior for Gringstroika*. Saint Paul, MN: Graywolf Press, 1993.

Grewal, Inderpal. *Home and Harem: Nation, Gender, Empire and the Cultures of Travel*. Durham: Duke University Press, 1996.

Holland, Sharon Patricia. *Raising the Dead: Readings of Death and (Black) Subjectivity*. Durham: Duke University Press, 2000.

Hurtado, Aida. *The Color of Privilege: Three Blasphemies on Race and Feminism*. Ann Arbor: University of Michigan Press, 1996.

Lorde, Audre. *Sister Outsider*. Trumansburg: The Crossing Press, 1984.

Lowe, Lisa. *Immigrant Acts*. Durham: Duke University Press, 1997.

McCracken, Ellen. *New Latina Narrative: The Feminine Space of Postmodern Ethnicity*. Tucson: University of Arizona Press, 1999.

Omi, Michael and Howard Winant, eds. *Racial Formation in the United States*. New York: Routledge, 1994.

Stanley, Sandra Kumoto, ed. *Other Sisterhoods: Literary Theory and U.S. Women Of Color*. Urbana: University of Illinois Press, 1998.

Trinh T. Minh-ha. *Woman Native Other*. Bloomington: Indiana University Press, 1989.

Vannoy Adams, Michael. *The Multicultural Imagination: Race, Color and the Unconscious*. New York: Routledge, 1996.

Reviews

Hannan, Jim. Review of *Geographies of Home*. *World Literature Today* 74, no. 3. (summer 2000) 596.

Sanders, Erica. "Miserable in Brooklyn." *New York Times Book Review*. Accessed April 1999. http://www.nytimes.com/books/99/04/18/bib/990481.rv091537.htm.

Taylor, Robin. *Fiction Book Page*. *www.bookpage.com*

Lesley Feracho

Ana Lydia Vega, *True and False Romances*

Trans. Andrew Hurley. New York: Serpent's Tail, 1994.

Textual Overview

The collection of short stories entitled *True and False Romances: Stories and a Novella* is the first collection of works by Puerto Rican writer Ana Lydia Vega to be published in English. It brings together several short stories and one novella from her last three works in Spanish: *Encancaranublado y Otros Cuentos de Naufragio* (1997), *Pasión de Historia y Otras Historias de Pasión* (1994), and *Falsas Crónicas del Sur* (1991). The short story "Deliverance from evil" ("Despojo") comes from her first solo collection, *Encancaranublado*, while the stories "True Romances" ("Pasión de Historia"), "Aerobics for Love" ("Tres aerobicos para el amor"), "Solutions, Inc." ("Ajustes, S.A"), "Just One Small Detail" ("Caso Omiso"), and "Série Noire" ("Serie negra") are included in *Pasión de historia*. The last two short stories, "Consolation Prize" ("Premio de Consolación") and "Eye Openers" ("Cuento en Camino"), come from Vega's last collection, *Falsas Crónicas*. The work ends with the novella "Miss Florence's Trunk" ("El baúl de Miss Florence: Fragmentos para un novelón romántico"), which opens her work in Spanish. This collection provides an introduction for English-speaking readers to Ana Lydia Vega's oeuvre by presenting stories that deal with themes like relationships between men and women, women's empowerment, parodies of the detective novel, questions of reality and perspective—particularly in the transmission of history (both written and oral), slavery, and representations of nineteenth-century Creole society in Puerto Rico. Each story is introduced by an epigraph that dialogues with the themes of the story. These epigraphs range from quotes by Alfred Hitchcock, Roland Barthes, V. S. Naipaul, Stephen King, Cornell Woolrich, La

Rochefoucauld, Chaucer, and Samuel and Susan Morse to refrains from popular songs by M. J. Canario. The diversity of these epigraphs, coupled with the themes of the stories, display how Vega fuses popular culture and classic literature to treat issues of love, desire, loneliness, and representations of truth in contemporary Puerto Rican society with resonance for readers of all nationalities.

Historical Context

Puerto Rican history has been most shaped by four major forces: its indigenous past, European colonialism, slavery, and U.S. foreign policy. The Taíno indians (originating in America) who inhabited the island in the fifteenth century called it "Boriken" or "Borinquen" which means "the great land of the valiant and noble Lord." In 1493 Christopher Columbus arrived on the island on his second voyage and found not only the more than 50,000 Taíno inhabitants but also the gold that was in rich supply. For this reason the town where Columbus arrived was called "Puerto Rico" (rich port). This name would later be given to the island, replacing "San Juan Batista" (St. John the Baptist), which would be shortened and used as the name of the capital city.

The African presence in Puerto Rico dates back to 1503–1513 when the first slaves were brought by the Spanish. The slave trade would be abolished three hundred years later in 1873. The colonization of the island by the Spaniards would not really begin until about 1508. Like many other Caribbean islands, African slaves were used primarily on the sugar cane plantations, and by 1530 sugar had become Puerto Rico's most important agricultural product (it would remain so until 1598). Despite several attacks by the British in 1598, 1702, and, 1797 it was 1898 that marked Puerto Rico's next most significant encounter with a major political and economic power—the United States. In July of this year U.S. troops set sail from Guantánamo, Cuba for Puerto Rico in order to combat Spanish troops there. Within a month almost the entire island was under U.S. control. By the end of the Spanish-American War the United States had ended Spanish colonial rule in the Americas and was given the territories in the western Pacific (Guam, the Wake Islands), the Philippines, Cuba, and Puerto Rico. As a result of the treaty that ended the war (The Treaty of Paris—1898) Puerto Rico became a U.S. protectorate, giving the United States political control of the island. This status as an unincorporated territory was finalized in the Foraker Act of 1901, which also established trade and political ties between the United States and Puerto Rico.

Politically, the first half of the twentieth century would bring about many changes for Puerto Ricans. In 1917 all Puerto Ricans were granted U.S. citizenship, and in 1948 Luis Muñoz Marín became the island's first elected governor. In 1952 a new constitution was drafted, making Puerto Rico an autonomous part of the United States called the Commonwealth of Puerto Rico (Estado Libre Asociado). As a result Puerto Ricans not only were official U. S. citizens (although they do not vote in U.S. elections) but were granted tax exempt status and access to governmental economic aid. Puerto Rico's current status as commonwealth has been and continues to be debated. The three political options discussed are: commonwealth status, statehood (annexation by the United States), and independence (as an autonomous nation).

Economically, Puerto Rico's history has been marked by the problems created by its initial agricultural dependence on a one-crop (sugar) economy, outside control of the factories producing sugar by United States corporations; unemployment; and low wages. The effects were especially felt between 1900 and 1940, resulting not only in the migration of many Puerto Ricans from the countryside to the city, but also to the mainland, particularly in the 1940s. This was heightened by the implementation of "Operation Bootstrap" after World War II, which sent Puerto Rican workers (especially from rural areas) to the United States in large numbers. By 1950 one-third of the population had relocated to the United States (especially New York City and Hawaii), becoming the largest migration of the island up to that point and creating a community that would be the base of what some historians loosely call the "Puerto Rican diaspora." Over time the community in New York in particular would develop a bicultural identity that tied them culturally, politically, economically, and linguistically to the mainland and the island. As a result, they would use the name "Nuyorican" to describe their dual identity. As a result of these cultural, political, economic, and linguistic ties, the issues of migration and its impact, Puerto Rican identity (in the U.S. and on the island), and independence have become central themes in the history of Puerto Rican literature.

Biographical Background

Ana Lydia Vega was born in Santurce, Puerto Rico on December 6, 1946. Both her mother and father were from the interior of Puerto Rico (Arroyo and Coamo respectively) and moved to the capital in the 1940s in search of better economic opportunities. (Flores 1992, 875) From early on Vega was influenced by her father's love of oral poetry and particularly the *décimas* (poems) that he composed as well as her mother's stories from Arroyo. These stories and the oral tradition of Arroyo in general would later serve as the springboard for her collection *Falsas Crónicas del Sur*. As a result of these influences Vega began writing poetry from early on in her childhood and then short stories and scripts in high school. (Hernández and Springfield, 816) She attended the University of Puerto Rico and the University of Provence, France and received her degree in French and Caribbean Literature. She currently teaches at the University of Puerto Rico, Rio Piedras campus.

Vega's short fiction includes: *Vírgenes y mártires* (Virgins and Martyrs) in collaboration with Carmen Lugo Filippi (1981), *Encancaranublado y Otros Cuentos de Naufragio (Encancaranublado and Other Shipwrecked Stories)* (1982); *Pasión de historia y otras historias de pasión (A Passion for History and Other Stories of Passion)* (1987), *Cuentos Calientes* (1992), and *Falsas crónicas del sur (True and False Romances)* (1994). She has also published essays that have been included in the collection *El Tramo Ancla: Ensayos Puertorriqueños de Hoy* (1988) and compiled in *Esperando a Loló y Otros Delirios Generaciones* (Waiting for Lolo and Other Generational Deliriums) (1994).

Vega has been awarded numerous national and international awards for her short stories. Her national awards include: the Emilio S. Belaval Prize for "Pollito Chicken" (1978), third prize in the Certamen de Navidad, Ateneo Puertorriqueño for "Despedida de Duelo" (1975), the Nemesio Canales Prize for *Cuatro Selecciones por una Peseta, Bolero a Dos Voces Para Machos en Pena* (written in collaboration with Carmen Lugo Filippi), as well as the P.E.N Club of Puerto Rico and Institute of Literature Prizes for the same work (1983). Her international awards include the Guggenheim Fellowship for Literary Creation in 1989, the Juan Rulfo International Prize for *Pasión de Historia* (1984), the Casa de las Américas Prize for *Encancaranublado* (1982), and the Circle of Iberoamerican Writers and Poets Prize for "Puerto Príncipe Abajo" (1979).

Reception of the Text

As the first collection in English of Ana Lydia Vega's work, *True and False Romances* was received with positive reviews in magazines and newspapers in the United States and Europe ranging from *Cosmopoli-*

tan to the *Times Literary Supplement.* Her combination of humor, irony, parody, and popular culture and language deals with women's lives, gender constructions, and political critiques, including analysis of American influence on the island. This was appreciated by reviewers who saw her fiction as an intricate, unconventional juxtaposition of different styles and techniques that contributed greatly to Latin American and Caribbean literature in particular, to women's narrative, which some critics called post-feminist, and to the literature of the Americas in general.

Major Themes and Critical Issues

The stories in *True and False Romances* come from three of Ana Lydia Vega's short story collections and can be placed into four general (and slightly overlapping) categories: stories that parody detective fiction ("True Romances," "Just One Small Detail," and "Solutions, Inc."), stories based on the oral traditions of the southern part of the island ("Eye Openers," "Consolation Prize," and "Miss Florence's Trunk"), stories dealing with Spiritism ("Deliverance from Evil"), and stories of women dealing with love, desire, and loneliness with at times unconventional behaviors ("Aerobics for Love" and "Série Noire"). These categories are particularly overlapping because they deal with overarching themes that connect all these stories. Of these themes some of the most noteworthy are: a critique of gender roles and particularly the constricting roles proscribed for women in Puerto Rican society; the attempts by women to break society's limitations and engage in empowering behavior where they are subjects and not objects; a critique of other forms of discrimination including racism and classism; a valorization of popular Puerto Rican (and on a larger scale Caribbean) culture, language, and beliefs while also critiquing the areas of North American (U.S) influence on culture and behavior; a representation of history from the point of view of previously silenced groups (women, blacks , etc.) that opens up discussions on truth, official history, and their connection to questions of power relations; and the use of humor (parody, satire) in cultural and political critiques.

The first theme, analyzing women's roles in society, is one that is frequently commented on when discussing Vega's works because it stands out so clearly in her short stories. In this collection one can point to any short story as an example. The opening story, "True Romances," parodies the detective novel by recounting the story of writer Carola

Vidal's fascination with two stories of women's victimization: the murder of a young woman (called the "Malén case") and the possible oppression of her friend Vilma by Vilma's husband Paul. These two stories are further compounded by the plot twist at the end, which reveals the tragic end to Carola's own life as a result of being stalked by her ex-boyfriend Manuel. It is this twist that converts the once-distanced reader into a detective him/herself, trying to piece together the last mystery of the narrator's life. As in the case of Vilma, Paul, and a potential lover, several of the short stories give a female perspective on restricting relationships that frequently end in betrayal and affairs. Examples include the betrayed wives in "Consolation Prize" and "Deliverance from Evil" and the women in the stories told in "Eye Openers." However, it is "Solutions, Inc." that serves as one of the most creative parodies of this problem. In this short story Vega creates a fictional advice agency that handles problems in women's relationships by giving advice and setting up scenarios that play on traditional and, to an extent, stereotypical roles where women are submissive, ideal wives and partners.

Nonetheless, many of these stories are not content with just presenting the problems of women's oppression but also critically look at ways in which they attempt to break out of these proscribed roles. In "Aerobics for Love," for example, Vega presents a divorced protagonist who engages in a nonconventional relationship as a counter to her feelings of loneliness and frustration. In the whodunit "Just One Small Detail" the female protagonist, Dalia, is not content to stand on the sidelines when she suspects her neighbor of killing his wife but instead investigates him in an attempt to arrive at the truth. Lastly, the reader is also given examples of how women use writing itself (like the author) as a tool to assert their voices and chronicle important issues in the stories "True Romances," "Eye Openers," and "Miss Florence's Trunk."

Vega's critical eye in her stories in not solely focused on gender issues but also looks at racial and class discrimination and the ways in which these behaviors sometimes overlap. This is most evident in the romantic novella "Miss Florence's Trunk," set on a sugar hacienda ("La Enriqueta") in nineteenth-century Puerto Rico. Through the voice of an "objective" observer, Miss Florence, the reader is given a glimpse into the lives of the European elite in Puerto Rico and their treatment of the slaves on the hacienda, the servants, and the mulatta women in town (Selenia). What stands out is her treatment of not only racial discrimination but also classism (particularly in the remarks by both Miss Florence herself and the ways in which women and men characters such as Susan and Charles Morse were also placed in restricting roles.

Throughout these short stories Vega's love of popular culture (including refrains and oral tales in general) is evident by the language she uses. She places popular sayings side by side with more literary references and expressions in Spanish, French, and English to create a linguistic pastiche in which no one style is dominant or more valued than the other while showing the place popular culture has in "literature." Her valorization of the oral tradition is especially evident in the short stories from *Falsas Crónicas del Sur*: "Eye Openers," "Consolation Prize," and "Miss Florence's Trunk." These stories grew out of her mother's tales from her hometown, Arroyo, and Vega's desire to capture, preserve, and yet transform these stories in her own creative way. While the use of various linguistic codes shows the heterogeneity of Puerto Rican identity, the references to American popular culture (as evidenced by the references by the protagonist in "Just One Small Detail" to Tom Cruise, Mick Jagger, W. C. Fields, Brian de Palma flicks, and *The Texas Chainsaw Massacre*) are a humorous critique of the sometimes subtle, sometimes explicit ways in which it has infiltrated Puerto Rican consciousness.

Of the nine stories in the collection, eight are told from the point of view of a female protagonist. This in itself is one of the ways in which Vega gives her readers another perspective—that of the once-silenced female voice. A larger study of the subjectivity of history can be found once more in "Miss Florence's Trunk." By placing the story of the real life hacienda "La Enriqueta" in the words of a woman and critically showing the treatment of both women and blacks, Vega forces us as readers to examine the ways in which histories once taken as objective truth are constructed, and the ways in which a change in perspective may bring to light previously unknown facts. This difference of perspective is dealt with on a more humorous level in "Consolation Prize" and "Eye Openers," where the short story is introduced as ". . . a true story, historical fact, and not some eye-opener made up to entertain . . ." and some of the tales are told differently by the male and female passengers traveling in a van.

Lastly, I would like to highlight Vega's use of humor, irony, parody, and satire to comically deal with serious issues of gender, class, race, and politics, to name a few. "Consolation Prize" for example highlights a neighbor's humorous retelling of a young woman's betrayal by her husband and the revenge she carries out that forever changes her life and his. Similarly, the use of humor and irony in "True Romances" and "Just One Small Detail" underscores the very real problems of women's physical and emotional abuse. On a political level, the comic cultural and political clash depicted in the first story, "Eye Openers," gives the reader a glimpse at the sometimes tense relationship of Puerto Rican citizens (as part of a commonwealth) with U. S. governmental institutions like the I.R.S. Vega's use of parody is especially strong in her treatment of the whodunit ("True Romances," "Solutions, Inc.," "Just One Small Detail") and the romantic novel ("Miss Florence's Trunk"). It is important to note that this intention is hinted at in the subtitle of "Miss Florence's Trunk" given in the original Spanish version: "Fragments for a Romantic Novella." The impact of Vega's sharp wit is especially felt when the more comical short stories are placed alongside the more sinister ones ("Deliverance from Evil" and "Série Noire") and in the stories like "True Romances" that combine a humorous and somber tone.

Pedagogical Issues and Suggestions

Because of the variety of short stories presented in this collection, one of the first strategies I recommend is to identify the different thematic levels on which they operate. In an attempt to give a general understanding of this range I have grouped the stories on a primary, intermediate, and advanced level based on subject matter treated (including sexual content and explicit language) and the complexity of the material. Of the nine short stories in the collection, "Eye Openers" is the one that I would place in the primary category (with some more intermediate situations) because of its relatively light treatment of deception, betrayal, and revenge. In the intermediate category I would place the stories "Solutions, Inc.," "Série Noire," and "Consolation Prize" because of their adult references to sexuality and their use of some explicit language. The stories "True Romances," "Deliverance from Evil," and "Miss Florence's Trunk" are three that I would place in the intermediate-advanced category because of their more explicit and sometimes sinister references. However, in the case of "Miss Florence's Trunk," the complex story of the nineteenth-century hacienda in Puerto Rico also invites a knowledge of that society that goes beyond just a basic textual reading. Finally, I would place "Aerobics for Love" in the advanced category because of its at times explicit sexual references.

One of the qualities contributing to Vega's distinctive style involves the ways in which she mixes theme, language, and tone to entertain and critique not only Puerto Rican culture but also women and men's relationships and Puerto Rican–U.S. relations in general. This combination is both innovative and challenging and needs a reading approach that takes all these elements into account. One of the first steps therefore, would be to identify the plot(s), identify the narrative voice of each story, and then establish the relation of each character to the basic plot(s). Is the story told in first person or third person? Is this person an eyewitness to the story she or he will tell? This is an important factor, for example, in stories like "Consolation Prize," "Eye Openers," and "Miss Florence's Trunk" because perspective/ point of view is one factor that influences our understanding of the events.

Secondly, I would recommend that links be made between the title of each short story, the epigraph preceding each one, and the themes covered. What does each title imply? What expectations does it possibly place in the reader's mind? At the end of the story what relationship can be drawn between the epigraph and the story? Are the reader's primary expectations validated or rejected? Turning again to "Miss Florence's Trunk," the epigraphs by Samuel and Susan Morse are an ironic commentary on slavery, women's oppression, and the very idea of history. These quotes are attributed to real people that in Vega's story become fictionalized. In some cases the epigraphs are easier to identify because they come from popular culture and fiction (like Alfred Hitchcock, M. J. Canario, Stephen King, and Cornell Woolrich, "father of noir fiction") while others are from historical figures (Samuel and Susan Walker Morse), theoreticians (Roland Barthes), or from classic and modern classic literature (Geoffrey Chaucer, La Rochefoucauld, and V. S. Naipaul). Not only is the relationship between each particular epigraph and story important but also the very diversity of the sources themselves. What does this intertextuality say about Vega's ideas on literature, history, and culture? How does it influence our perceptions of these areas?

Vega's adept use of humor entertains and challenges her readers. Therefore, an understanding of each story's tone is a key to our appreciation of the texts' themes. Some steps that are useful in establishing her tone(s) are first identifying irony, parody and satire as narrative techniques and then seeing where they are used in the stories. Once that is done there can be an analysis of the effect of the irony or parody on the reader's perception of the character(s): Does it distance us and reveal a more critical side to the character's behavior or does it draw us in as readers and reveal something about ourselves? The study of these techniques can be complemented by an understanding of Vega's language. As with the epigraphs, she uses a variety of registers (popular culture, French, English, etc.) that are at times comical and at other times more sarcastic. It is also important to note that in many cases Vega will use different tones and registers within a story (as in "True Romances" and "Deliverance from Evil"). Because Vega incorporates so much oral tradition in her stories it is at times helpful (if not highly recommended) to read some sections of her stories out loud (i.e., "Just One Small Detail," "Consolation Prize," or "Eye Openers") in order to get an aural understanding of her tone and cultural references.

An analysis of Vega's use of tone and irony can also help in our understanding of her commentaries on issues like women's oppression and empowerment, class relations, and racism, to name a few. The protagonist Carola Vidal, for example, is a complex character whose motives for researching and writing the story of the "Malén Case" and listening to her friend Vilma are not always clear cut. Some helpful questions for the reader are: Why does Carola Vidal want to write this story? In the case of the murder of Malén, how does she recreate the crime? Whose point of view does she take and is this consistent throughout? How does she feel when she listens to Vilma tell of her life? Knowing what we do about Carola's own life and death, does this change how we assess her motivations as a writer? Equally important to a study of female behavior in a male-dominated society is an understanding of the role of irony in "Solutions, Inc.," particularly with its surprise ending. In this short story the reader can begin by discussing the various "suggestions" given the client of case 600 and what type of female behavior they represent. Why are those specific behaviors suggested and what do they say about the society in which the client lives? How does that portrayal of men and women in society contrast with our own society?

This last question is one that can be applied not only to "Solutions, Inc." but, to a certain extent, to all of Vega's short stories. This is because some (if not many) of the themes she discusses are relevant not only to Puerto Rican society but to individuals across cultures as well. However, it is always important to remember the fine line between cultural specificity and universality. In some cases ("Miss Florence's Trunk" being the most obvious example) there is a specific cultural and historic context that informs the characters' behavior and must therefore be recognized, along with the ways in which these behaviors reveal at times more widespread human actions. This understanding can also help us see the different communities that Vega speaks of and to whom she addresses her texts.

Literary Contexts

Puerto Rican literature, both on the mainland and in the United States, has historically dealt with the tension between the political, economic, and social forces that shaped the nation from colonization in 1493 to its transferal to an American protectorate in 1898 and the assertion of an autonomous national identity. After 1898, in contrast to earlier emphasis on a creole, Hispanic American nationalism, writers asserted a sociopolitical, cultural, and literary independence from the United States through their use of the Spanish language as a counterpoint to the American (and therefore English-based) influence on the island, and their literary ties with trends in Latin American literature (Kanellos 1987, x). Puerto Rican identity was initially represented in literature by the *mestizo,* which bridged indigenous, European, and, to a lesser extent, African cultures, followed by the exaltation of the *jíbaro* (rural peasant) as a figure that valorized the principles and resistance of the Puerto Rican people and their rural past (Acosta-Belén, 222). Contemporary writers have emphasized the tripartite aspect of Puerto Rican identity stemming from its indigenous, European, and African roots in an urban setting that links the island with the mainland through postwar migrations (creating the Puerto Rican diaspora). Among the many literary generations that have represented the diversity and innovation of Puerto Rican literature, three groups stand out: the generation of 1930, the generation of 1950, and the generation of 1970. The first generation included writers like Luis Llorens Torres and Luis Palés Matos, who dealt with indigenous (Creole) themes like the life of the exploited peasant *(jíbaro),* rural life, and the legacy of Africa in Puerto Rican culture. This latter theme was particularly evident in the Negrista poetry of Luis Palés Matos, whose collections like *Tun Tun de Pasa y Grifería* (1937) invoked a black African heritage as part of Puerto Rican identity and as part of his critique of Europe and the United States. (Kanellos 1987, xi-xii).

The next generation of writers, the first postwar generation, focused less on the rural sector and instead explored the daily issues of the Puerto Rican working class in an urban setting, as well as the displaced rural subject trying to survive in the city. These urban studies were part

of the overall analysis of the effects of industrialization and urbaniza-
tion on Puerto Rican society and were accompanied by a change from
the traditionalist narrative style of the previous group of writers to the
use of flashback and a more experimental fluid style that included
stream of consciousness and interior monologue. Despite these thematic and structural shifts, this generation did continue to explore
issues of national independence and cultural autonomy and critique
North American colonialism. Among the more well-known writers of
this generation are José Luis González, Pedro Juan Soto, Emilio Diaz
Valcárcel, and René Márques. The playwright René Márques and the
poet Julia de Burgos are particularly important in the history of linking
the experiences of Puerto Ricans on the island and on the mainland.
René Márques's play *The Oxcart* (*La carreta*,1961) was a literary
representation (along the lines of Steinbeck's *The Grapes of Wrath*) of
the effect of emigration to the United States on the values, religious
beliefs, language, and culture of rural Puerto Ricans and the need to
return both physically and morally to the island. Julia de Burgos's
poetry praised the beauty of the Puerto Rican countryside and the need
for national liberation while also exploring her identity as a woman,
writer, and Puerto Rican living in the United States. For many critics her
work was a bridge between the ". . . late vanguard of the 1930s with the
existentialist anguish of the 1950s" (Smith, 682). Her poetic chronicles
of her identity and displacement from the island are even more telling
when placed within the context of her life and tragic death in New York
(Kanellos 1987, xi-xii).

The last generation, the generation of 1970, includes writers like
Luís Rafael Sánchez, Edgardo Rodríguez, Juliá and Manuel Otero.
However, this generation has also been marked by the significant
presence of women writers like Rosario Ferré, Carmen Lugo Filippi,
Magali García Ramis, and Ana Lydia Vega. While continuing the
critique of the political crisis of Puerto Rico's status as a free associated
state and of the false morality of the Puerto Rican bourgeoisie, this
generation broke with the model of social realism and used their
narrative to take a more critical look at the construction of history as it
related to Puerto Rican national identity and culture (Smith, 684–685).
As part of this project these writers, publishing in the 1970s and 1980s,
stress the need to recognize African-Caribbean elements as part of a
national identity and Puerto Rico's link to a larger Caribbean community. This was complemented by the use and valorization of popular
speech and oral tradition as a foundation for their literary visions and a
search for new esthetic forms that included realist-experimental styles,
magical realism, and elements of the marvelous as well as the use of the

comic and grotesque. The women writers of the generation of 1970 in particular used the narrative to explore issues like women's socialization, the social and economic struggles they face, relationships between men and women, negritude, and homosexuality as part of a general project that attempted to question and subvert traditional relations of power between different social groups (Acosta-Belén, 226). These issues among others are being addressed by other Puerto Rican writers like Mayra Montero and Mayra Santos-Febres, who fall outside the generation of 1970 chronologically yet share thematic ties.

The history of Puerto Rican literature on the mainland dates back to the end of the nineteenth century and Spanish-language newspapers that continued until the 1950s. For Puerto Rican writers in the United States, particularly in cities like New York, Puerto Rican identity took on a different meaning than that of their island counterparts. While incorporating elements of the island identity these writers were predominantly bilingual, writing their poetry in Spanish and English and their prose in English. Their literary influences also included aspects of popular culture like salsa music, Hispanic folklore, roving bands, and American popular culture. For these writers their community stretched beyond Puerto Rican ties to blacks, other Latino groups and multiethnic writers in the United States who explored issues of American identity, marginality, displacement, and cultural pride. Among the mainland writers who most impacted and continue to impact Puerto Rican literature are: Miguel Algarín (founder of the Nuyorican Poet's Café), Tato Laviera, Ed Vega, Piri Thomas, Sandra María Esteves, Miguel Piñero, and Esmeralda Santiago (Kanellos 1987, xiii-xiv). However, it is important to note that contemporary mainland Puerto Rican literature is not just concentrated in New York but explores the Puerto Rican diaspora found throughout the United States, as in the writing of Judith Ortiz Cofer.

Comparative Literature

Ana Lydia Vega's use of popular and classic culture, language, and literature combined with the use of humor and irony in order to deal with gender, social, and political issues make her short stories unique in not only Caribbean but Latin American literature. As a result, comparisons with mainstream American literature have to be made with care, taking into account a variety of ethnicities and even genders. In some ways her treatment of everyday people can be found in narratives by Southern women writers and ethnic writers like African American and Native American women writers. Five writers in particular come to mind: An African American writer of the 1940s, Zora Neale Hurston, who used humor and sharp character portrayals to represent rural communities in Florida in novels like *Their Eyes Were Watching God,* Southern writers Flannery O'Connor and Tillie Olsen, and Native American writers Louise Erdrich and Leslie Marmon Silko. In O'Connor's short story "A Good Man Is Hard to Find," for example, the use of humor and irony allow her to critically look at gender, class, and race in Southern culture. Olsen's characters in works like *Tell Me A Riddle* show people representing the spectrum of gender, class, and race who have been marginalized and look for ways to survive and even flourish. The particular use of humor mixed with tragedy in some of Louise Erdrich's representations of Native American life is also a link between her and Vega, while the connection with Leslie Marmon Silko is seen more in both women's valorization (although in different ways) of oral tradition. If we compare across gender as well as ethnicity, one can add the style of Sherman Alexie (author of *The Lone Ranger and Tonto Fistfight in Heaven*) to the list because of his use of humor, oral tradition, and popular culture in Native American portrayals. Comparisons to Vega's work can also be made across literary genres. As a lover of detective fiction, Vega's parodies of the genre make some of her stories comparable to those of contemporary detective writer Sara Paretsky, who penned the V.I. Warshawski series. Paretsky's emphasis on a sharp-talking female private detective show the ways in which she too uses wit and sarcasm to explore women's empowerment in a male-dominated society.

It is important to note that these comparisons are at best approximations. Just as each writer ultimately has a unique style, the same can be said of Ana Lydia Vega. When placed in the multicultural (indigenous, European, and African) and contemporary bicultural (island-mainland) context out of which she comes, Vega's works treat issues of everyday people and at times critiques of the more elite classes with a sense of humor and irony that goes beyond more traditional American works. This multiplicity in her subject and her language has at times been called postmodern by some critics because of the ways in which this fragmentation questions notions of power, privilege and objective centralized voices. Her mixture of popular culture and more classical references along with her manipulations of narrative voice also serve to reflect critically on the text itself and how it represents individuals and their place in history and society.

BIBLIOGRAPHIC RESOURCES

Primary Sources

Hurston, Zora Neale. *Their Eyes Were Watching God.* New York: Lippincott, 1937.

O'Connor, Flannery. *A Good Man Is Hard to Find.* Madison, WI: Turtleback Books, 1999.

Olsen, Tillie. *Tell Me A Riddle.* Piscataney, NJ: Rutgers University Press, 1995.

Vega, Ana Lydia. *Encancaranublado y Otros Cuentos de Naufragio.* Ciudad de la Habana: Casa de las Américas, 1982.

———. *Falsas cronicas del sur.* Rio Piedras, P.R.: Editorial Universidad de Puerto Rico, 1991.

———. *Pasión de Historia y Otras Historias de Pasión.* Buenos Aires: Editiones De la Flor, 1991, c. 1997.

Secondary Sources

About Puerto Ricans and Puerto Rican Literature

CELAC, ed. *Adiós, Borinquen querida: The Puerto Rican Diaspora, Its History and Contributions.* New York: Center for Latino, Latin American and Caribbean Studies, 2000.

Colón, Jésus. *The Way It Was and Other Writings: Recovering the U.S. Hispanic Literary Heritage.* Edna Acosta Belén, Virginia Sánchez Korrall, eds. Houston: Arte Público, 1993.

Flores, Angel. *Spanish American Authors: The Twentieth Century.* New York. H.W. Wilson Company, 1992. 875–876.

Flores, Juan. *Divided Borders: Essays on Puerto Rican Identity.* Houston: Arte Público Press, 1993.

Foster, David William. *Puerto Rican Literature: A Bibliography of Secondary Sources.* Westport, CT: Greenwood Press, 1982.

Kanellos, Nicolás. *Images and Identities: The Puerto Rican in Two World Contexts.* New Brunswick: Transaction Books, 1987.

———. *Biographical Dictionary of Hispanic Literature in the United States: The Literature of Puerto Ricans, Cuban Americans and Other Hispanic Writers.* New York: Greenwood Press, 1989.

Sánchez-González, Lisa. *Boricua Literature: A Literary History of the Puerto Rican Diaspora.* New York: New York University Press, 2001.

Smith, Verity, ed. *Encyclopedia of Latin American Literature.* Chicago: Fitzroy Dearborn Publishers, 1997.

About Ana Lydia Vega

Boling, Becky. "The Reproduction of Ideology in Ana Lydia Vega's *Pasión de Historia* and *Caso Omiso.*" *Letras Femeninas* 17, no. 1–2 (1991): 89–97.

———. "What's Wrong with This Picture? Ana Lydia Vega's *Caso Omisp.*" *Revista de Estudios Hispánicos* 23 (1996): 315–324.

Den Tandt, Catherine. "Tracing Nation and Gender: Ana Lydia Vega." *Revista de Estudios Hispánicos* 28, no. 1 (March 1996): 341–356.

Fernández Olmos, Margarite. "From a Woman's Perspective: The Short Stories of Rosario Ferré and Ana Lydia Vega." Doris Meyer and Margarite Fernández Olmos, eds. *Contemporary Women Authors of Latin America*. Brooklyn: Brooklyn College Press, 1983.

Hernández, Elizabeth and Consuelo López Springfield. "Women and Writing in Puerto Rico: An Interview with Ana Lydia Vega." *Callaloo* 17, no. 3 (1994): 816–825.

Puleo, Augustus. "Ana Lydia Vega, the Caribbean storyteller." *Afro-Hispanic Review* (fall 1996): 21–25.

"Social Criticism in the Contemporary Short Story of Selected Puerto Rican Women Writers." *MACLAS: Latin American Essays* 3 (1989): 113–123.

Vega, Ana Lydia. "To Write or Not to Write?" Trans. Rosemary Geisdorfer Feal. *Philosophy and Literature in Latin America: A Critical Assessment of the Current Situation*. J. E. Jorge Garcia and Mireya Camurati, eds. New York: Albany State University of New York, 1989.

Contributors

Frances R. Aparicio, born in Santurce, Puerto Rico, came to the United States at the age of eighteen to pursue her college education. She has been a faculty member at Stanford University, University of Arizona, Tucson, and University of Michigan, where she directed the Latino studies program during the 1990s. She is currently professor and director of the Latin American and Latino studies program at University of Illinois at Chicago, where she established the Lectures in the Community series. Professor Aparicio's works include a number of books and anthologies on Latino/a literatures and cultures. Her book *Listening to Salsa: Gender, Latin Popular Music and Puerto Rican Cultures* (1998) has not only been an influential text on popular music and on Latino/a cultural studies but also the recipient of two awards. She has also published critical anthologies, literary translations, and an anthology of Latino literature for young readers. She has been a member of national committees, advisory boards, and guest editor of *Latino Studies,* a new Palgrave journal edited by Suzanne Oboler at University of Illinois at Chicago. Professor Aparicio is currently writing on bilingualism, cultural identity, and Latino cultural productions in the Chicago area.

Barbara Brinson Curiel is an assistant professor at Humboldt State University. Her poetry has been published in a variety of anthologies featuring Hispanic literature. In addition she has published three poetry collections: *Nocturno* (Berkeley: El Fuego de Aztlán Press, 1978), *Vocabulary of the Dead* (Oakland: Nomad Press, 1984), and *Speak to Me From Dreams* (Berkeley: Third Woman Press, 1989). Her recent scholarly publications include "My Border Stories: Life Narratives, Interdisciplinarity, and Postnationalism in Ethnic Studies," which appeared in *Post-national American Studies* (2000) and "The General's Pants: A Chicana Feminist (Re)Vision of the Mexican Revolution in Sandra Cisneros's 'Eyes of Zapata,'" in *Western American Literature* (winter 2001).

Norma Cantú currently serves as professor of English at the University of Texas at San Antonio. She is the editor of a book series, Rio

Grande/Rio Bravo: Borderlands Culture and Tradition, at Texas A & M University Press. Currently a member of the Board of Trustees of the American Folklife Center at the Library of Congress, she also serves on the board of the American Folklore Society, the Federation of State Humanities Councils, and the Mexican American Cultural Center. Author of the award-winning *Canicula: Snapshots of a Girlhood en la Frontera* (Albuquerque: University of New Mexico Press, 1997), and coeditor of *Chicana Traditions: Continuity and Change,* (Champaign: University of Illinois, 2002), she is currently working on a novel and ethnography of Matachines de la Santa Cruz, a religious dance drama from Laredo, Texas.

Theresa Delgadillo is an assistant Professor of women's studies at Notre Dame University. She is at work on two projects: a book manuscript titled "Hybrid Spiritualities: Resistance and Religious Faith in Contemporary Chicana/o Narratives" and a monograph titled "Racial Memory, Mestizaje, and Miscegenation: The Case of 'Angelitos Negros.'" Her publications include: "Race, Sex, and Spirit: Chicana Negotiations of Catholicism," forthcoming in *Reconciling Feminism and Catholicism;* "Forms of Chicana Feminist Resistance: Hybrid Spirituality in Ana Castillo's *So Far from God*" in *Modern Fiction Studies* 44, no. 3 (1998); "Exiles, Migrants, Settlers, and Natives: Literary Representations of Chicano/as and Mexicans in the Midwest," published by the Julian Samora Research Institute at Michigan State University (1999); and "Gender at Work in Laguna Coyote Tales" in *Studies in American Indian Literatures* 7, no. 1 (1995). She has been the recipient of a University of California, MEXUS Dissertation Research Grant, a Ford Foundation Dissertation Fellowship, and a UCSB Center for Chicano Studies Rockefeller Postdoctoral Fellowship. Delgadillo serves on the Executive Committee for the Chicana and Chicano Literature Division of the MLA and is a board member of the Institute for Women, Spirituality and Justice.

Dionne Espinoza is an assistant professor in the Department of Chicano Studies at California State University, Los Angeles. She teaches courses on Chicana/Latina feminisms, activism, and cultural production. Her articles have been published in *Other Sisterhoods: Women of Color and Literary Theory; Aztlan; A Journal of Chicano Studies;* and *Velvet Barrios: Popular Culture and Chicana/o Sexualities* (forthcoming). She is currently completing a manuscript entitled "Revolutionary Sisters: Chicana Activism and the Cultural Politics of Chicano Power," which is forthcoming from the University of Texas Press, Chicana Matters series.

Lesley Feracho is an assistant professor in the Department of Romance Languages and the Institute of African-American Studies at the University of Georgia at Athens and a current postdoctoral fellow of the Rodney/Mandela/DuBois Postdoctoral Fellowship. Her research interests include identity politics and migration in contemporary Latin American narrative and in particular cross-cultural literary narrative and poetry of women writers of African descent from the Hispanophone and Lusophone Americas. Professor Feracho has published in *Afro-Hispanic Review, Hispania,* and *PALARA* on the poetry of Carolina Maria de Jesus, Miriam Alves, and Nancy Morejon as well as the importance of oral tradition in Afro-Cuban and Afro-Ecuadorian narratives. She is currently working on the book *Linking the Americas: Hybrid Discourses and the Reformulation of Feminine Identity,* which studies women's redefinitions of the self in narratives from Brazil, Cuba, and the United States. For her fellowship, she's exploring the identity politics in the original and published autobiographies of Afro-Brazilian writer Carolina Maria de Jesus and African American (U.S) writer Zora Neale Hurston.

Rosa Linda Fregoso, professor in the Department of Latin American/Latino Studies at the University of California, Santa Cruz teaches courses in culture and cinema at UCSC and has published widely in areas of cinema, culture, and feminist theory. Her major publications include: *The Bronze Screen: Chicana and Chicano Film Culture* (Minneapolis: University of Minnesota Press, 1993), *Miradas de Mujer,* coedited with Norma Iglesias (Juarez, MX: CLRC & Colegio de la Frontera-Norte, 1998), and *The Devil Never Sleeps and Other Films by Lourdes Portillo* (Austin: University of Texas Press, 2001). At this time, she is revising her manuscript, *Mexicana Encounters: The Making of Social Identities on the Borderlands* (Berkeley: University of California Press, forthcoming). Professor Fregoso is currently working on issues of cultural representation, transnational feminism, and gender/sexual violence.

Karen Gaffney is a doctoral candidate, completing her degree in the English department at the University of Delaware. She has taught courses in English and women's studies and has presented her research on American women writers and the intersection between feminist and critical race theory at a number of national conferences. Her article "Excavated from the Inside: White Trash and Dorothy Allison's *Cavedweller*" is forthcoming in *Modern Language Studies.*

Michelle Habell-Pallán is an assistant professor of American ethnic studies at the University of Washington. Currently a Mellon/WWNFF research fellow, she is coeditor of *Latino/a Popular Culture* (New York:

New York University Press 2002), and she has published several articles on U.S. and Canadian Latino culture production, including "'*El Vez* is Taking Care of Business': The International Appeal of Chicano Popular Music," which appears in *Cultural Studies* (April 1999). She is currently completing her book manuscript, *The Travels of Chicana and Latino Popular Culture and the New Transnational Imaginary* and serving as chair of the Chicana/o literature division of the Modern Language Association. She can be contacted at mhabellp@u.washington.edu.

Andrea O'Reilly Herrera, professor at the University of Colorado at Colorado Springs, serves as the director of their ethnic studies program. She is a published poet and the author of a number of essays on writers ranging from Charlotte Bronte to Sandra Cisneros. She has also edited a collection of essays on the image of the family in British and American literature and an anthology of short stories written by Latin American women writers. Her most recent projects include a collection of testimonials, *ReMembering Cuba: Legacy of a Diaspora* (Austin: University of Texas Press, 2001), drawn from the Cuban exile community and their children residing in the United States, and a novel *The Pearl of the Antilles* (Tempe: Bilingual Press, 2000), which chronicles the lives of five generations in a single family of Cuban women and takes up the interrelated themes of exile, loss, and the preservation/perpetuation of cultural memory.

Juan Felipe Herrera, one of the pioneers in Chicano literature, is professor of Chicano and Latin American studies at California State University in Fresno. He is a poet and *teatrista* with nineteen books: poetry, fiction, young adult novels, children's books, and new media. His recent work includes *Giraffe on Fire* (Tucson: University of Arizona Press, 2001) and *Notebooks of a Chile Verde Smuggler* (Tucson: University of Arizona Press, 2001). He lives in Fresno with his soul partner and poet, Margarita Luna Robles.

Tiffany Ana Lopez is associate professor of English and director of CASA—Chicano Arts and Social Action at the University of California at Riverside. Her book *The Alchemy of Blood: Critical Witness in U.S. Latina Drama* is forthcoming from Duke University Press. Her publications include the anthology *Growing Up Chicana/o* (New York: William Morrow, 1993); "Violent Inscriptions: Writing the Body and Making Community in Four Plays by Migdalia Cruz," *Theater Journal* (March 2000); "A New Mestiza Primer: Borderlands Philosophy in the Children's Books of Gloria Anzaldúa," in *Such News of the Land: American Women Nature Writers* (Hanover, NH: University Press of New England, 2001); and a new book in progress on U.S. Latina/o children's literature. She serves as editorial advisor to *American Thea-*

ter, editorial board member for *Aztlán: A Journal of Chicano Studies*, and co-chair of the Latina/o literature affiliate for the American Literature Association. She may be reached at Tiffany.Lopez@ucr.edu.

Rosa Morillas-Sánchez is an associate professor of American literature at the University of Granada in Spain. She has published several articles on Chicano literature and is coeditor of the volume *Literatura Chicana: Reflexiones y Ensayos Críticos* (Granada, Spain: Editorial Comares, 2000). She is currently working on an anthology of Chicano Literature.

Ifeoma C. K. Nwankwo is an assistant professor of English and Afroamerican and African studies at the University of Michigan at Ann Arbor. Her research focuses on inter-American intraracial encounters in the languages, identities, and ideologies of people of African descent in the Americas. Her in-progress book project focuses on ideological, identificatory, and material relations during slavery, particularly in the wake of the Haitian Revolution. She has also written articles on the mechanics of memory in Panamanian West Indian texts, the politics of intraracial translation, and the traveling market women in the Jamaican patois poetry of Louise Bennett. A Ford Foundation Fellow, Professor Nwankwo has presented her work to U.S. and international audiences in a variety of sites including Liverpool, England; Panama City, Panama; Antigua, West Indies; Havana, Cuba; and Tuscaloosa, Alabama.

Alvina E. Quintana is an associate professor in the Department of English and women's studies at the University of Delaware. She is the author of *Home Girls: Chicana Literary Voices* (Philadelphia: Temple University Press, 1996). Her research and reviews on cultural/cinema studies, feminist theory, and ethnic American literary production have appeared in a number of journals and anthologies that include but are not limited to: *American Quarterly, Amerasia Journal, Aztlán, Cineste, Cultural Studies*, and *Signs*. Professor Quintana is presently completing a book-length study, tentatively entitled *Borders Be Damned: Creolizing Literary Relations*.

Claudia Sadowski-Smith is an assistant professor in the Department of English at Texas Tech University. She is the editor of *Globalization on the Line: Culture, Capital and Citizenship at U.S. Borders* (New York: Palgrave Press, 2002), and has published essays in journals like *Arizona Quarterly, Diaspora*, and *Postmodern Culture*. Professor Sadowski-Smith is currently working on a book-length study on representations of globalization in border literature.

Lisa Sánchez González is an assistant professor of English, women's studies, and African American studies at the University of Texas at Austin. She is the author of *Boricua Literature: A Literary History of* *the Puerto Rican Diaspora* (New York: New York University Press, 2001). Her essays have appeared in a number of journals and critical anthologies, including *American Literary History, Cultural Studies, Recovering the U.S. Hispanic Literary Heritage,* and *African Roots/ American Cultures.* She also produces community-based news and public affairs programming for public radio.

Index